The Moral Architecture of World Peace

Helena Cobban

The Moral Architecture of World Peace

Nobel Laureates

Discuss Our

Global Future

University Press of Virginia

Charlottesville and London

Publication of this book was assisted by a grant from the
Page-Barbour Lecture Fund.

The University Press of Virginia
© 2000 by the Rector and Visitors of the University of Virginia
Printed in the United States of America
First published in 2000

⊗ The paper used in this publication meets the minimum
requirements of the American National Standard for Information
Sciences—Permanence of Paper for Printed Library Materials,
ANSI Z39.48-1984.

Library of Congress Cataloging-in-Publication Data
Cobban, Helena.
    The moral architecture of world peace : Nobel laureates dis-
cuss our global future / Helena Cobban.
        p.   cm.
    Includes bibliographical references and index.
    ISBN 0-8139-1987-8 (alk. paper)
    1. Peace.   2. Pacifists—Biography.   3. Nobel Prizes.
4. Political violence—Prevention.   I. Title.

JZ5538.C63 2000
327.1'72—dc21   99-056608

For all those whose hearts and lives

may be touched by these laureates' words

Contents

Acknowledgments

I would like to acknowledge first, and with great humility, the immense honor the University Press of Virginia bestowed on me by inviting me to write this text, and the unprecedented inspiration I received from listening to, and working closely with, the utterances of these laureates. Obviously, I want to express gratitude for the work done by Professor P. Jeffrey Hopkins, Bryan Phillips, and their associates in the University of Virginia's religious studies department, and by Ms. Michele Bohana, director of the Institute for Asian Democracy, in organizing the 1998 Nobel Peace Laureates Conference.

The sponsors of the conference included—from the University of Virginia—the Office of the President, John T. Casteen III; the Office of the Dean of the College and Graduate School of Arts and Sciences, Melvyn P. Leffler; and the Page-Barbour and Richard Lecture Series Committee. Additional sponsors included Dr. Inder and Vera Vaswani Chawla, Terrence D. Daniels, PMD International, Inc., Wallace Stettinius, and GFW Intelos.

In writing this work, I have drawn firstly on the inspiration that came from the laureates' words, and also on the large amounts of help and encouragement I have received from mentors, friends, and colleagues over the years. Two great figures in international news coverage, Geoffrey Godsell and Joseph C. Harsch of the *Christian Science Monitor*, started challenging me, back in 1976, to probe more deeply behind global headlines; and my editors at the paper have continued to support my explorations until today. Catherine M. Kelleher and Michael MccGwire were my first mentors in strategic studies. My understanding of the challenges and importance of international human rights work has been helped along by numerous rights advocates, especially in the Middle East, and by my colleagues at Human Rights Watch. My spouse, William B. Quandt, and many other friends here in Charlottesville have given me conceptual and stylistic help as I pulled this book together in 1999.

All those associated with organizing the 1998 conference gave generously of support and insight that proved critical to the success of the writing project. P. Jeffrey Hopkins and Michele Bohana provided advice and textual comment. Melvyn P. Leffler provided background materials obtained during his research at the Norwegian Nobel Institute. Donna L. Packard transcribed the proceedings of the conference on behalf of the Press; some clarifications also came from a second transcript prepared by Steven Weinberger, and from referring directly back to the excellent audio-tapes prepared by the University Relations office. Britt H. Krivicich gathered some needed research materials.

Geir Lundestadt, director of the Norwegian Nobel Institute in Oslo, graciously answered some questions about committee procedures. George Lopez of the University of Notre Dame and Harold H. Saunders of the Kettering Foundation provided helpful critiques of a first draft of the manuscript. This work is truly the result of many minds. However, it is certain that inaccuracies, infelicities, and misapprehensions still remain in the text. For them, I alone remain responsible.

The Moral Architecture of World Peace

1

A Gathering of Framers of the Future Global Culture

They came from homelands in five different continents. They came from different generations and from widely varying cultural and religious backgrounds. They came at midpoints along personal journeys that had taken each of them through the fire of conflict and the wasteland of searing loss—journeys that had also taken them toward a greatly increased awareness of both the interconnectedness of all humankind and the negative consequences of the use of violence. They came bearing personal stories that showcased the power of the human spirit.

They came together, these eight Nobel peace laureates and the representative of one other, for public discussions that probed to the heart of what it will take to build world peace in the twenty-first century. Only a week before the conference, Archbishop Desmond Tutu, the head of South Africa's groundbreaking Truth and Reconciliation Commission, had presented the commission's final report to then-President Nelson Mandela. At the conference, Tutu delivered one of his first lengthy public reviews of the commission's work. Jody Williams, a woman from Vermont who led a successful, globe-girdling citizen campaign for a treaty to ban landmines, explained how that campaign had been run, and she explored the potential for increasing the involvement of citizen groups in global affairs. And His Holiness the Dalai Lama gave a full explanation of his thinking on the need for both external and internal disarmament.

These presentations were just some of the highlights of an unprecedented public conversation on the challenges of building world peace that was hosted by the University of Virginia, an institution founded by Thomas

1

Jefferson two centuries ago with the aim of exploring and affirming the "illimitable freedom of the human mind."[1]

Those November days in 1998 were biting cold, and the world the peace laureates were discussing was filled with uncertainties. The straightforward (though always risky) polarities of the planet's forty-five-year cold war had melted away, and no stable new framework for dealings among human communities had yet won acceptance from the peoples of the world. Many regions of the world were wracked with intergroup conflict or with the repressive policies of brutal dictators. A vast financial crisis had recently spread its hand of misery over most of east Asia; and all around the globe poverty, disease, environmental degradation, and corrupt governance robbed millions of children of their right to life, health, education, and basic human dignity.

The conversations that the peace laureates conducted in the university's amphitheater-style Cabell Hall touched on all these challenges. But they differed from many of the other discussions that political leaders or other "experts" conduct on world affairs in two important ways. First, these conversations moved seamlessly from the global to the intimately personal, weaving into the discussions on, for example, strategic affairs or the requirements of diplomacy such subjects as the need for personal transformation and forgiveness at all levels of human society and the need for community organizing. Second, these conversations stressed the centrality of the agency of individual men and women in building increased understanding among peoples, and in working to build a just and hope-filled society for the future of all humankind.

Such a society may seem far from the situation we face today. But what these laureates were engaged in added up to no less than sketching out a moral architecture for a future world at peace.

WHO ARE THEY, these visionary leaders? Taking them in the order of their awards, they are:

Betty Williams, born in Northern Ireland in 1943, was awarded the 1976 Nobel Peace Prize jointly with Mairead Maguire Corrigan, a neighbor with whom she had founded a grassroots peace movement called the Community of Peace People earlier that year. With the province then deeply entangled in the intercommunal troubles that had reignited in the late 1960s,

these two young homemakers helped form a movement that sought to promote nonviolent alternatives in the relationship between the province's
Protestant and Catholic communities.

After receiving her peace prize, Williams helped to establish Lagan College, one of a very small number of schools in Northern Ireland organized
along nonsectarian lines. And she extended her concern for the situation of
children in crisis-ridden communities by traveling on aid missions to war
zones and famine-struck localities in numerous other countries.

In the 1980s, she moved to Texas, where, in 1992, she was named to the
state's Commission for Children and Youth. Some years later she moved to
Florida, where she continued her work in activism. In 1997, she founded
the World Centers of Compassion for Children, whose aim is to establish
safe havens for children in zones of war and crisis.

Archbishop Desmond Tutu, the former head of the Anglican Church in
South Africa, was awarded the peace prize in 1984. Egil Aarvik, the chair of
the Norwegian Nobel Committee, in his presentation of the prize to Tutu
referred to the prize awarded twenty-three years earlier to the black South
African leader Albert Luthuli.[2] Aarvik explained, "It is the Committee's
wish that this year's award should be seen as a renewed recognition of the
courage and heroic patience shown by black South Africans in their use of
peaceful means to oppose the apartheid system."[3]

Tutu was born in 1931 in Klerksdorp, Transvaal. An early aspiration to
become a doctor was abandoned because of his family's limited means,
so he followed his father in becoming a teacher. In 1957, however, the
apartheid government imposed tough new limitations on the segregated
(and severely underfunded) black education system. At that point, Tutu
decided to become an Anglican minister, hoping to continue serving his
people effectively in that role. Twenty-one years later, he was named the
first black general secretary of the South African Council of Churches,
which became a major force in the country's antiapartheid movement: it
ministered to thousands of survivors of the system's violence, challenged
white church-people to examine their role in the apartheid system, and
mobilized international support for the antiapartheid movement.

In the early 1990s, the apartheid system was overturned in a transition
from minority rule to egalitarian democracy that was remarkable for its
orderliness. (In 1993, African National Congress (ANC) head Nelson Mandela and apartheid-era President Frederik W. de Klerk were jointly named

peace laureates for their leadership in negotiating that transition.) In 1995, as part of the transition, the new democratic administration under President Mandela fulfilled a promise to establish the Truth and Reconciliation Commission, with a mandate to investigate the violence committed by all sides during the apartheid era. Tutu was named its chair.

Oscar Arias Sánchez, former president of Costa Rica, was named a laureate in 1987. He was cited for his pioneering role in sponsoring the Esquipulas-II agreement among five Central American states that were then snared in one of the most horrific regionwide systems of violence associated with the latter years of the global cold war.

Born in 1941, Arias trained as an economist and became a protégé of Costa Rica's legendary president José Figueres Ferrer, the man who abolished the country's standing army in 1948. Arias won his first cabinet post in 1972; fourteen years later he was elected president. Immediately, he plunged into the challenge of regional peacemaking.

After receiving the peace prize, he established the Arias Foundation for Peace and Human Progress, whose main aims are to promote gender equality, to strengthen civil society, and to resolve or defuse military conflicts in the developing world. In 1997, Betty Williams, the Dalai Lama, and the 1986 peace laureate, Elie Wiesel, joined Arias in his project of issuing the International Code of Conduct on Arms Transfers, which they asked all arms-exporting nations to sign. This code—which was later endorsed by thirteen other peace prize winners, as well as the former president Jimmy Carter and other personalities—seeks to link the international transfer of "conventional" weapons in seven main categories to the recipient countries' records in assuring human and democratic rights (see chapter 8).

Tenzin Gyatso, His Holiness the Fourteenth Dalai Lama, is the spiritual head of the Tibet-based Mahayana strand of Buddhism and head of the Tibetans' India-based government-in-exile. He was awarded the peace prize in 1989. The Dalai Lama was (re-)born a simple country boy in eastern Tibet in 1935, and two years later he was recognized as the fourteenth incarnation of his country's historic Dalai Lama line. Raised in Tibet's capital, Lhasa, the Dalai Lama studied to become a spiritual and community leader. He was still a minor in 1950 when the Chinese communists, flushed with power after seizing control of nearly all their own country the previous year, moved to take over Tibet's mountain fastnesses too. For nine years, the young Dalai Lama and his advisors tried to find a formula for coexistence with the forces from Beijing; but in a series of bloody clashes in 1959, the Chinese made clear that they wanted to control Tibet and integrate it fully into their communist, "new" China. The Dalai Lama and thousands of other Tibetans escaped to India. Over the decades that followed, they kept alive there a good portion of their twenty-five-hundred-year-old Buddhist culture. Meanwhile, their compatriots back home were subjected to some of the worst depredations of the Mao Tse-tung years, including the Great Leap Forward, which devastated Tibetan (and Chinese) agriculture, and the Cultural Revolution, which sought to exterminate all traces of noncommunist thinking, including religious thinking.

In 1987, the Dalai Lama presented to the U.S. Congress a breakthrough peace plan. It called for establishing the whole of Tibet as a "zone of *ahimsa*" (zone of nonviolence) and giving a democratic Tibetan administration jurisdiction over all spheres of life except security and foreign affairs.[4] On awarding the peace prize to the Dalai Lama the following year, Aarvik noted, "It would be difficult to cite any historical example of a minority's struggle to secure its rights, in which a more conciliatory attitude to the adversary has been adopted than in the case of the Dalai Lama."[5]

Aung San Suu Kyi (pronounced Ong-san sue-chee) was born in Rangoon, Burma, in 1945.[6] She was the youngest child of General Aung San, a legendary leader of the movement to win Burmese independence from British colonial rule.[7] She was two years old when her father was killed, on the eve of Britain's withdrawal from Burma. She was then brought up by her mother, Daw (Aunt) Khin Kyi, a pioneer of female participation in independent Burma's strongly male-dominated political leadership who was named Burma's ambassador to India in 1960.

In 1962, General Ne Win mounted a coup against Burma's democratic administration and instituted an increasingly brutal form of leftist dictatorship over the country. Daw Khin Kyi sought refuge in India and Aung San Suu Kyi stayed with her. Aung San Suu Kyi completed her education in India and Britain, earning a degree in philosophy, politics, and economics from St. Hugh's College, Oxford, in 1967.

In 1988, Daw Khin Kyi, now back in the Burmese capital, Rangoon, suffered a stroke. Aung San Suu Kyi was allowed to return home to help nurse her mother, and so she was in Burma when vast demonstrations against military rule broke out there later that year. The demonstrations caught the

military by surprise: after restoring a semblance of order, the military reluc-
tantly agreed to hold elections for a new parliament. These elections were
held in May 1990, and the National League for Democracy (NLD),
headed by the youthful Daw Suu, won a stunning 82 percent of the seats.
The military (which had reorganized its administration under the Orwellian name of the State Law and Order Restoration Council—SLORC)
immediately backtracked: the new chamber, they said, would have only a
consultative function but no real powers of governance. Later the election
results were summarily annulled. They also kept Daw Suu under the tight
house arrest to which they had confined her the previous year.

The Nobel selection committee named Daw Suu as its laureate in 1991,
citing her commitment to democracy and nonviolent political reform.
She was unable to travel to Norway to accept her prize. (Or rather, the
SLORC may have been happy to see her leave the country but would give
her no guarantee she would ever be allowed back.) Her elder son received
the prize on her behalf.

Throughout the 1990s, Daw Suu and her colleagues in the NLD continued to seek negotiations with the SLORC, but the SLORC kept her
under near-total house arrest and forbade her husband and sons to visit
her.[8] Elsewhere in the country, numerous other NLD organizers, including 235 of its elected parliamentarians, were thrown into jail; many of them
died under torture.[9]

Daw Suu did not attend the University of Virginia gathering. While the
military would—as always—have been glad to see her leave Burma, once
again, they gave no guarantee that she would be allowed to return. She chose
to remain in Rangoon, maintaining what contact she could with her people.

Harn Yawnghwe spoke on behalf of Aung San Suu Kyi at the conference. He was born in 1948. His father, Sao Shwe Thaike, was hereditary
prince of one of Burma's many ethnic minorities, the Shan: in that capacity,
the prince had negotiated (with Daw Suu's father) the terms of minority-
majority relations in the soon-to-be-independent, federated country. Sao
Shwe Thaike was then the first president of independent Burma, and in
1952 he became speaker of its upper house. His wife, too, was a pioneer in
Burmese politics: she was elected to Parliament in 1956. Then, during the
1962 military takeover, Sao Shwe Thaike was killed. His widow left for the
family's homeland in Shan state, where she headed one of the many groups
fighting against Burmese military domination.

Harn Yawnghwe received the rest of his education in Thailand and Canada. From there, he contributed to relief efforts for Indochinese refugees, and helped to translate the Bible into the Shan language, while becoming increasingly involved in pro-democracy activism. In 1997, he was named head of the Euro-Burma Office in Brussels—a project sponsored by the European Union to help prepare Burmese citizens and their institutions for a future transition to democracy.

Rigoberta Menchú Tum was awarded the peace prize in 1992. She is a K'iche'—a member of one of Guatemala's twenty-one Mayan groups. A radiant figure in traditional K'iche' dress, and with a ready smile, she was accompanied to the conference by her husband and her young son, Mash.

Born in 1959, Menchú was easily the youngest of the laureates participating. Her growing-up years were scarred by recurring intercommunal violence that—often with some stoking from the U.S. Central Intelligence Agency—marked Guatemalan life for many decades. She grew up extremely poor, working for a pittance on coffee plantations.

In 1979, she and her brothers joined an organization of peasant activists that her father had helped found. Her younger brother Petrocinio was betrayed to brutal local *jefes* later that year and was tortured badly before being killed in a mass public execution. Soon after that, her father and other activists were mown down inside the Spanish Embassy, where they had sought asylum, in an assault by Guatemalan troops that violated every international norm of diplomatic immunity. Three months later, her mother was kidnapped, raped, tortured, and left for dead on a remote hillside.[10]

A grief-stricken Menchú fled to Mexico. Starting in 1982, she became deeply involved in UN activities related to the rights of indigenous peoples: she attended UN General Assembly sessions on indigenous rights issues and participated in the annual sessions of the UN's Commission on Human Rights. In 1992, when she became the youngest person ever to be awarded a peace prize, the new chairman of the Nobel committee, Francis Sejersted, declared that "by maintaining a disarming humanity in a brutal world, Rigoberta Menchú Tum appeals to the best in all of us, wherever we live and whatever our background. . . . There is a most urgent need to define the rights of aboriginal peoples and to respect those rights. . . . To succeed in this, we need people like Rigoberta Menchú Tum."[11]

Since becoming a laureate, Menchú has continued to work for the rights of indigenous peoples around the world and in her native country. She also established the Rigoberta Menchú Tum Foundation, which conducts social-welfare, education, and conflict-resolution projects in Guatemala and other parts of Central America.

José Ramos-Horta of East Timor was awarded the peace prize in 1996, jointly with East Timorese Bishop Carlos Ximenes Belo. In his citation that year, Sejersted noted Ramos-Horta's "efforts to unite the various East Timorese groups into a single national front, while constantly seeking opportunities for a peaceful solution to the conflict with Indonesia."[12]

Ramos-Horta was born in East Timor's capital, Dili, in 1949. At that time, the country was still part of Portugal's far-flung global empire. Until 1974, Portugal and its imperial holdings continued to be ruled by one of Western Europe's two surviving 1930s-era military/fascist dictatorships; but that year, a peaceful pro-democracy coup overthrew the dictatorship. The new Portuguese administration immediately started to dismantle the imperial system.

Portugal's former dictators had done nothing in any of their former colonies to prepare the tightly subjugated local people for independence. In East Timor, the result was that a highly vulnerable community of around 800,000 people was left to the mercy of neighboring Indonesia. With its population of 200 million and a strong, U.S.-backed military, Indonesia was able to overrun the tiny (but mineral-rich) territory of East Timor easily in December 1975.

In the weeks preceding the Indonesian invasion, the East Timorese tried to establish their own independent government. The young Ramos-Horta was named its minister for external relations and ambassador to the United Nations.[13] When Indonesia invaded, he was able — in a narrative now depressingly familiar — to escape into exile. Those of his compatriots who stayed in East Timor faced grisly retribution from the Indonesian military. Over the next four years, an estimated one-third of East Timoreans were massacred or lost their lives to war-related starvation or disease.[14] Ramos-Horta himself lost three of his siblings to Indonesian assaults in those years.

In 1992, Ramos-Horta launched a new peace initiative, calling for a three-phase process leading to a verifiable act of self-determination by the people of East Timor.[15] But the long-time Indonesian dictator, President

Suharto, always refused to discuss these demands. Then, in the spring of 1998, mass demonstrations in Indonesia forced Suharto to resign. By late 1998, Ramos-Horta and his compatriots had reason to hope that their long campaign for independence might be gaining momentum.

There remained, however, much potential for violence in East Timor. In late August 1999, the United Nations held a territory-wide referendum in which all adult East Timoreans were able to choose between independence and a continued tie to Indonesia. After 78.5 percent of them voted for independence, the Indonesian troops who were still supposedly responsible for security went on a punishing anti-independence rampage that was halted only two weeks later, after the UN Security Council finally agreed to send in international peacekeepers.

Jody Williams won the peace prize in 1997 jointly with the International Campaign to Ban Landmines (ICBL), of which she had been the coordinator. She was born in Vermont in 1950 and grew up with a strong interest in international affairs. In 1976, she went to Mexico for two years as an English-language teacher; then she returned to the United States to earn a master's in international affairs from Johns Hopkins University. From 1986 through 1992, she was deputy director of the nonprofit group Medical Aid of El Salvador, with special responsibility for its child health programs.

In 1992, the Vietnam Veterans of America Foundation (VVAF) hired Williams to coordinate a new international campaign that the foundation and medico international, a German nongovernmental group, hoped to launch. The campaign sought to cut off *at their source* the miseries inflicted by antipersonnel landmines on numerous communities around the globe. The groups planned to achieve this goal by securing an international ban on the production, sale, export, and deployment of this devastating form of weaponry.

For five years, Williams devoted her considerable organizational flair to coordinating the ICBL's network of nongovernmental organizations (NGOs) around the world. By 1998, the network comprised some twelve hundred organizations, operating in more than fifty different countries. As each NGO mounted increasing political pressure on its own government, some smaller and midsized governments started competing to demonstrate their leadership in the relentlessly escalating campaign.[16] In October 1996, Canadian Foreign Minister Lloyd Axworthy stunned some of his more staid counterparts by laying down an open challenge to governments around the world to complete negotiations on a total landmine ban and to open the resulting treaty for signatures—all within the unprecedentedly short period of twelve months.

Many other governments—but not, in the end, that of the United States—took up Axworthy's challenge. Axworthy, the ICBL, and their allies brought the negotiations to a successful conclusion at a meeting in Oslo, Norway, in September 1997. By the end of April 1999, a total of 135 governments had signed the treaty, which entered into force on March 1, 1999.

Bobby Muller was cofounder of the ICBL, which had received the peace prize jointly with Jody Williams in 1997. Born in Austria in 1946, Muller migrated to the United States with his family at a young age, and grew up on New York's Long Island. He graduated from Hofstra University in 1967 and immediately fulfilled a strong ambition to enlist in the U.S. Marines. "I chose infantry, and I chose Vietnam," he said, adding that he had been quite aware of the dangers faced by young infantry officers there. In 1969, he suffered a combat injury to his spine: that injury left him unable to use his legs.

At the University of Virginia conference, as Muller wheeled himself onto or off the stage in his wheelchair, his paraplegia served to underline the continuing personal and social costs being paid by *all* the victims of the Vietnam War. As he came to grips with his injury after his return to the United States, Muller joined other Vietnam veterans in an increasingly effective veterans rights campaign. In 1980, he helped found the VVAF, and in 1987, he became its president. Under his leadership, the foundation reached out to fellow victims of the war from what had been the "other" side of the firing line in Southeast Asia. One of the foundation's first outreach projects helped to establish physical rehabilitation programs in Cambodia, where Muller saw firsthand the devastating legacies of the U.S. bombings of the 1970s, of the internal genocide later launched under dictator Pol Pot, and of landmines. In the 1990s, those mines, which had been sown during earlier decades of upheaval, continued to kill and maim civilians and to deny vast swaths of otherwise usable land to Cambodia's land-poor peasantry.

Muller, the VVAF, their counterparts in Cambodia, and others active in postwar rehabilitation movements around the world soon decided that dealing with the *effects* of the millions of landmines still planted in numerous countries around the world was no longer enough. That was when they launched the ICBL. When the Nobel committee awarded the peace prize to the ICBL and Jody Williams, committee chair Sejersted noted, "You have helped to rouse public opinion all over the world against the use of an arms technology that strikes quite randomly at the most innocent and most defenseless."

Moderating the interactions among the laureates was *Julian Bond*, the chair of the National Association for the Advancement of Colored People (NAACP) and a history professor at the University of Virginia.

THE CONSTRUCTION OF a robust moral self, philosopher Charles Taylor tells us, depends crucially on the elaboration of a satisfactory narrative of and for that self.[17] At the level of that curious social construction known as a nation, elaboration of a national narrative, or a national "story," is equally required. It provides an explanation of national origins and exceptionalism. It builds solidarity among otherwise disparate groups who are considered part of the nation. And it seeks to increase the sense of identification that individual citizens feel with the nation of which they are part.[18] Any nation-level culture requires its own panoply of national stories, and equally important, its individual national heroes: its George Washington, forever avowing to his father that he cannot tell a lie; its Jeanne d'Arc; its fearless Voortrekkers; its "Heroes of Soviet Labor"; and so on.

But what of the future *globewide* human culture that people might hope to build over coming decades? Who are its heroes to be; what narratives, its stories?

Just over a century ago, the Stockholm-born inventor of dynamite found that he had accrued a considerable personal fortune, largely in the arms-production business, and he undertook what may be considered a supremely redemptive act: he wrote a will dedicating much of his fortune to funding five annual prizes, to be awarded to "those who, during the preceding year, shall have conferred the greatest benefit on mankind." One of these prizes, he wrote, should be given to "the person who shall have done the most or the best work for fraternity between nations, for the abolition or reduction of standing armies and for the holding and promotion of peace congresses." Thus, in the closing years of the nineteenth century, was born the Nobel Peace Prize. Alfred Bernhardt Nobel, their originator, died in 1896. Five years later, on December 10, 1901, the first Nobel Peace Prize was awarded.[19]

From the very beginning, the five Norwegian nationals who make up the peace prize selection committee have shone their spotlight of recognition primarily on individuals and organizations operating outside the networks of formal, intergovernmental relations. These prizes have been awarded both to individuals and—in a slight amendment to Alfred Nobel's will—to groups of individuals working together in nongovernmental associations. In its first year, 1901, the prize was divided equally between French national Frédéric Passy, the founder of his country's first peace society, and Swiss national Jean-Henri Dunant, the founder of the International Committee of the Red Cross.[20] In 1906, U.S. President Theodore Roosevelt became the first of only a handful of heads of state to be named laureates over the years. The first of the dozen woman laureates, Baroness Bertha von Suttner, from Austria, received her award in 1905.

During the early decades of the peace prize, the purview of the selection committee still seemed bounded by the concerns of the Euro-American "first world." In 1936, the committee took a first, tentative step further south, naming a laureate from Argentina, Carlos Saavedra Lamas. In the 1940s, India's charismatic guru of nonviolent change, Mohandas Mahatma Gandhi, was on the shortlist for the prize "several times," according to selection committee secretary Geir Lundestad. In 1948, the committee finally came close to awarding the prize to Gandhi. But he was assassinated before the award could be made, and the committee decided against making a posthumous award.[21] In 1960, ANC head Albert Luthuli, from South Africa, was the second laureate to be named from outside the Euro-American heartland. In 1973, North Vietnamese Foreign Minister Le Duc Tho was the third laureate named from the "developing world," being named a colaureate with Henry Kissinger for the respective roles they played in fashioning the Paris Peace Accords—but Le declined the award.

It was not until the late 1970s that the awards became anything like truly global in their scope. Since then, many of the laureates—including those at the University of Virginia gathering—certainly must be considered among the heroes of the global culture of the future.

Alfred Nobel's visionary act in funding the peace prize has had, over the century since then, the notable effect of shining a spotlight of recognition and publicity on numerous people and organizations whose labors for peace might otherwise have gone underacknowledged. In addition, in more recent decades, it has created an increasingly *global* context within which many laureates have come to reframe their own concerns and activities in an increasingly global way, while it has also provided a globewide bully pulpit from which they could share and further promulgate these ideas.

It was notable that nearly all of the laureates represented at the University of Virginia conference named among their own heroes both Mahatma Gandhi and Dr. Martin Luther King Jr., the visionary African American advocate of equal rights and nonviolent social change who won the peace prize in 1964.[22]

True, a different kind of grouping of Nobel peace laureates could have been assembled in Charlottesville—one that, by including such figures as Henry Kissinger, South Africa's Frederik de Klerk, or Palestinian leader Yasser Arafat, might have ensured a stronger voice for practitioners of the "realist" brand of politics that still dominates most of the daily conduct of, and discourse about, world affairs. Indeed, a public dialogue between the Dalai Lama, or Bishop Tutu, and such a figure could have been a highly instructive encounter. But it would have been a very different encounter from that which occurred. For although the participating laureates expressed widely differing opinions on a number of issues, still, the overarching tenor of the gathering was that of a collaborative, group effort to think out loud about the moral parameters of a future world at peace. P. Jeffrey Hopkins, the professor in the University of Virginia's religious studies department who organized the conference with Michele Bohana, the director of the Institute for Asian Democracy in Washington, D.C., explained that "of the twenty-one living Nobel peace laureates, we invited several whom we knew had participated in group efforts before. . . . We also invited the most recent Nobel Peace Prize recipients."[23]

The individuals and organizations that have won a Nobel Peace Prize have often, throughout the one-hundred-year history of the prize, networked with one another on collaborative ventures. A number of the laureates who came to the Charlottesville gathering had made a joint attempt in 1993 to visit Aung San Suu Kyi in Burma. (The SLORC would not let them enter the country, stopping them at the border with Thailand.) In 1995, Oscar Arias invited all fellow Nobel peace laureates to join him in developing an International Code of Conduct on Arms Transfers and providing moral leadership for the code campaign. Among those who joined the commission Arias established were Betty Williams, Archbishop Tutu, the Dalai Lama, Rigoberta Menchú, José Ramos-Horta, and Jody Williams. In July 1997, four of the laureates who attended the University of Virginia conference were among a broader group who called on the world's governments to declare the first decade of the twenty-first century the Decade for a Culture of Nonviolence.[24]

In the short valedictory remarks he made at the end of the conference, University of Virginia President John Casteen III told the participating laureates, "Certain common threads run through the dialogue of these two days. Each of you has in some way exhorted us to individual action. Both words — 'individual' and 'action' — matter. We must transform ourselves as individuals before we can think of transforming the world. . . . You have told us to . . . recognize our responsibility, but also our power, as individual persons; to turn that recognition to fruitful action, and to conceive that action out of a sense of love and forgiveness."

He added, "You are the peacemakers of our time, revered by every people, by every religion. We see your strength and your courage as models for those whose lives you've touched in these short days, and I want to acknowledge that those qualities of yours are special contributions to education as we practice it here and at universities around the world. . . . Your lives are arguments that humankind is capable of making ethical progress."

Arguments, yes, but more than that: arguments backed up by powerful and thought-provoking stories. If, in the decades to come, the peoples of the world should prove willing to make the series of Copernican leaps that will be needed to build a world at peace, then these stories can provide some of the building blocks for the future global culture.

THERE THEY WERE then, gathered on the stage in Cabell Hall: three women and seven men of great talent and vision, and with striking — and often, strikingly interlocking — stories to tell.

The format of the two days of conversations had — by the conscious design of Michele Bohana and Jeffrey Hopkins — been kept as open-ended as possible. The conversations were as remarkable for the breadth of their purview as for the interweaving of their many common threads. The moral architecture that the laureates sketched out was built on the following broad imperatives:

- to pay continuing attention to the human and civil rights of people in *all* the world's communities
- to work to build constructive and respectful modes of coexistence among all groups, peoples, and nations
- to find robust and workable alternatives to violence as a means of resolving disputes at every level of human interaction
- to turn away from continued reliance on armed force
- to escape from all systems of suspicion and violence, including those that have placed the profit, claimed property rights, and personal convenience of people in the rich world far ahead of the basic needs of our fellow humans in poor countries.[25]

THE DISCUSSIONS CARRIED out by the laureates were an important current strand in the deliberations that have preoccupied political thinkers and philosophers since the dawn of human life. What is the role of the individual in public life? What does the individual owe to the varying levels of community of which he or she is a part: to family, "nation," government, his or her own conscience—or to all of humanity? How can people from different cultural groups, faiths, worldviews, or traditions, try to get along? How can people deal with, but also get beyond, the gross injustices of the past? How can individuals even start to define some of these terms like *justice, nation, culture,* or *humanity?*

While the laureates were wrestling with these issues, all of them—all of us—gathered in Cabell Hall started to engage actively in the process of *imagining a future world at peace.* Such imagining is important.[26] For example, many people today consider the system of nation-state governance "natural": beyond that, many also consider the underlying "fact" of the division of the world's people into discrete "nations" to be an equally natural state of affairs. But sociologist Benedict Anderson is only one of many scholars who have charted out the very concrete mechanisms through which, in numerous different cases around the world, these "national communities" were constituted in the first place.[27] Anderson's key insights are that the idea of a national community is always in some way first *imagined,* even before it is constituted, and that the dimensions of this *imagining* help powerfully to define those of the later constituted entity.

Since the end of the cold war, numerous policymakers and high-level analysts have engaged in public discussion of the "security architecture" or the "financial architecture" of the world of the twenty-first century. But few of these suggested "architectures" propose doing much beyond fiddling at the margins of the world system as we know it today. Few ask the deeper questions about what kinds of responsibilities people in different human groups should have toward each other. Few even start to tackle the complex problems raised by the issue of state sovereignty; few question the state-dominated, political assumptions on which most of the Western theory of international relations has been built until now. Pitifully few have gone on to reexamine the existential and moral underpinnings of those assumptions; few, therefore, have done anything that can be said to contribute to sketching out the moral architecture of a future world at peace.

The laureates gathered in Charlottesville started to do just that. In doing so, they aptly illustrated Kant's dictum, "Though politics is a difficult art, no art is required to combine it with morality. For as soon as the two come into conflict, morality can cut through the knot which politics cannot untie."[28]

In addition, these men and women brought to the forum a wealth of engaging human stories—stories whose telling can inspire us and help us think through the issues of human governance that lie behind them.

2

The Dalai Lama and the Need for Internal
and External Disarmament

A person forced to flee his country at a young age and live in
exile for more than forty years. A leader who daily hears news
of the sufferings inflicted on his people and the ongoing destruction of
their ancient religion and culture. How do we expect such a person to be?

When Tom Sitzman, a second-year math and biology major at the
University of Virginia, learned in July 1998 that the Dalai Lama was coming to the university later that year, he knew he wanted to see him. In
early November, Sitzman was first in line for the free tickets being
handed out for the laureates' event. Though the weather was freezing and
the ticket booth would not open until early the following Monday, Sitzman and others set up their tents beside the booth around midnight the
preceding Saturday.

Soon enough, the line snaked clear around the football stadium. Students adapted quickly to the new lifestyle: tents, textbooks, boom boxes,
barbecue grills, guitars, old pizza boxes, and inert figures in sleeping
bags were strewn all around the stadium. The faces—African American,
European American, Asian American—were sleepy, but eager. "As soon as
I heard about the conference, I knew it was a once-in-a-lifetime experience," Sitzman said on Monday morning. Other denizens of the line nod-
ded their bleary-eyed agreement.

So what did those who were encountering this global figure for the first
time see? A physically large man of undefinable presence. A man draped in
elegant burgundy robes. But also—and this was evident from the laureates'
very first photo call outside Thomas Jefferson's historic rotunda—a person
stripped of all bitterness; a person of great playfulness, gentleness, and

17

humor. "What I like about the Dalai Lama," Archbishop Tutu said later in the conference, "is that, really, he is very *naughty*."

Indeed he was. At times throughout the gathering, both these laureates —men from whom a high degree of public decorum might be expected— would horse around behind the table like a couple of eight-year-olds. Thinking about this afterward, I guessed that perhaps people who have to bear the aching, lifelong burdens these two have carried find that humor and a childlike quality can help them to endure.

Archbishop Tutu's daughter Naomi has written of her father, "There is some truth to the theory that he laughs and tries to get others to do so to stop himself from crying. However, I think there is also the realization that no situation is completely devoid of any joy or hope, for once that becomes true, then there is no reason to struggle or live. In addition, he believes that humor is liberating because once you begin to take yourself or your situation in life too seriously, you become a prisoner of your self-perception."[1]

These qualities of lightheartedness and self-awareness are also among those enjoined by the respective religious traditions in which these men have been schooled: Christianity and Buddhism. From the Christian perspective, Dr. Martin Luther King Jr. reminded us in one of his sermons that "we must not stop with the cultivation of a tough mind. The gospel also demands a tender heart."[2]

The Dalai Lama learned the teachings of Mahayana Buddhism first in the natural piety of his parents' modest home in northern Tibet. After the two-year-old was discovered to be the reincarnate Dalai Lama, he was taken in a vast, horse-mounted cavalcade to the Tibetan spiritual and administrative capital, Lhasa, where he was installed in a suite of rooms high up in the towering, centuries-old Potala Palace. At the age of six, he started his formal religious education in Lhasa through intensive study of ancient Tibetan-Buddhist texts, debate and discussion with other monks, and lengthy periods of personal and group meditation. These studies have continued ever since and have been supplemented by His Holiness's interest in many other branches of learning. From the Buddhist perspective, lightheartedness is considered valuable since it helps to further the important goals of self-transcendence and increasing compassion with all sentient beings.

THE DALAI LAMA did not deliver his main presentation to the conference until the end of the second day. But what he said in his presentation about the relevance of nonviolent action and nuclear disarmament in today's world provided a sturdy conceptual foundation for the entire, two-day-long deliberation. Therefore, it makes sense to bring those words to the front of the book while presenting what His Holiness said about the situation of his people in Tibet in chapter 5.[3]

His Holiness focused most of his presentation on his theory of nonviolent action. He started his discussion by changing the terms of the visual interaction between himself and the hushed audience awaiting his words: he asked hall managers to turn up the house lights. Then, speaking in forceful, staccato bursts laced with periodic exclamations of "So!" he took the audience to the heart of the theory of nonviolence: the need for what he called "inner disarmament." Most advocates and practitioners of nonviolent social action believe that violence is an interpersonal or intercommunal *system* into which any of us can easily become locked, but that with an increase in awareness—of the existence and dynamics of this system, and of our own role within it—we can start to take actions that will help to transform the relationships involved into more productive, less harmful ties. Often, as many of the laureates illustrated at the conference, that increase in awareness will involve making a Copernican leap beyond an individual's previous, more self-bounded view of various issues.

His Holiness's first focus was on the importance of considering the motivation of the person or persons against whom you are struggling for your rights:

I believe that in human actions, the prime mover is *motivation*. So of course, the immediate result, it is very, very important to tackle the symptoms of these things. Then, in the long run, it is very, very important, I feel, to look at motivation: whether there is a possibility to change that motivation. . . . You see, so long as the negative motivation or negative emotion does not change, then . . . human beings have the ability to find some ways to express their negative feeling. So therefore, in the long run, looking at motivation: try to *change* that motivation. That means, try to cultivate the *right* kind of motivation, and try to *reduce* the negative motivation. . . .

Now I think of the horrible climate condition that happened in Central America [Hurricane Mitch, of 1998]. Such sort of violent things . . . are without any motivation—so we call it a natural disaster.

That, we can't avoid. But other types of violence, which are created by humans, ourselves: there, motivation is involved. So that kind of violence, which is a result of human motivation, now there, we can change [it], we can reduce [it]. And I mean, there is a possibility to eliminate it. So, there, I think, we should try to change the attitude. Try to cultivate the right kind of motivation.

How? Through which method? I feel that prayer or religious belief in some extent is useful, and can be helpful. But, basically, I feel, simply awareness: awareness of the consequences of long-term, short-term effects. If we make clear the negative consequences for the long run . . . I think that eventually people can develop a clear realization of these negative things.

Violent activities are bad because they bring a painful experience and unhappiness.

His Holiness then asked a question that has been central to advocates of nonviolent social and political change throughout the years: what is it, precisely, that distinguishes violence from nonviolence? His answer:

We can't judge. We can't make a clear demarcation on violence and nonviolence on a superficial basis, it has to do with motivation. . . . Certain verbal action, as does physical action, looks more dreadful, looks more violent, harsher. But essentially, because these activities come out of sincere motivation, or compassion, or sense of caring, they are, essentially, nonviolent. On the other hand, with negative motivation, try to cheat, try to exploit, try to deceive, and . . . use nice words, a big smile (although artificial smile), some kind of smile, like that, and [come] with some gift: it *looks* like a nonviolent, friendly gesture, but because of the motivation, I think it is the worst kind of violence!

So, the violence can [claim that it is a] manifestation or expression of compassion; but nonviolence is *actually* the expression of compassion. So therefore, the concept of nonviolence and compassion is something very, very close.

Other theorists of nonviolence have expressed slightly varying views on this question. Mahatma Gandhi's Hinduism-based, social action strategy of *satyagraha* is related in many ways to the Dalai Lama's Buddhism-based view of nonviolence. Like the Dalai Lama, Gandhi also stressed the role of motivation in defining violence. For him, it was *an intention to coerce another living being* that constituted violence. "Coercion," he said, "is violence to the soul."[4] But while Gandhi, like Quakers and members of other Christian peace churches, all agree with the Dalai Lama that motivation is important, they also consider that a "good" motivation can never render an inherently violent act acceptable. For example, Gandhi wrote in 1921, "It is my firm conviction that there is an intimate connection between the end and the means, so much so that you cannot achieve a good end by bad means."[5]

But certainly, neither the Dalai Lama nor any of these other advocates of nonviolence has ever equated pacifism with "passive-ism." His Holiness noted in his talk,

> When we talk about nonviolence, peace, this does not mean that we remain indifferently, passively. Problems and contradictions always remain there. I believe, so long as human beings remain there, as long as human intelligence remains there, some kind of conflict, some kind of contradiction always remains there. . . .
>
> We need some kind of method or technique to overcome that contradiction. That, I feel, is compromise. Today's reality: the only way to solve a problem is compromise. Since my interest is very much related with the other's interest, so therefore you can't sacrifice the other's interest. And therefore, compromise, 50-50. If possible, one's own side 60 percent, other side 40 percent! If possible! I think that's the best. Otherwise, in reality there is no possibility of 100 percent victory for oneself.

Turning to the present-day world, the leader of the hard-pressed Tibetans said he believes that wars have become unwinnable, mainly, he said, because of the close economic connections existing even between states that may be political rivals. "Under these circumstances, destruction of your enemy is actually destruction of yourself!" he said. "Judging from that viewpoint, the concept of 'we' and 'they' no longer exists. So the concept of war, destruction of the other side, is not relevant to today's situation."[6]

The view that large-scale warfare has become unwinnable in the modern age is one shared by many other major thinkers around the globe. American strategic analyst Bernard Brodie noted, after his government's successful use of atomic weapons in 1945, that the nature of warfare—and the mission of the American military establishment—had both been entirely transformed. From that moment on, Brodie said, the primary goal of the American military would be not to win, but to *avert* the outbreak of another "total" war.[7]

In a seminal sermon delivered in the mid-1950s, Dr. King recalled that he had once thought that "war, horrible as it is, might be preferable to surrender to a totalitarian system." But he said he later came to believe that "the potential destructiveness of modern weapons totally rules out the possibility of war ever again achieving [even] a negative good. If we assume that mankind has a right to survive, then we must find an alternative to war and destruction."[8]

At the level of large-scale warfare between major modern states, the Dalai Lama's judgment that wars have become unwinnable may indeed be correct. But as he pointed out, popular perceptions regarding war have too frequently lagged behind this reality. He urged his listeners to make the kind of transcendental leap beyond their present system of thinking that would enable them to look at the world's conflicts from a broader, more holistic—and more realistic—standpoint:

> We are carrying a certain way of thinking which is essentially an old way of thinking. . . . "My nation/their nation," "my religion/other religion." Sometimes, these have the beautiful name "patriotism." Patriotism! Too much narrow-minded patriotism, what you call "nationalism": from this, sometimes, people become mad!
>
> Therefore, the situation in which we live is much changed, but the *people* who are in that situation, their thinking still is something a little different. That, sometimes, I feel is one of the causes of our unnecessary pain, unnecessary problems.
>
> Therefore, we need education that the concept of violence is very bad, that it is not a realistic way to solve the problem, and that compromise is the only realistic way to solve the problem. I think that *the answer is in the child's mind*, the younger generation, the new generation. Right from the beginning we have to make clear this reality. In that way, I think our whole attitude toward oneself, toward the world, toward the "other," can be a more healthy attitude. This, I usually call "inner disarmament." Without inner disarmament, it is very difficult to achieve genuine, lasting world peace.[9]

Notably, he did *not* ask his listeners to turn completely away from self-concern. Instead, in a move similar to Western thinkers' exhortations to pursue an "enlightened" self-interest, he urged his listeners to develop a greater sense of caring for others, arguing that this compassion would bring increased well-being to the self:

A sense of caring for others is actually the *best* way of caring for oneself! Because [the] human [by] nature is a social animal. I think in simple things, we need human companions. We need human companions, with a genuine human smile. That provides us comfort, satisfaction. . . . The moment you think of others, this automatically opens your inner door. Through that way you can communicate with others very easily, without any difficulties.

The moment you think just of yourself and disregard others, then because of your own attitude, you also get the feeling: oh, other people also have a similar attitude toward you. That brings suspicion, fear. Result? You yourself lose inner calmness.

Therefore, usually I say if we are selfish, selfishness is basically right. Happiness of the self: it's our right. Also, we have every right to overcome suffering. . . . But selfishness which leads to no hesitation to harm one another, to exploit one another: that kind of selfishness is a blind selfishness! Therefore, I sometimes jokingly describe: if we are selfish, then we should be "wise-selfish" rather than "foolish-selfish." I feel that the moment you take a sense of caring for others, that brings inner strength. Inner strength brings us inner tranquillity, more selfconfidence.

So, through these things, even though your surroundings may not be friendly or may not be positive, still you can sustain your peace of mind. That much, according to my own little experience, I can tell you.

He contended that this process of self-transcendence, or "inner disarmament," is also beneficial to one's physical health: "With peace of mind, a calm mind, your body elements become more balanced. Constant worry, constant fear, agitation of mind, are very bad for health. So, therefore, peace of mind not only brings peace and tranquillity in our mind, but also has a very good effect for our body!"

At one point in the conference, Jeffrey Hopkins asked the Dalai Lama this question, relayed to him by an audience member: "Does His Holiness find from his personal experience that philosophical ideas affect people's behavior? For example, does he see that an overemphasis on oneself, as opposed to an emphasis on helping others, affects one's behavior?"

"I don't know!" the Dalai Lama replied.

First of all, I don't know what is the exact meaning of "philosophy." So anyway, it is a certain way of thinking—of vision, or certain deeper meanings: such a belief, or viewpoint. Certainly, it is *widened* view toward oneself, toward others. Now, for example, one Buddhist view or philosophy: interdependency. Now that view is very, very helpful to widen our perspective. . . . [It is] the view or the theory that one thing depends on many other factors. So one should see that sort of viewpoint or understanding there. And [when] one event happened here, immediately you see the sort of desire to look for wider implications, or the *causes* of conditions. So you see, "these things," rather than "this event itself." That way [of philosophizing], I can use. But otherwise, I don't know.

A little later, His Holiness returned to the second half of the question:

Now again, "individualism": that, I don't know the exact meaning [of]. But in any case, I want to say something: the moment one thinks of oneself, the whole mental focus is very narrow. So, within that narrow area, even small problems appear very big. The moment you should think about others, the mental level becomes very wide. So, one's small problem then, it appears [to have] no significance. That I think makes a big difference.

And then, another thing. When we develop a strong sense of caring of others, then when we hear or see pain or unfortunate experiences of others, then that also . . . a little disturbs your peace of mind, or your calm mind. But then, if you look down, or look deeper, there are big differences. Some kind of disturbances, or feeling of burden, out of a sense of caring for others: *that*, in deep there, that is a kind of volunteer[ism]. *You take care of others. You are taking someone's serious concern of others directly.*

So, deep inside, it is something voluntarily you accept. And, on the basis [of] that feeling, there is inner strength. You have selfconfidence. And on that, you have the *courage*, you see, to take *care* of others.

So the other ones just think of "myself, myself," and some kind of unfortunate things happen. That's really provable. So, in a deep sense, deep down, there are big differences. So I think that in thinking about others, actually, is a *great* benefit to oneself.

ALONGSIDE INNER DISARMAMENT, His Holiness argued strongly for the need for *external* disarmament. He based this part of his argument first on the conclusion he'd expressed earlier that war in the present age has become unwinnable. He also argued that even today's enemy, "if you treat them well, the next day will be a good friend." (Forty years earlier, Dr. King described the impression he had received, during a visit to India, of the aftereffects of Gandhi's successful nonviolent struggle against the British: "The aftermath of hatred and bitterness that usually follows a violent campaign was found nowhere in India, and *a mutual friendship*, based on complete equality, existed between the Indian and British people within the Commonwealth."[10])

The Dalai Lama argued that the peoples of the world should start cooperating with each other for another reason, too, the emergence of transnational problems like overpopulation, and the degradation of the natural environment. "These are not a question of my nation's survival," he said. "These are a question of the survival of humanity! These bigger issues, I think, these are our *common* responsibility to tackle. Compared to these bigger things, small, small things within ourselves are minor."

He noted that some progress had been made toward "external" disarmament, but not yet nearly enough. He urged his listeners to start working for nothing less than a totally demilitarized world:

My dream is that one day the whole world should be demilitarized. But you cannot achieve that overnight. Also, you cannot achieve that without a proper, systematic plan. However, *it is very important to make some kind of clear target!* Even though it may take one hundred years, or fifty years, that doesn't matter. But make some kind of a clear idea, or clear target; then, try to achieve that step by step.

I think as a first step, we have already started the elimination of antipersonnel mines, and the biological [weapons]: these things are now starting. Also, now, already now [we are] reducing nuclear weapons. Now eventually, there should be the total ban of nuclear weapons. I think these things now are foreseeable, now are possible. These ideas are coming now. I think these are great, hopeful signs.

So, that is external disarmament!

AT THE CONCLUSION of his presentation, all present rose to their feet in a lengthy ovation that seemed to express both a recognition of the strength of His Holiness' presence, and overwhelming support for what he had said. In Cabell Hall that afternoon, it seemed that no one made the judgment that has sometimes been leveled against the Dalai Lama—that his ideas are "too idealistic" or "not practical."

And perhaps his listeners were right. The past couple of decades have (as the Dalai Lama noted) seen remarkable strides toward nonviolent resolution of some—though by no means all—previously bitter conflicts, as well as some progress on the disarmament front. How "realistic," though, are the two key arguments he voiced in his presentation: that nonviolent solutions are always better than violent solutions, and that we can and should work for total world disarmament, including at the nuclear level?

On the broader point—that concerning the superiority of nonviolent solutions—can it honestly be said that the tactics of nonviolence would be any more effective, or long-lasting, than the tactics of military engagement used to confront a figure like Saddam Hussein or Slobodan Milosevic? Or how about the fight against the apartheid regime in South Africa: fine though the Dalai Lama's words may have been, was it not the armed struggle initiated by Nelson Mandela and the African National Congress (ANC) that ended up toppling apartheid?

These are not easy issues to untangle. In the case of South Africa, it might be valid to conclude that it was a combination of three things that ended up toppling apartheid. There was the ANC's armed struggle, yes. But the periodic sabotage attacks carried out by the ANC and other opponents of apartheid never, by themselves, came close to toppling the system. Alongside them, however, was the massive participation by South Africa's non-"White" peoples in prolonged campaigns of classic civil disobedience, as well as the broad embargo maintained by the international community on any economic dealings with the apartheid regime. Those latter two were classic tactics of nonviolent struggle—descended from nonviolent tactics developed within South Africa in the early 1900s by Mahatma Gandhi, himself. And as the apartheid system became weaker and more isolated during the 1970s and 1980s, the two nonviolent strands of the struggle came to assume an increasingly important role in bringing pressure on the architects of *apart-hood* that resulted, in the 1990s, in the victory of the democratic forces.[11]

In the case of Milosevic or Saddam Hussein, "realists" have continued to argue that the use of force may prove "necessary." And yes, past uses of forces against those dictators may have seemed—temporarily, at least—to solve some of the problems that they posed. But they notably have not resolved the core issue of bringing a lasting stability to the regions in which those two men rule.

For his part, His Holiness is no stranger to the terrible problems a community can face when it comes under the rule of a brutal dictatorship; indeed, the whole topic of the practicability and effectiveness of nonviolent struggle in confronting extreme governmental repression—in various countries around the world, including Tibet—is one that recurred often during the laureates' conference, and therefore forms a major theme in the present book. In this context, it is worth recalling that Gandhi even urged people living under Hitler's fascism to try to develop ways of sustaining nonviolent resistance to it; during some of the mostly sharply polarized years of the global cold war, there were numerous researchers in the United States and Western Europe who were planning for a nonviolent defense of Western Europe against any future Soviet invasion. (Many of them used the term *social defense* for this concept.) Then, when the peoples of Eastern Europe did finally throw the yoke of Soviet control from their backs, they did so *not* through NATO's military might, but through the "velvet power" of their own mass civilian movements.[12]

But what about the prospects of using nonviolent strategies to deal with gross instances of repression *in countries far from our own?* When we hear about gross human rights abuses in places like Bosnia, Rwanda, or Kosovo, what options do those of us lucky enough to live in wealthy, secure Western nations have to intervene?

One immediate response is often the humanitarian response. And during the past century, literally millions of people from scores of different national communities have had their lives saved—or immeasurably improved—through the efforts of the modern age's globe-circling network of humanitarian organizations. Sometimes, though, those successes have been accompanied by troubling side effects. The effect of some purely humanitarian interventions can—as the United Nations High Commissioner for Refugees, Mrs. Sadako Ogata, has pointed out—serve to prolong and deepen conflicts, or to institutionalize the results of previous instances of "ethnic cleansing." Sometimes, too, well-meaning foreign-based NGOs can have devastating effects on local commodities markets and governance structures, by temporarily flooding a needy community with inappropriate forms and amounts of relief aid. *Long-term capacity building* is the watchphrase that the more farsighted and effective international NGOs have adopted for overseas relief aid; but it is one that is applied too rarely by some of the less responsible actors in the international aid field.[13] Meanwhile, there is tragically little that even the best humanitarian organizations can do to *prevent the forces of repression from continuing their attacks*, and even less they can do to roll back the consequences of earlier abuses such as the "ethnic cleansing" of huge swathes of land.

Those around the world who are appalled by the seeming impotence of purely humanitarian interventions have felt rightly frustrated. Throughout the 1990s, one common response in the West to this frustration was to call for bringing in the military. These cases, surely—the thinking goes—must be ones where the vast technological capabilities of NATO forces can make a difference. This thinking is the origin of the phenomenon that some observers have dubbed "militarized humanitarianism." Clear examples in recent times include the dispatch of mainly Western military forces to Bosnia, Somalia, or Kosovo.[14]

There are numerous different points on the spectrum of militarized humanitarianism. All such efforts are described by their originators in humanitarian or salvationist terms. But in only a few of the cases seen in the 1990s has the military deployment in question succeeded in changing even the *behavior* of the rights abusers enough to bring about the establishment of a stable, rights-respecting, political order, let alone changing their deeper human motivations. Instead, most of those parts of the world where a major humanitarian effort has become militarized continue to suffer from deep-seated instability and ongoing large-scale rights abuses. Refugees continue to be denied the basic right to return to their homes in peace. Ethnic militias on all sides continue to arm and to prepare for the next round of bloodshed.

In this latter regard, the "demonstration effect" of the use of military force by the powerful-seeming Western nations should not be underestimated. Resorting to the use of highly destructive (and too often, carelessly applied) levels of force by the United States and its allies against various targets around the world sends a powerful message to everyone—including dictators and rights abusers—that the use of force to resolve differences with others is *quite okay*. Many Western policymakers seem to listen carefully to the Dalai Lama when he talks about Tibetan issues. But few seem to pay much heed when he gives more general advice like that which he reiterated during the discussion period at the conference: "Through nonviolence, whatever we achieve, the result, there is no negative side effect. Through violence, negative side effects. Through violence, even though we may get some kind of satisfaction, but negative side effects [are] also immense."

If militarized humanitarianism has generally registered little success in persuading (or *coercing*, to use a term of art of U.S. strategic planners) rights abusers to change their ways, is there something else that well-meaning outsiders can do to help that goes beyond forever applying the bandages of the humanitarian?

Possibly one of the best longer-term suggestions is that first proposed in 1993 by John Paul Lederach, an experienced citizen-mediator from the historically pacifist Mennonite tradition: the creation of a multicultural, global Peaceforce, which within seven years could consist of as many as 250,000 well-trained individuals committed to nonviolent activism. "The members would be paid and would enlist for five-year assignments following a full year of training," he explained. "The Peaceforce would accompany relief deliveries in settings of armed conflict, provide protection to vulnerable populations, and secure and monitor cease-fires while negotiations are pursued and implemented."[15] One would hope that the members of this force would also be charged with engaging in a direct and friendly fashion with members and leaders of the politically *dominant* communities in the areas of their deployment, in a concerted attempt to "reduce the negative motivation"—to borrow the Dalai Lama's words—that these people feel toward their neighbors.

If Lederach's suggestion had been taken up at the time he proposed it, we might already have the Peaceforce that he envisaged fully established and ready to deploy in crisis points like Kosovo or East Timor. Numerous additional problems would need to be addressed—like the key question (also faced by military forces) of gaining access to the crisis points in anything like sufficient numbers to get the job done. But already, even before the creation of a force as large as the one he proposed, groups like Peace Brigades International, Witness for Peace, or the Christian Peacemaker Teams, operating in small numbers in various crisis points, have demonstrated the kind of work that a future Peaceforce could do.[16]

It should be noted, meanwhile, that the stress His Holiness placed on the value of *caring*, or *compassion*, as a central tool in the tough task of conflict resolution has significant resonance with the contributions many Western feminist scholars have started making to the fields of political philosophy, ethics, and social and international affairs. Echoing the Dalai Lama's insistence that the human is, by nature, a social being, such scholars as Carol Gilligan, Martha Minow, Joan Tronto, and Nancy Chodorow have criticized the tendency of (male-dominated) traditional Western philosophy to consider the human person as a self-sufficient monad. Instead, these feminists have emphasized that interdependence is a constitutive part of the human condition, and they have created a conceptual framework for an "ethics of care." Building on this work, too, other feminist scholars (of both genders) have started to explore the global implications of this view.[17]

FINALLY, WHAT CAN be said about the Dalai Lama's vision of a world stripped of all of its weapons, including nuclear weapons? At a general level, it is evident that throughout human history the technological level of any group's armaments has been a major factor determining its ability to protect itself, and beyond that, to dominate other groups. The history of the Europe-based global empires was no exception to that. But with the United States' use in warfare of history's first two nuclear weapons, a terrifying new threshold was crossed. Over the decades that followed, as two nations built ever larger and more deadly nuclear arsenals, and others built their own somewhat smaller versions, it became evident that humankind could now, for the first time, with the pressing of a few nuclear hair-triggers, *wipe out all traces of life on earth.*

After the collapse of the Soviet Union in the early 1990s, the United States had a unique opportunity to lead an effort toward world nuclear disarmament. But so far it has chosen not to do so, despite the fact that as long ago as 1968, the United States and all other signatories of the Nuclear Non-

Proliferation Treaty (NPT) promised, in Article VI, to "pursue negotiations in good faith on effective measures relating to . . . nuclear disarmament, and on a treaty on general and complete disarmament under strict and effective international control."[18]

True, during the last third of the twentieth century, the two nuclear superpowers did engage in an effort first to control the growth of their nuclear arsenals and then to start reducing them. But as of the end of 1998, the second Strategic Arms Reduction Treaty (START-II) was still far from entry-into-force. And even that treaty would still allow Russia and the United States each to maintain between three thousand and five thousand "strategic" nuclear warheads—many times the number that would eliminate all human life on earth.[19]

Back in 1995, the government of the generally staid and always pro-American nation of Australia established the international Canberra Commission and charged it with examining the plausibility of eliminating nuclear weapons worldwide. The group's seventeen members included General Lee Butler, who as head of the U.S. Strategic Command from 1992 to 1994, had commanded two legs of the "triad" of American strategic nuclear weapons; Field Marshal Lord Carver, who was Chief of Britain's General Staff and Defense Staff in the 1970s; and Robert McNamara, who was U.S. Secretary of Defense under Presidents Kennedy and Johnson.[20]

In its final report, the Canberra Commission stated that "in the post–cold war environment, the argument for [nuclear] deterrence is largely circular. . . . The only military utility that remains for nuclear weapons is in deterring their use by others. That utility implies the continued existence of nuclear weapons. It would disappear if nuclear weapons were eliminated." The report noted that even if existing disarmament agreements were fully implemented, in 2003 the United States and Russia would still have large stocks of both strategic and tactical nuclear warheads (and the six other nuclear-capable nations would still be outside any agreements to reduce their nuclear arsenals). "The proposition that large numbers of nuclear weapons can be retained in perpetuity and never used—accidentally or by decision—defies credibility," the report stated. "As long as any state has nuclear weapons, there will be others . . . who will seek to acquire them." The commission called on the five "declared" nuclear states—the United States, Russia, Britain, France, and China—to "give the lead by committing themselves, unequivocally, to the elimination of all nuclear weapons."

It called for this elimination to be achieved "at the earliest possible time" and described several useful steps to be taken along the way. However, it chose not to set a target date either for the final elimination or for any of the intermediate steps.[21]

Despite that one final failure of nerve on the part of commission members, their work showed that denuclearization is considered a plausible as well as a necessary step by people from the heart of the Western nations' strategic-planning community. In April 1998, the editor of the prestigious annual *Strategic Survey* published by the London-based International Institute for Strategic Studies (IISS) noted that "in the last few years there has been a dramatic change and remarkable upsurge of interest in, and support for, abolishing nuclear weapons. . . . Since the mid-1990s there has been an unprecedented focus on nuclear abolition as a desirable policy objective. The view must now be taken seriously."[22] But clearly, considerable further political action would still be needed to push the nuclear-abolition campaign forward.

At the level of chemical and biological weapons, the major governments of the world have already strongly committed themselves to zero production, zero holdings, zero transfers, and zero use. In those fields, the goal is to uphold the norms expressed in existing international agreements, and to seek to finish universalizing accession to them. Regarding so-called conventional arms, meanwhile, President Oscar Arias has been spearheading an effort to stop the transfer of deadly weapons to governments that are nondemocratic or otherwise abuse the rights of their own people or others. His proposal raises many serious questions about the responsibilities of people who engage in capitalist acts (in this case, arms sales—many of them government subsidized). Do people involved in such transactions—the people who produce or sell or such arms, or the taxpayers whose governments subsidize their export—bear any responsibilities to those who suffer from the use to which those commodities may later be put? These and other questions regarding arms control are considered more fully in chapters 8 through 10.

For now, it is enough to note that the goal of a general and complete disarmament of the whole world, as urged by the Dalai Lama, is something that is already an important and valid part of the existing global discourse. It is a goal, moreover, to which all the major governments of the world (except a few nonsigners of the NPT) long ago formally committed themselves. But it is a goal that still, as His Holiness noted, needs to be pinned down—as the anti-landmine treaty was—with fixed, agreed steps and, equally important, a timetable.

LOOKING BACK OVER the century just ending, His Holiness noted that it had been his own generation's century. He judged that a lot of progress had been made in the course of it in some regards, but that he still, on balance, sometimes described it as "a century of bloodshed." Nevertheless, he expressed continued optimism that humans were, in general, becoming more mature:

> Talking about nonviolence, this is becoming something more, a political force, or political idea. So, I think this is a very good sign. Therefore, the next century should be a century of dialogue. So we, the present generation, have to make some kind of . . . preparation for a happier, friendly, peaceful next century. So that when my generation is ready to say goodbye, and we can hand over to the next fresh, broadminded generation a more hopeful world. Then, they look after themselves. . . .
>
> It is very, very important to remain with hope and determination. If we lose hope, and remain with pessimism, that is the greatest of failure. So, in spite of difficulties: ah! remain with optimism. Ah! these things can change, can be overcome. So, that kind of determination and hope, I think, is the key factor for a brighter future.

He ended his presentation in a characteristically unassuming way. "That much, I wanted to share with you," he said. "If you agree, then try to think more and investigate, and eventually implement. If you feel these [ideas] are too much idealistic, not practical, then forget them. It's no problem!"

3

The Individual and the Totalitarian State:
Aung San Suu Kyi and the Question
of Human Rights in Burma

What is the condition of the individual confronting the power of an authoritarian state? Many people have written about the experience of being trapped inside this particular kind of a system of violence: survivors of regimes marked by religious or nationalistic intolerance, Holocaust survivors, survivors of Stalin's or Mao's gulags, those survivors of torture or other gross governmental abuses whose testimonies continue to be recorded by activists of the present-day human rights movement.

The Burmese democratic leader Aung San Suu Kyi has experienced the power and caprice of a totalitarian government up close. She did not expect to have to do this. When she returned to Burma in April 1988 to help her ailing mother, she knew there was some unrest fermenting against the military dictatorship that had ruled there for the past twenty-six years. But by her own account, she little imagined the role she would be called on to play during the years that followed. She later told an interviewer, "When I returned to Burma in 1988 to nurse my sick mother, I was planning on starting a chain of libraries in my father's name. A life of politics held no attraction for me."[1]

During her years in exile, 1962–1988, Daw Suu had kept up a strong interest in the culture, history, and current affairs of her native land. In Oxford, Japan, and India, she researched different phases of Burma's history, and published informative studies of different aspects of the national liberation movement in which her father, Aung San, had played such a strong leadership role. She married an Englishman, Michael Aris, an expert on Himalayan Buddhism. Later, the couple arranged for their two sons to participate in a traditional Theravada ceremony in a Buddhist monastery in Burma. She researched and published a delightful young people's guide to her country.

Daw Suu's years in exile allowed her to study and reflect deeply on the processes involved in winning a people's liberation from dictatorship, while also trying to ensure that the successor regime would not fall into the same old habits of authoritarianism as its predecessor. (This was the sad but all too common twist of history depicted in George Orwell's satire *Animal Farm*). During her teenage years, her mother, Daw Khin Kyi, was Burma's Ambassador to India: there, Daw Suu became an engaged student of the work of Mahatma Gandhi. Later, after she graduated from Oxford, she spent two years working for the United Nations in New York, and was able to learn more about Dr. Martin Luther King Jr. She was intrigued, in particular, with the relationship between the nonviolent strategies Gandhi and King had followed and the significantly (though not totally) different strategies followed by her beloved father.

So once she was back in Rangoon in 1988, at her mother's side in the gracious old family home on University Avenue, she was well placed to stay in touch with the political currents swirling all around her. One experienced correspondent has noted that during the demonstrations that gathered force in Burma that summer, "thousands of protesters had carried portraits of her father in demonstrations all over the country; his name was almost mythical and symbolised all that Burma was not but should be—free, democratic and prosperous."² When it became known in Rangoon that Aung San's daughter was back in town, many activists and leaders in the Burmese pro-democracy movement were eager to find out more about her.

U Tin U was a former military figure (indeed, a former minister of defense) who had been purged by the country's dictator, General Ne Win, in 1976; he then served four years in prison and later entered a Buddhist monastery. During that time, he became ever more committed to the notion that his country could and should become a democracy. In 1988, he was one of numerous people who came to the house on University Avenue to "check out" this forty-three-year-old daughter of his country's most beloved founding father. "It really struck me," he later recalled, "the way she talked, her complexion, her features and gestures were strikingly similar to those of her father. She resembled him in almost every way. I thought that she was a female replica. So inspired, I thought she was the lady who could carry on his work. Also, she had a very clear mind and a very strong head."[3]

On August 8, 1988, Rangoon and many other parts of the country witnessed vast popular demonstrations against the dictatorship, mounted by students, monks, and many other sectors of society. Even conscripts serving in different branches of the armed forces joined in. The response of the military leaders was swift and bloody. In Rangoon, elite forces entered the streets and cleared away the demonstrators by force. That day alone, 500 demonstrators were reported killed and many thousands more were wounded. Many of the wounded tried to receive treatment, and a degree of sanctuary, in Rangoon General Hospital, but the troops followed them there. Outraged citizens joined the hospital staff in a huge display of solidarity. Over the days that followed, the dictatorship tried a number of desperate maneuvers to help it regain control: these included numerous "dirty tricks" aimed at discrediting and dividing the pro-democracy activists, and naming a new president to serve as a fresh "front man" for aging dictator Ne Win.[4]

In retrospect, the events of mid-August 1988 looked like a truly prerevolutionary situation. If the pro-democracy movement had been better organized then, it might have had a chance of chasing the dictatorship out of the country. But it was not well organized. Many of its supporters were still looking for leadership, or even for a single leader who could coordinate all their efforts. Meanwhile, word had gotten out about the gifts of Aung San's daughter. When she agreed to give a public address—her first ever, in Burma—at the central Shwedagon Pagoda on August 26, 1988, more than half a million people turned out to see her!

The speech she gave that day was brief, forceful—and masterly. Addressing the throng in eloquent Burmese, she started with a strong call for discipline and unity: "Revered monks and people! This public rally is aimed at informing the whole world of the will of the people. Therefore at this mass rally the people should be disciplined and united to demonstrate the very fact that they are a people who can be disciplined and united. Our purpose is to show that the entire people entertain the keenest desire for a multiparty democratic system of government." She addressed head-on the dictatorship's main criticism of her: that her long stay abroad and her marriage to a citizen of once-hated Britain disqualified her from any leading role in

Burmese politics. She quoted her father as having stated that democracy was "the only ideology we should aim for," and that the armed forces should serve the people, rather than the other way round.

"There can be no doubt," she concluded, "that everybody wants a multi-party democracy system of government. It is the duty of the present government to bring about such a system as soon as possible. For the people's part they should continue to demonstrate for this through peaceful and disciplined means." She called for the holding, "as quickly as possible," of free and fair elections. And she reminded her listeners that fellow citizens who retained a sincere commitment to the single existing party, the (military-backed) Burmese Socialist Programme Party, should not be molested. "They should not be threatened or endangered. Each one should go forward towards his own goal. *Do not because of your greater strength be vengeful towards those who are of weaker strength.*"[5]

A new political star had been born. At the end of the following month, Daw Suu and U Tin U were among the leaders who registered the establishment of a new political party, the National League for Democracy (NLD). But already, the military was laying plans for a broad counter-attack. Early in September, they formed a new body, the State Law and Order Restoration Council (SLORC). Its declared mission was twofold: to restore "peace and tranquillity" and to prepare for the promised "democratic, multi-party elections." The military was seemingly confident that, if and when such elections might be held, it could find plenty of ways to "arrange" a resounding victory for its own party.

During the next twenty months, the SLORC lashed out at the NLD leadership. In July 1989, it arrested Daw Suu and U Tin U and confined them to a tight house arrest; hundreds of other NLD activists throughout the country were harassed and arrested as well. Throughout the remaining months of campaigning, it kept Daw Suu and U Tin U in solitary confinement. The SLORC finally scheduled elections for May 27, 1990. But in an odd turn, when the polls opened on that day, the SLORC ended up allowing what all observers agreed was a remarkably free and fair ballot.

Bertil Lintner, a journalist covering the election, described what ensued:

> There was a massive turn-out of voters. Entire families lined up outside the polling booths early in the morning on the 27th to make sure they would be able to cast their votes. And the outcome was an

astounding victory for the NLD. It captured 392 of the 485 seats contested. . . . The rest went to NLD allies from the various minority
areas while the military-backed National Unity Party captured a mere
ten seats. . . . There was not a single reported incident of violence or
misbehavior on the part of the public on election day. The Burmese
went to the polls with unity and dignity. The SLORC was probably as
taken aback as almost everyone else; it was totally unprepared for an
NLD victory of this magnitude. The NLD won even in Rangoon's
Dagon township, which includes the capital's cantonment [military
housing] area and the SLORC's headquarters.[6]

Recalling how he heard the election results, U Tin U said:

After six months [in prison], the authorities became paranoid that the
Americans would swoop in by helicopter and rescue me. So they
went to the trouble of having barbed wire strung around my hut—the
sides and over the top—like a cage. This was to be my home for the
next five years. In any case, it was the workers, who were also prisoners and constructed the cage, who secretly informed me of the election results. . . . As the election results came in [one of the workers]
scratched information on bits of thick sandpaper. Each line was a
township and an NLD victory. Eventually, it added up to 390 elected
MPs from the NLD. My cage was the harbinger of the greatest news
I received while in prison, and I was so thankful to those daring workers who freed my spirit, so to speak, while they caged me in![7]

Despite the NLD's huge victory at the polls, the SLORC was not about
to cede power to it. SLORC leader Khin Nyint immediately denied that
the body just elected had ever been intended to have any true legislative
powers. These, he said, would continue to be exercised solely by the
SLORC itself. The military leadership then sought vengeance for the
NLD's apparent popularity by stepping up its campaign of abuse and
harassment against it. Thousands of additional NLD leaders and activists,
in addition to those already in jail, were arrested and tortured. Entire communities suspected of sympathizing with the NLD—though not the military cantonments!—were forcibly relocated.

Repression continued. Indeed, after the brief, tantalizing era of partial
sunlight in the period 1988–90, the country returned to an even harsher

version of the one-sided system of internal violence that Burma's forty-four million people had known before 1988. In late 1997, the SLORC tried to change its image by changing its name to the more peaceable-sounding State Peace and Development Council, but these changes—like the SLORC's attempt to change the name of the country to Myanmar or to redenominate Burmese banknotes—had little effect in how citizens of Burma were actually treated.

Human Rights Watch noted of the Burmese situation during 1998 that "the government stepped up its practice of targeting villagers suspected of supporting ethnic insurgents. Forced relocations were especially prevalent in the central southern Shan state, Kayah (Karenni) state, Karen state and Tenasserim division, all of which were areas where peace talks or cease-fires had broken down in the previous three years." This report also referred to an International Labor Organization finding that "compulsory labor was 'pervasive' in Burma, widely performed by women, children and the elderly, especially forced on ethnic minority groups, and frequently accompanied by physical abuse, including beatings, torture, rape and murder." And after the NLD had reached yet another impasse in its request for talks with the SLORC, in August 1998, "over 700 NLD members were detained, bringing the number of elected parliamentarians in detention to 194."[8]

AND WHAT OF Aung San Suu Kyi, the reserved, thoughtful woman who remained the central figure of leadership for democrats throughout the country? In 1991, the legendary Czech dissident (and democratically elected president of then-Czechoslovakia) Václav Havel, nominated her for the Nobel Peace Prize. The Norwegian Nobel Committee enthusiastically endorsed this nomination. But Daw Suu remained incarcerated, impoverished, and isolated within her house in Rangoon. At the glittering annual award ceremony in Oslo that year, her son Alexander Aris received the prize on her behalf. Nobel committee chair Francis Sejersted noted soberly in his speech, "This is not the first time that political persecution at home has prevented a Peace Prize Laureate from receiving the prize in person. It happened to Carl von Ossietzky in 1936, ill in one of Hitler's concentration camps. It happened to Andrei Sakharov and to Lech Walesa. Ossietzky died before the regime fell, but both Sakharov and Walesa saw their struggles succeed. It is our hope that Aung San Suu Kyi will see her struggle crowned with success."[9]

In 1993, the Dalai Lama and many other Nobel laureates who would later come to Charlottesville attempted to visit Daw Suu at her home in Burma. But the SLORC would not even allow this illustrious group to enter Burma from the Thai border, where they had gathered.[10]

In 1995, Daw Suu was allegedly released from the tight house arrest to which she had been subject since 1989. Over the years that followed, the SLORC intermittently "allowed" her to hold meetings of the NLD leadership in her home, to address students and others who would come to the walls of her compound to hear her talk, or to receive visiting foreign dignitaries or journalists. But any of these so-called privileges could be, and were, capriciously withdrawn by the SLORC at a moment's notice, with no further explanation. And still, she was not allowed outside the family's compound.[11] All these restrictions were in strong violation of the Universal Declaration of Human Rights, of which Burma had been one of the earliest signatories back in 1948.

At the conference, Harn Yawnghwe, who spoke on behalf of Daw Suu, told the audience:

> She would have really enjoyed the company and fellowship of her fellow Nobel laureates, and she would have enjoyed the intellectual challenge. The fact that she is not here really highlights the situation in Burma. . . .
>
> The reality is that although she's supposed to be free, she's not. How can you say she is free when she cannot meet with her husband and her children?[12] They cannot visit her. They are not given visas by the military junta. She cannot get on the telephone to talk to them because not only is the telephone line tapped when it is working, but most of the time it is cut; and even when it is not cut, when she talks to people if the military thinks that the subject is not appropriate, they will cut the line.
>
> Apart from that, she cannot, as the leader of her party, move about freely to talk to members of her party or even with the executive of her party. . . . And not everybody can just walk in to visit her. There are troops around, the roads are blocked: there are security agents all over the place. Is that freedom?

But Daw Suu has always known that, unlike Burma's other democrats, she has enjoyed two significant forms of protection from the worst of the

SLORC's depredations. One was her status as daughter and intellectual heir to the man considered the father of the country's independence—and the man who was also the revered founder of the Burmese military. The other protection has been her standing in the international community, where her visibility increased considerably after she was awarded the Nobel Peace Prize in 1991. She has always, therefore, been at pains to point out that Burma's other pro-democracy activists have suffered far worse than her, and that though she has been the one to deal with the party's international contacts, in all its deliberations and actions inside Burma she is just one member of a collective leadership.

Throughout her decade in detention, however, Daw Suu's personal qualities have been tested. In the early years of her detention, the SLORC let her (British) husband and two teenage sons visit her periodically. But she suspected that those visits were allowed mainly to fuel her desire to be with her family, so that when their visas expired and they had to leave Burma, she would choose to go with them.[13] She always refused to go, and she kept up her spirits in Rangoon with her continued political engagement, reading, meditating, and a prolonged study of Buddhist texts. In 1996, she told an interviewer, "As a mother, the greater sacrifice was giving up my sons, but I was always aware of the fact that others had sacrificed more than me. I never forget that my colleagues who are in prison suffer not only physically but mentally for their families who have no security outside—in the larger prison of Burma under authoritarian rule. Prisoners know that their families have no security at all. . . . Because their sacrifices are so much bigger than mine I cannot think of mine as a sacrifice. I think of it as a choice."[14]

Ever since she and her colleagues established the NLD in 1988, the party has been strongly committed to the use of nonviolent methods to bring democracy to Burma. For Daw Suu, as for many of her comrades, that commitment sprang naturally out of their practice of Theravada Buddhism, the school of Buddhism that is most widespread in Burma. But during her years in exile from her country, Daw Suu had also been able to hone her understanding of nonviolent action by studying the works of other social activists. One of the key ideas she learned from Gandhi was the role that adherence to the strategy of nonviolence can play in helping its practitioners to overcome the sense of *fear* that could otherwise, for those confronting powerful authoritarian governments, become paralyzing. In 1991, she wrote,

It is not power that corrupts but fear. Fear of losing power corrupts those who wield it, and fear of the scourge of power corrupts those who are subject to it. . . .

Within a system which denies the existence of basic human rights, fear tends to be the order of the day. Fear of imprisonment, fear of torture, fear of death, fear of losing friends, family, property or means of livelihood, fear of poverty, fear of isolation, fear of failure. . . . It is not easy for a people conditioned by the iron rule of the principle that might is right to free themselves from the enervating miasma of fear. Yet even under the most crushing state machinery courage rises up again and again, for fear is not the natural state of civilized man.

The wellspring of courage and endurance in the face of unbridled power is generally a firm belief in the sanctity of ethical principles combined with a historical sense that despite all setbacks the condition of man is set on an ultimate course for both spiritual and material advancement.[15]

Numerous incidents in the laureate's own life point to the validity of this assertion. After the SLORC eased up its restrictions on her in 1995, she was able to record a number of revealing thoughts and reminiscences in some conversations she held in her home with an experienced observer of Burma (and University of Virginia graduate), Alan Clements. In one of those conversations, she described an incident that was already legendary among Burma's democrats. It took place in April 1989, in the brief period when the SLORC still allowed her and other NLD leaders to travel around the country to campaign for the promised elections.

Daw Suu took full advantage of this opportunity and traveled at a relentless pace from province to province, campaigning among both ethnic Burmans and members of the numerous other ethnic groups who make up one-third of the country's population. In several of the areas she went to, local army commanders were unused to the norms of democratic campaigning. One day, as she and a group of friends were returning from a day's campaigning to a temporary rest stop in the Irrawaddy delta town of Danabyu, they were met by a row of soldiers, kneeling, and with their guns ready to fire. A captain told the campaigners that if they continued walking down the center of the road, he would order the soldiers to fire. Daw Suu replied that in that case, they would walk along the side of the road. She recalled what happened next:

> He [the captain] replied that he would shoot even if we walked at the side of the road.
>
> Now that seemed highly unreasonable to me *(laughing)*. I thought, if he's going to shoot us even if we walk at the side of the road, well, perhaps it is me they want to shoot. I thought, I might as well walk in the middle of the road. While I was walking . . . the major came running up and had an argument with the captain. We just walked through the soldiers who were kneeling there. And I noticed that some of them, one or two, were actually shaking and muttering to themselves, but I don't know whether it was out of hatred or nervousness. . . .
>
> I was quite cool-headed. I thought what does one do? Does one turn back or keep on going? My thought was, one doesn't turn back in a situation like this. I don't think I'm unique in that.[16]

Clements's conversations with Daw Suu delved deeply into the spiritual and intellectual bases of her political activism. In the very first conversation, he asked a question a Burmese student had asked him to pass on to her, about whether the country's democracy movement should join those other Burmese opposition movements that had taken up arms, instead of continuing on its existing path of nonviolence.

> DAW SUU: I do not believe in an armed struggle because it will [perpetuate] the tradition that he who is best at wielding arms, wields power. Even if the democracy movement were to succeed through force of arms, it would leave in the minds of the people the idea that whoever has the greater armed might wins in the end. That will not help democracy.
>
> CLEMENTS: Daw Suu, how effective is non-violence in the modern world, and more specifically, with regimes that seem devoid of sensitivity or any sense of moral shame and conscience?
>
> DAW SUU: Non-violence means positive action. You have to work for whatever you want. You don't just sit there doing nothing and hope to get what you want. It just means that the methods you use are not violent ones. Some people think that non-violence is passive-ness. It's not so.[17]

Later, he asked whether she considered nonviolence to be "an immutable ethical and spiritual principle that will never alter in your approach to the struggle?"

DAW SUU: We have always said that we will never disown those students and others who have taken up violence. We know that their aim is the same as ours. They want democracy and they think the best way to go about it is through armed struggle. And we do not say we have the monopoly on the right methods of achieving what we want. Also, we cannot guarantee their security. We can't say, "Follow us in the way of non-violence and you'll be protected," or that we'll get there without any casualties. That's a promise we can't make. We have chosen the way of non-violence simply because we think it's politically better for the country in the long run to establish that you can bring about change without the use of arms. This has been a clear NLD policy from the beginning. . . . [Gandhi] did say at one time that if he had to choose between violence and cowardice, he would choose violence. So, even Gandhi, who was supposed to be the great exponent of non-violence, was not somebody who did not make exceptions. . . .

CLEMENTS: But what about choosing violence out of compassion, if it's the right word, rather than using it as an option instead of cowardice? Nelson Mandela writes: "Leadership commits a crime against its own people if it hesitates to sharpen its political weapons where they have become less effective." Isn't he saying that one's attachment to non-violence becomes in fact an act of violence towards one's own people, when the non-violent approach is no longer effective?

DAW SUU: It depends on the situation and I think that in the context of Burma today, non-violent means are the best way to achieve our goal. But I certainly do not condemn those who fight the "just fight," as it were. My father did, and I admire him greatly for it.[18]

Like all the twentieth century's great proponents of nonviolence, Daw Suu always paid great attention to the need not to "demonize" or dehumanize her opponents. "I do think of SLORC as people," she told Clements. "They do not always think of us, who oppose them, as people. They think of us as objects to be crushed, or obstacles to be removed. But I see them very much as people."[19] She also showed a deeply sympathetic understanding of how hard it might be for the leaders of an oppressive, authoritarian system to be forced, through a democratic opening, to come to terms with the gravity of their past misdeeds:

> I read somewhere that it is always more difficult for the perpetrator of a cruel deed to forgive the victim, than for the victim to forgive his tormentor. I found that very strange when I first read it, but I think it's true. The victim can forgive because he has the moral high ground as it were. He has nothing to be ashamed of. Of course he may be ashamed if he had behaved in a very bad way, or if he had groveled. Then he may acquire a hatred towards his tormentor, based not really on what the tormentor had done to him, but on what he had done to himself.
>
> It was Shcharansky who said that when he was in prison he had to keep reminding himself, "Nobody can humiliate me but myself, nobody can humiliate me but myself." I think if you haven't done anything that is shameful then you can forgive your tormentor. But the tormentor finds it difficult to forgive the victim because he knows that he has committed an act of shame.

Clements asked if she could actually envision SLORC's members sitting down with her and saying, "Daw Suu, we're going to work this out together." She smiled and replied, "Oh, very much so. I have no trouble envisaging such a thing. That might just be wishful thinking, in some people's interpretation, but it will have to happen some day."[20]

THE UNIVERSAL DECLARATION of Human Rights, of which independent Burma was one of the founding signatories back in 1948, marked the consolidation of a radical new trend in international politics: the launching of a global-level challenge, in the name of the *rights of individual humans*, to the traditional, absolutist notion of state sovereignty. An "opening shot" in that campaign had already been evident three years before, when—at U.S. insistence—the Charter of the United Nations made explicit reference to the concern of the new world body for the "human rights and fundamental freedoms" of all the peoples of the world. The United Nations then set up the Commission on Human Rights, chaired by Eleanor Roosevelt, which worked hard to conceptualize—or "imagine" the shape of—and then draft the text of the Universal Declaration of Human Rights. (Mrs. Roosevelt received much useful help from

René Cassin, a French specialist on international law. He later became president of the European Court of Human Rights. In 1968, he was awarded the Nobel Peace Prize.)

The Universal Declaration was adopted by the United Nations on December 10, 1948. The intention of the drafting committee had been to supplement it with first one, and later two, separate International Covenants. These covenants dealt with more detailed aspects of the human rights issue that, as Mrs. Roosevelt understood, might be controversial texts for many member states—including the United States—to ratify. Her strategy was therefore to secure, first, as universal as possible an adherence to the Universal Declaration and then to proceed to the subject matter of the covenants. One of these covenants—which the United States still had not ratified in 1999!—deals with economic, social, and cultural rights; the other addresses civil and political rights. Mrs. Roosevelt's strategy looked successful. By the end of the century, all the world's states except Saudi Arabia had ratified the Universal Declaration.[21]

In many countries, including Burma, there remains a distressingly wide gap between the actions of states in initiating or maintaining their adherence to the Universal Declaration, and the actions they take that affect their own people. Nevertheless, as Mrs. Roosevelt understood, the mere *assertion* of global norms and standards by an authoritative international body can, of itself, start to reframe people's thinking and to empower marginalized or repressed communities, even before these communities become strong enough to enforce actual respect of the norms.

From that point of view, the whole text of the Universal Declaration deserves to be widely read and understood. Among its thirty articles are several of particular relevance to the case of Burma:

Article 3
Everyone has the right to life, liberty and security of person.
Article 4
No one shall be held in slavery or servitude; slavery and the slave trade shall be prohibited in all their forms.
Article 5
No one shall be subjected to torture or to cruel, inhuman or degrading treatment or punishment. . . .
Article 9
No one shall be subjected to arbitrary arrest, detention or exile. . . .

Article 20

1. Everyone has the right to freedom of peaceful assembly and association.
2. No one may be compelled to belong to an association.

Article 21

1. Everyone has the right to take part in the government of his country, directly or through freely chosen representatives.
2. Everyone has the right to equal access to public service in his country.
3. The will of the people shall be the basis of the authority of government; this will shall be expressed in periodic and genuine elections which shall be by universal and equal suffrage and shall be held by secret vote or by equivalent free voting procedures.[22]

Burma's early adherence to the declaration did not count for much after General Ne Win seized power in the name of the military in 1962. After the SLORC was established in 1988, it continued the military's tradition of thumbing its nose at the global norms contained in the declaration. The SLORC was able to join with a number of authoritarian regimes in Asia, including those of China, Malaysia, and Singapore. These regimes raised the specific charge that the declaration was in some way inappropriate to their societies since on a number of (generally undefined) points it was incompatible with what they described as "Asian values."

At the conference, Daw Suu's representative, Harn Yawnghwe, devoted his main presentation to an impassioned refutation of this charge, and the allied charge (made by Malaysia's dictator, Mahathir Muhammad) that the declaration was formulated by rich governments that did not understand the needs of poor countries. Harn noted, "The initial text for the declaration did not start with governments. It was American civic organizations and nongovernmental organizations which lobbied for human rights to be recognized within the UN so that it would not fall into the same trap as the League of Nations.[23] Because of that, human rights became a major component of the UN Charter, and from that it led to the formation of the UN Commission on Human Rights." He noted that the committee that had drafted the declaration included China, meaning that "Asian values" were represented. (Lebanon, which also had a distinguished specialist on the drafting committee, is also technically an Asian country.)

Harn recalled that the Asian countries that supported the declaration in 1948,

> were Burma, China, India, Iran, Iraq, the Philippines, and Thailand. In actual fact, it was the smaller countries in the third world who were very enthusiastic about the declaration because this was the first international agreement that recognized the equality and dignity of all people regardless of the size of their country, regardless of their geographic or ethnic origin. And U Thant, a Burmese who was the secretary-general of the United Nations in the sixties, said that the Universal Declaration is the Magna Carta of mankind. And yet, today, we have the generals in Burma saying that "the UN Declaration doesn't fit our values. It's being imposed on us by Westerners."

> Another argument used by the people who push "Asian values" is that they were not members when the declaration was adopted, so they shouldn't be forced to accept it. Their argument is not valid, because if you join an organization, you should know what the organization stands for . . . and you cannot say that you were not a member when it was adopted!

Harn argued, too, that there is no consensus on the meaning of "Asian values." But, he noted, that has not prevented Singapore's longtime strongman Lee Kuan Yew from trying to explain—in reference to Japan, China, Taiwan, Singapore, and Hong Kong—that "these countries have done well economically because of Asian values and that means that, according to him, they place group interests over individual interests. And that is the debate." He recalled that Lee's arguments had gained some credibility at the time of the 1993 World Conference on Human Rights in Vienna: Asian government representatives who took part in a preparatory meeting in Bangkok, Thailand, adopted Lee's view and issued a declaration stating that "human rights must be considered in the context of national and regional peculiarities."

"That's what the governments say," Harn countered, "but we do not agree!" He recalled that various Asian NGOs had held an alternative conference, which rejected Lee's notion.

"Is there really a distinct set of Asian values that are different from 'Western values'—if there is such a thing?" he asked. He noted that among the countries of the "West," there were evident differences in culture and values between the United States and Europe, even within Europe, and between Slavic countries and Mediterranean countries.

So what Western values are we talking about? And what Asian values are we talking about? . . . Lee Kuan Yew was only talking about the so-called East Asian countries. What about south Asian values— India, Pakistan, Sri Lanka, Bangladesh? What about the Malay-Polynesia values from Indonesia, Malaysia, Papua New Guinea, all these countries? And even in Burma, where we have many ethnic groups, we have very different values. If you're living on the plain and being a rice farmer or if you're living in the hills and you are a hunter, you have very different values, so what values are we talking about?

Some of the people who argue about different values also say, well, it's really Western Christian values being imposed on Asian. But, again, you have to remember that the Asian values debate that Lee Kuan Yew used really was based only on Confucianism, which is very different again and does not touch on the values that the rest of Asia have, which are Buddhist, Muslim, Hindu, Christian and also animist. . . .

And if you really look at Christian values, basic Christian values without all the cultural overtones, it's not a Western value. It's from the Middle East. It has the same root as Islam and Judaism, and on top of that, there are more Christians today in Asia and Africa than in the Western world so-called, and there are many Hindus, many Buddhists, and many Muslims in the Western world. So what are we really talking about?

Daw Suu has also devoted a lot of attention throughout the years to the question of whether the Universal Declaration and its supplementary covenants can be considered compatible with traditions indigenous to Asia. In 1988–89, when she and her colleagues were hard at work building their new political party—and she was also, until her mother's death in December 1988, helping to look after her—Daw Suu still made time to start pulling together her reflections on the "Asian values" question. These reflections were later published in her volume *Freedom from Fear.* "There is nothing new in Third World governments seeking to justify and perpetuate authoritarian rule by denouncing liberal democratic principles as alien," she wrote. "By implication they claim for themselves the official and sole right to decide what does or does not belong to indigenous cultural norms."[24]

Most of her essay deals specifically with the cultural-values arguments then being made in Burma. Asking (rhetorically) why her country, with its abundant natural and human resources, now found itself mired in poverty, she wrote, "The Burmese people, who have had no access to sophisticated academic material, got to the heart of the matter by turning to the words of the Buddha on the four causes of decline and decay: failure to recover that which had been lost, omission to repair that which had been damaged, disregard of the need for reasonable economy, and the elevation to leadership of men without morality or learning." Within the Buddhist tradition, she noted, there has never been a concept similar to that which dominated Europe for so many centuries: that of the "divine right" of rulers to rule as they pleased. Instead, in Buddhist tradition, the ruler is expected to observe a set of rules called the Ten Duties of Kings. These, she wrote, "are widely known and generally accepted as a yardstick which could be applied just as well to modern government as to the first monarch of the world. The duties are: liberality, morality, self-sacrifice, integrity, kindness, austerity, non-anger, non-violence, forbearance and non-opposition (to the will of the people)."[25]

Of this crucial last duty, she wrote:

> The royal duty of non-opposition is a reminder that the legitimacy of government is founded on the consent of the people, who may withdraw their mandate at any time if they lose confidence in the ability of the ruler to serve their best interests.
>
> By invoking the Ten Duties of Kings the Burmese are not so much indulging in wishful thinking as drawing on time-honoured values to reinforce the validity of the political reforms they consider necessary. It is a strong argument for democracy that governments regulated by principles of accountability, respect for public opinion and the supremacy of just laws are more likely than an all-powerful ruler or ruling class, uninhibited by the need to honour the will of the people, to observe the traditional duties of Buddhist kingship. *Traditional values serve both to justify and to decipher popular expectations of democratic government.*[26]

In his presentation, Harn Yawnghwe also pointed to interpretations of other major Asian traditions that show a strong compatibility between an insistence on human, civil, and political rights and traditions that are broadly followed in different parts of Asia, like Confucianism or Islam. He argued, however, that in any culture, Eastern or Western, there may be values that ought to be rejected—like support for slavery or the degradation of women.

He dealt head-on with the accusation frequently repeated by the SLORC that democracy is, along with the whole notion of human rights, another "Western import" into his country:

> Burma has been a country isolated for the last thirty-five years. The military took over in 1962 and they blocked off contact with the rest of the world. So how can the people of Burma who have had no contact with the Western world for over thirty years be influenced by Western values? The media? All media in Burma is controlled by the military! We have no cable television, we have no satellite TV. It's illegal to have a satellite dish. You have no access to the Internet. In fact, a Burmese citizen who was the consul-general of Denmark was arrested for having a fax machine! They arrested him, denied him treatment, and he was an old man. He had a heart condition; they denied him medical care. He died in prison—and this is a person who is a diplomat, accredited to a foreign government, not only Denmark, but several European governments!
>
> So, how were the Burmese people influenced by Western values? They have no access to the West, but yet they want democracy.

He also argued that the broad support the democracy movement had won in Burma debunked the theory that "you can't have a democracy without a middle class." He said,

> The people of Burma are peasants. I would say about 85 percent of the country live off agriculture. We have very few people in the cities and a very small middle class, but yet, the people . . . knew what they want. Why is that? That is because through their own experience they have seen . . . that a small elite should not be left to make all the decisions and be unaccountable for their actions. What is good for the generals has not been good for Burma and the people. . . . So, people in Burma want democracy because they want to limit the power of their rulers. They want to be able to have rulers who are accountable,

who are responsible, and people who will be responsive to the needs of the people. It has nothing to do with being a middle class or being influenced by Western values.

Harn reminded his listeners that "the largest and one of the longest functioning democracies in the world today is India. It's an Asian nation which has traditions going back many thousands of years, and yet it is a democracy. It's not perfect, but it functions. So I would like to say, this is ample evidence that democracy and human rights are not at odds with Asian values, and not at odds with Asian cultures and traditions." He added that he found it difficult to understand "why it is so difficult for some of these rulers to accept that people should be treated equally regardless of who or what they are."

AFTER HARN FINISHED his presentation, Julian Bond asked him about the seeming paucity of demonstrations or other expressions of popular dissatisfaction in Burma in the preceding months. There had been some signs of protest, Harn replied, "but it's been small, and it has not caught the attention of the media." He explained that one of the reasons Burma had not witnessed the kind of large-scale demonstration witnessed in Indonesia and other East Asian countries during 1998 was that all the country's universities had been closed since December 1996:

> Can you imagine that? One university demonstrated then, and the whole country is shut down! There are no universities operating in Burma today. At the time of those student demonstrations, they also closed down the high schools because the high school students were supporting the university students. This is the extent of their control.
>
> The labor movement? It doesn't exist in Burma. It's illegal to have a union. It is illegal for anybody to gather, to have more than four people. The military intelligence is everywhere, and the priesthood, the Buddhist *sangha*—many of their leaders are also in prison. Also, as I said, the media is controlled, so it is very difficult, because Aung San Suu Kyi, whose party is recognized as having won the election, cannot move around. She cannot talk to ordinary people, so that's why it has been very difficult, but we know there have been protests now and again and students have tried to protest. But they are very quickly put down.

Rigoberta Menchú asked Harn about the Burmese refugees in Thailand. "Some years ago I had the opportunity of being with them," she explained. "I was very struck by the condition of their life, by the lack of liberty that they have in Thailand. And many of us want to read all about this but we have a very difficult time."[27]

He told her that the refugees' situation had gotten worse since her visit:

There have been attacks from across the border and refugee camps have been burned. People have been kidnapped from refugee camps, and the Thai government has tried to make conditions safer by consolidating camps, so the restrictions have increased on those refugees. This year the Thai government invited the United Nations High Commission for Refugees [UNHCR] to be present on the border. In one way, it could help if the UN is present on the border, but we are also concerned because we know that among the Thai military . . . they feel that if the refugees were not in Thailand, there would be no problems. . . . So the idea to secure Thailand's border is to push the refugees back into Burma.

Those portions of international humanitarian law dealing with political refugees are very explicit on this point: governments of countries hosting refugees are not allowed forcibly to repatriate refugees to homelands in which they face a well-founded fear of persecution. Harn, who worked on refugee-aid issues for many years, said he judged that the presence of UNHCR representatives on the Burmese-Thai border might not, in itself, provide a sufficiently strong guarantee for the refugees' safety:

We are not so sure, because in the early 1990s we had 300,000 refugees from the Arakan state [one of the constituent states of the Burmese federation]—Muslim Rakhinjas, who had fled to Bangladesh. They were repatriated to Burma by the UNHCR. The UNHCR said it was a voluntary repatriation, but we have heard that the refugees were not really told that they had any choice.

The other problem with repatriation is that, in theory, when you repatriate a refugee, he or she really should be able to reintegrate back into their community and be able to live in freedom. Nobody in Burma lives in freedom! They are subject to forced labor. The brutality from the military: women are raped, people are killed on the spot for small offenses. And then, people are not really reintegrated into society. They live in camps on the Burmese side of the border, so what is the sense of repatriation? We would like the UNHCR to be there, but they need to protect the refugees. They need to monitor the situation, not [just to] oblige governments or armies.

GIVEN THE STRONG predominance of sovereign state "rights" and interests within the UN system, the question of whether any outsiders—other governments, nongovernmental organizations, or indeed the United Nations itself—have any "rights" to help beleaguered individuals or populations like those in Burma remains a complex one. Indeed, the situation is worse even than it might seem from a consideration of the simple issue of "state sovereignty." For in addition to trying generally to adhere strictly to that principle, the United Nations is also hamstrung by another profoundly antidemocratic rule. In the Security Council, which is the place where most of the decisions about peacekeeping and other UN interventions are made, each of the five declared nuclear weapons states has a permanent seat, and therefore has the power to veto any decision the council might want to make. These states are commonly known as the P-5. Since two of them are China and Russia—each of which has its own profound human rights problem—they are generally very unlikely to support any effective Security Council action in support of human rights.

Mohamed Sahnoun, the wise Algerian diplomat who was the UN secretary-general's special representative in charge of the (relatively successful) early phases of the United Nation's humanitarian deployment in Somalia, has reflected deeply on how to resolve the conflict between humanitarianism and the claims of state sovereignty. In his book *Somalia: The Missed Opportunities*, he made a strong case that, although the global system continues to be based on the extensive sovereignty of states, still, this sovereignty has some significant limits. He pointed to the continuing relevance of the Universal Declaration and other international instruments that the United Nations adopted in its formative first six years, such as the four Geneva Conventions of 1949, the Convention for the Prevention and Punishment of Genocide, and the 1951 Convention on Refugees. He concluded, "More than any Security Council resolution, this initial, comprehensive, and fully persuasive body of international legislation gives the right and obligation to both the UN and regional organizations to come to the rescue of endangered populations by providing relief and actively contributing to the resolution of the conflict itself."[28]

International humanitarian interventions need not always have a military dimension. (One relatively successful phase of the international humanitarian intervention in Kosovo occurred when the Organization for Security and Cooperation in Europe—OSCE—deployed civilian monitors in the region in 1998. But their work was never given a full test before the intervention became dramatically militarized in March 1999.) Nor, indeed, need humanitarian interventions always involve the deployment of personnel to the affected area. One tool of international intervention that was adopted by the United Nations in the 1960s and proved very effective in buttressing the fight for democracy in South Africa was the imposition of economic sanctions on the apartheid regime. It is this same tool of sanctions that many in the West have sought more recently to use against Burma's dictators.

Archbishop Tutu had witnessed the effectiveness of UN sanctions on South Africa's apartheid regime. During the conference, one of the audience members asked him to evaluate the sanctions that the United States and other governments maintained against SLORC-ruled Burma in the 1990s, based on his experience in his own country. He replied,

> We would not have succeeded quite to the extent that we did, and perhaps with so much less bloodshed than would otherwise have been the case, had it not been for the sanctions. And we have said— I mean, as laureates, when we went to Thailand on behalf of our sister laureate, Aung San Suu Kyi—that we were calling on Western countries and Asian countries [to impose sanctions], that this is a nonviolent strategy for changing an unjust system. And we went also to the White House and made the same plea, and we have to say that President Clinton was very good to have responded positively to our particular plea.
>
> You get all sorts of people saying all sorts of things about sanctions —that they will hurt the persons, the people, you are trying to help. Twaddle! It is baloney on the first order because you are speaking about people who are already suffering, you know, and you're saying that you're trying to find some way that is a nonviolent strategy for bringing about the change that everybody says they want. . . .

I would want to say as firmly as I can that it is a moral issue. . . . I mean, it's asking are you on the side of right or the side of wrong? Are you on the side of justice or the side of injustice, or on the side of freedom or oppression? It's very clear, and everything else is obfuscated and I would plead that we do all we can to put the screws on that military junta that they should accept the results of the election.

Tutu seemed to be expressing a consensus among the participating laureates, both in his support for the sanctions against the SLORC, and in his appreciation of the stand the Clinton administration took in support of these sanctions. East Timor's José Ramos-Horta asked Harn Yawnghwe why he thought the administration did not go even further and try to impose the same kind of "secondary sanctions" on countries doing business with Burma that, under the Helms-Burton Act, the U.S. Congress had called for against countries doing business with Cuba.

Harn replied,

In the case of Burma, we have no complaints about U.S. government policy. They have been very, very supportive. When the U.S. ambassador who was in Burma finished his term after 1988, the U.S. did not replace him. They downgraded relations with Burma. There's no foreign aid to the regime. There is an arms embargo, and since early '97 President Clinton has enacted legislation which prevents Americans from making new investments in Burma. So we have sanctions from the U.S. In addition to the sanctions, we have visa bans. High-level military junta officials and their families cannot visit the U.S.

The U.S. lead has caused other nations, including the European Union, to adopt similar measures. The only thing we don't have in Europe is the investment ban. We almost got it. The European Union was willing to enact a similar ban, but France vetoed it . . . because they have a major investment in Burma with Unocal in southern Burma, building a gas pipeline. And that gas pipeline actually has caused untold miseries to the people living in that area.

Harn said he thought that one of the reasons the administration was not pushing for something like the Helms-Burton legislation for Burma was that under the rules of the World Trade Organization, governments are not supposed to take any steps to hinder world trade. (Indeed, several European governments had protested the Helms-Burton Act, along with the Iran-Libya Sanctions Act that paralleled it, on precisely these grounds.) He noted that the Commonwealth of Massachusetts and several U.S. cities have adopted selective purchasing rules, under which they would not award contracts to companies doing business in Burma, and that "many, many companies have pulled out [of Burma] because of this legislation." But the European Union and Japan sued the Commonwealth of Massachusetts for contravening World Trade Organization rules, and they were joined in the suit by a number of American corporations who feared that other states or cities might adopt similar rules against companies doing business with Indonesia or China. "It's currently before the court," he said. (Subsequently, Massachusetts lost its case.)

DURING HIS DISCUSSION of the Universal Declaration of Human Rights, Harn argued that in addition to providing a basis for the protection of individual rights that was as valid in Asia as it was in Europe, the declaration also provided an excellent basis on which to design systems of rule in countries—like his own—which contain communities from a number of widely differing cultures. "I would like to give you a practical example of how applying the Universal Declaration really can work."

You may not be aware of it, but I am not from the same ethnic group as Aung San Suu Kyi. She is a Burman; I am a Shan. Apart from that, my father and her father were on opposite sides of the table when they were negotiating to form modern Burma. They were able to agree, in 1948, '47 actually, before the Universal Declaration, that the basis for all the different ethnic groups joining Burma to gain independence from Britain . . . would be equality: all the races of Burma would be equal, and they would participate voluntarily in the union of Burma. So that is right in line with the Universal Declaration.

Unfortunately, Aung San Suu Kyi's father was assassinated before we got independence and in a sense, the ethnic [i.e., non-Burman] people were betrayed because the agreement with General Aung San was not fully implemented. In the aftermath of independence, my father tried to bring about agreement, but the military said that amending the constitution peacefully would break up the country. So, instead, they launched a coup. . . . We were the only house that the military surrounded and opened fire on! One of my brothers was killed. My father was arrested, taken to the prison, and he died eight months later in solitary confinement. My mother was also nearly arrested but she was luckily away and she escaped, and we all escaped finally. I have been a refugee. The only thing I possessed was the clothes on my back.

But I have recovered—and now I'm working with a Burman! You could say, the agreement with my father was not honored, and maybe I could accuse Aung San Suu Kyi and the Burmese leadership of betrayal, but that is not the way it works. I know that she stands for the universality of human rights. She stands for democracy, for people to decide, and I am proud to have been asked by her to represent her today.

For her part, the visionary Burmese laureate still confined to her house on University Avenue wrote in 1994 that "it is precisely because of the cultural diversity of the world that it is necessary for different nations and peoples to agree on those basic human values which will act as a unifying factor."[29]

His Holiness the Dalai Lama, Tenzin Gyatso (Photo by Jim Carpenter)

Archbishop Desmond Tutu (Photo by Jim Carpenter)

Oscar Arias Sánchez (Photo by Jim Carpenter)

José Ramos-Horta (Photo by Jim Carpenter)

Harn Yawnghwe (speaking on behalf of Aung San Suu Kyi)
(Photo by Jim Carpenter)

Rigoberta Menchú Tum (Photo by Jim Carpenter)

Betty Williams (Photo by Lynne Brubaker)

Jody Williams (Photo by Jim Carpenter)

Bobby Muller (Photo by Bill Sublette)

A plenary session (Photo by Jim Carpenter)

Rigoberta Menchú Tum commenting (Photo by Bill Sublette)

An exchange between the Dalai Lama and Desmond Tutu
(Photo by Lynne Brubaker)

4

The Challenge from the Indigenous World: The Powerful Voice of Rigoberta Menchú Tum

It would be hard to recall Rigoberta Menchú Tum's presence in Cabell Hall without describing the colorful, intricately embroidered *huipil* (blouse) and headband that she wore. In many places around the globe, however, the "norm" for participants in public discourse on international affairs has been for a long time the clothing style of the Western professional man.

The situation might have been different. If the balance of power and, crucially, the balance of military technologies between different parts of the world had been the reverse of what it was at the end of the fifteenth century, then today's norm for the dress code at a discussion of this nature, being held in this same spot, might have been that of, say, the Mattaponi Indians, who used to control vast areas of land in the region now known as Virginia. Indeed, maybe the Mattaponi would have used the last five hundred years to establish and build a globe-circling empire: vast, Mattaponi-peopled colonies might have dominated the whole landmass of Europe. The "indigenous" question could then have been represented at this conference by someone from the struggling remnants of a small European tribe or people. The English, perhaps.[1]

But enough of counterfactuals. At the laureates' conference at the University of Virginia, Rigoberta Menchú Tum stood at the podium, showing a little of the shy demeanor that, she notes in her two books, is a common habit of Mayan women—and also, smiling, beaming in her bright K'iche' Mayan dress. These colorful embroideries carry many significations for many different audiences. "On the few occasions that I have received an invitation to an official government function [in Guatemala]," the laureate has written, "it always specifies that I should wear a dark-colored dress."[2]

She started her presentation with an invocation in K'iche' Mayan. Then she switched to Spanish:

> I am Maya, and I was born Maya. And I was born in a country where indigenous people are the majority, and where we have had to wage war, and have had to wage peace.
>
> Over above feeling like an indigenous person, I believe that the indigenous peoples of the world are a fount of inspiration for a multicultural world. The indigenous peoples have a message to give in the prevention of conflict because for many years our peoples used dialogue, conversation, and peaceful means for the resolution of interethnic differences, familial differences, and intercultural differences. And overall, the contribution of the indigenous peoples is one of education, one of education in the word, and education in which the values of the word will give the opportunity to the other to express himself, and to be heard. To us it was given as people, not as famous men and women, but as a *people*: an experience of dialogue, an experience of conversation.
>
> And we were able to contribute to peace, to negotiation, and we were able to contribute so that the war would come to an end in Central America. But from a collective conviction, as a raw, painful experience as part of the victims of armed conflict. We've also contributed to peace as exiles, as displaced people, as refugees.
>
> And [I speak] also from the standpoint of indigenous women and indigenous peoples who are not always listened to, not only in our country but also throughout the world.

During the second day of the conference, each of the laureates met for a short discussion with a different class of University of Virginia students. Menchú met with Professor Herbert (Tico) Braun's Spanish studies class. "Guatemala is a fount of multicultural education," she told the students. "The majority of indigenous women are at least bilingual—and most of this is self-taught. In our own lives, we are very technical and professional. I didn't go to school, but I consider myself a well-prepared individual. I have seventeen doctorates!"

Braun asked her how, with the multiple identities she has to deal with—

K'iche', Maya, Guatemalan, Central American—she sets about identifying herself. "I don't just *identify* myself as Mayan," she replied. "I *am* of the Mayan people. I am of the Mayan women, and part of Mayan spirituality. And I also love to learn about other cultures. I think the world belongs to all of us. . . . I don't stop being Mayan because I go to Japan. The most important thing is that you don't try to impose one culture on another. And nor do I think that you can't be my friend until you think like me. The most important thing is to recognize that the world *is* multicultural, and to see that you can have friends who are not the same as you."

She gave an example: "I sometimes have a feeling that something is going to happen in the future. That is how I am. But I can't expect that you have to have the same ability before you can be my friend!"

MENCHÚ'S HUSBAND, Angel Francisco Canil, and their four-year-old son, Mash, accompanied her to Charlottesville. The father and son watched most of the formal part of the proceedings from the front of the auditorium—and Mash was remarkably patient with the adults' habit of wanting to sit still for such lengthy periods of time.

Throughout Menchú's two books, one recurring theme is the importance, to her and all Maya, of close family and community ties. In *Crossing Borders*, she wrote of her feelings for "the humble village where I was born and grew up, where the elders taught us the meaning of the different kinds of birdsong, the meaning of darkness, the place where I learned what it meant to be a descendant of the Mayans of Guatemala."[3]

"Our community," she wrote, "is the reason why we are still alive, why we are still here five hundred years after the Conquest. We have survived amid the rubble of endless massacres. If our people had disintegrated, if they had lost their languages, if they had lost their communities, their collective way of life, their concept of leadership, they would have died out. . . . We also discovered that we have not simply been spectators during these five hundred years. We have been protagonists as well."[4]

She grew up in a poor K'iche' family that had to take seasonal jobs in exploitative coastal plantations, since the hard work they did cultivating their own land in Guatemala's thickly forested altiplano mountains never offered them any assurance of survival. From the age of eight, the young Rigoberta joined her family in doing backbreaking plantation work. There, uprooted from their home community and its familiar altiplano environment, the family was housed in huge sheds with migrant workers from many of Guatemala's twenty-two other language groups. Communication with non-K'iche' was often difficult.

In *I, Rigoberta Menchú*, the future laureate devoted two chapters to explaining the multilayered links that, under these circumstances, she built up with each of her parents. Her father was one of the founders of a peasant group that sought to organize cultivators from indigenous communities around social justice issues, and on occasion apparently used arms in furtherance of their aims. He was killed in the Spanish Embassy, along with several of his compañeros. Of the violent deaths of her parents, Menchú has written:

> When my father was about to die, I dreamed of a little room full of light and heat. He was wearing strange clothes. He looked sad. He told me, "Take care of yourself because I am no longer with your mother. We are no longer together." Then, weeping with sadness, I replied "But why, Papa? I believe in you and I believe in Mama. We shall only be happy if the two of you are together."
>
> "You must trust me," he replied. It was only a dream. Three days later he was dead.
>
> When my mother died, I had a similar dream. I dreamed that I was coming down the hill of Cholá, the crag on the hillside near our village. I saw my mother coming up the hill. She was carrying a heavy basket on her head. Suddenly I saw that the basket was full of rotten meat. I was terrified. About five days after my dream, I heard that my mother had been abducted and was being tortured at the army barracks in Xejul. I knew then that she would not come back.[5]

After her mother's death, the traumatized young woman arrived at the convent in Huehuetenango to find temporary shelter. She thought she was the only one of her entire family who had survived. She was twenty years old. Many months later, she was delighted to be reunited with two of her sisters, ages ten and thirteen; and later still, she discovered that her brother Nicolás had also survived.

From Huehuetenango, sympathetic church people helped her to flee to a safer refuge in Mexico. It was 1980. Working with church organizations to provide aid to other Guatemalan-Maya refugees in southeast Mexico, she was soon able to regain her self-confidence. Over the next couple of years, she became an eloquent and fluent Spanish-speaking voice for democracy and the rights of indigenous peoples. She started to travel to New York, Geneva, and elsewhere, working with a broad coalition of indigenous peoples to lobby a not-very-responsive United Nations.

Over the years, activists in the various indigenous rights organizations registered some worthwhile, if still modest, achievements. The United Nations established the Working Group on Indigenous Peoples (UNWGIP), which tried to raise the sensitivity of all UN bodies to indigenous rights issues. In 1991, the UN-affiliated International Labor Office adopted a convention concerning Indigenous and Tribal Peoples in Independent Countries, which stated that "the peoples concerned shall have the right to decide their own priorities for the process of development as it affects their lives, beliefs, institutions and spiritual well-being and the land they occupy or otherwise use, and to exercise control, to the extent possible, over their own economic, social and cultural development."[6] On December 18, 1992, just eight days after Menchú received her Nobel Prize, the UN General Assembly adopted the Declaration on the Rights of Persons Belonging to National or Ethnic, Religious or Linguistic Minorities. The new declaration seemed to offer some valuable protections to the world's indigenous communities. Among other things, it stated that "persons belonging to minorities may exercise their rights including those set forth in this Declaration individually as well as in community with other members of their group, without discrimination" and that "states should, where appropriate, take measures in the field of education, in order to encourage knowledge of the history, traditions, language and culture of the minorities existing within their territory."[7] But it also made a number of paralyzing concessions to the sovereign-state system—as one might expect, in a text adopted by representatives only of sovereign states. It also failed to make any specific mention of "indigenous peoples" as such, or to take into consideration the very special interests of indigenous communities.[8]

While working in the indigenous rights movement during the 1980s, Menchú had the chance to learn more about the experiences of other rights struggles around the world, and to find new sources of inspiration. At the conference, an audience member asked Menchú who her role models were. Her reply:

Beyond the indigenous communities themselves and beyond the indigenous women that I've always known in my life, I have been very much inspired by Mandela. Not only have I been inspired by him, but I continue to be inspired by him—and I expect that next year I will be able to speak with him a lot because I cannot let the century end without being with him! But I also have other idols. Martin Luther King, I've always been very, very positively impressed by his struggle against racism in the United States; and also Gandhi. And then also many, many people in Central America that I have known all my life, who lost their lives in the wars of the last decade.

Asked what had given her strength to endure the tragedies she had experienced, she replied:

I've always thought that when one . . . lives through something, one *must* live through that thing. One has no alternative but to do so. People who are victims have had no alternative but to be victims. The hope that one has that the world will one day be different has to do with one's hope that no one will have to live through the things that one has experienced. So this becomes a profound conviction: that human beings must find a way to live with each other, find a way to live together.

But I also gain strength from people, from women and from those people who work in little corners that go unrecognized, but where they are sure of a new future. And I have seen that when people obtain something, a school or something like this, this gives them the energy to keep on going. Every success gives them new strength. What gives people the strength to carry on are mutual interests, and the possibilities for the future.

Above all I am a Maya, and we Maya believe that all of us are but passers-by on this earth—and that we must do something while we pass through.

IN THE 1980S while Menchú and her colleagues in the indigenous rights movement were trying to draw international attention to the plight of their peoples, the situation back home in Guatemala continued to be one of terror and extreme vulnerability. As had been the case there for decades already, the violence of the 1980s pitted a U.S.-backed central government that was dominated by mixed-race, Spanish-speaking *ladinos* against the country's Maya and other indigenous communities—some of whose members had taken up arms against the government.

In the early 1980s, government forces launched what Menchú has described as a "scorched-earth" campaign in the rural areas of the country.

> The reasoning behind the campaign was that the destruction of whole villages would lead to the elimination of all witnesses to their crimes. Witnesses included people from the villages who, by chance, happened not to be there at the time. Like me. If the soldiers had caught me, I could not have told my story. It's as simple as that. . . .
>
> The aim of the scorched-earth policy was annihilation. They didn't care if they sacrificed fifty people in order to eliminate ten potential guerrillas. They knew they were not destroying actual guerrilla bases, but they wanted to prevent them from being created. They shot pregnant mothers, children, men and women of all ages. They killed them in the vilest manner, and deliberately tortured them as an example to others. There were numerous clandestine prisons and cemeteries. The regime considered every poor person, every indigenous person, to be an enemy.[9]

The climate of psychological terror induced by the scorched-earth campaigns lived on for many years after the massacres. In numerous communities torn apart by the violence, the *jefes*, who were the local arm of the government's rule, denied families even the ability to give loved ones who had been tortured to death the proper burial that Mayan beliefs demand. Instead, the tortured bodies were frequently thrown into informal burial pits in ravines whose existence and whereabouts were kept secret from surviving family members. The jefes then maintained a continuing reign of terror in the remnants of the villages, threatening and brutalizing survivors into not challenging the "official" version of what had happened—that the guerrillas had tortured and killed the menfolk.

During the scorched-earth campaign, many Mayan women lost *all the male members of their families* to the government-backed killers. British anthropologist Judith Zur spent a long time living with Mayan widows in a K'iche'-Maya village, between 1988 and 1993. She has written movingly about the long struggle these women had to undertake in order to survive in, and make sense of, a physical and spiritual universe that had been ripped apart by the terror. "The dead cannot be remembered properly; they are left unmourned and their kin are unable to release their grief. Survivors are unable to forget [the dead's] ineluctable, wandering, and malicious spirits, left in a liminal state of living death, haunting the living and threatening the society with further death. . . . The sense of persecution is pervasive."[10]

Throughout the 1980s and early 1990s, numerous organizations and individuals—including Oscar Arias—worked hard to try to end the (highly one-sided) system of violence that had become so deeply engrained in Guatemala. All such efforts were exhausted or failed until at last, in December 1996, the United Nations succeeded in brokering a cease-fire between the government of President Alvaro Arzú Irigoyen, a center-right civilian, and the country's main opposition group.

But alongside the still-lingering *climate* of terror, which continued so long as Guatemala's judicial and police systems continued to be subject to the often brutal pressures of the military, Guatemala continued—even after 1996—to see many continuing *acts* of terror. In April 1998, Bishop Juan José Gerardi presented the archbishop of Guatemala with a painstakingly researched report that concluded by attributing responsibility for *90 percent* of the civil-war killings to the Guatemalan military: two days later, Gerardi was bludgeoned to death outside his own house by an "unknown" assailant. In June 1998, the annual report on the human rights situation prepared by the UN Mission for Guatemala (MINUGUA) revealed an increase in extrajudicial executions and torture over the previous year. The report did also, more optimistically, find some decline in violations of the right to liberty, due process, and freedom of association.[11]

Under the terms of the 1996 cease-fire, the United Nations was mandated to establish its own truth commission to investigate the causes of the violence that had plagued the country for more than three decades. The commission's report, submitted in early 1999, found that during those decades of the civil war, about 200,000 of Guatemala's 11 million people had been killed or made to "disappear." Of the 42,000 killings of civilians that the panel was able to investigate, it found the army responsible for 93 percent. (The country's guerrilla movements were blamed for 3 percent, and 4 percent were unattributable.) "The massacres that eliminated entire Mayan villages . . . are neither perfidious allegations nor figments of the imagination, but an authentic chapter in Guatemala's history," the UN report stated. It documented a total of 626 massacres that the army carried out during the 1980s, judging that in the north of the country, where the Mayan population was largest, the campaign had amounted to a systematic "genocide."[12]

Soon after the UN report was released, President Clinton expressed his regret for the decades of support that the U.S. government had given to the Guatemalan military—support that stretched as far back as the CIA-engineered overthrow of the democratically elected President Jacobo Arbenz Gúzman in 1954. "It is important that I state clearly that support for military forces or intelligence units which engaged in violent and widespread repression of the kind described in the [UN] report was wrong," Clinton said. "And the United States must not repeat that mistake."[13]

Jody Williams asked Menchú about the situation of previously marginalized groups in Guatemala since the 1996 cease-fire: "Have they had to lower their voice to maintain peace on the surface, or do they still struggle with the same determination to make sure that the beautiful words on the piece of paper is a reality for everybody in society?"

Menchú replied,

So that you don't hear me as being very pessimistic, I'm going to say some of the most optimistic things that I believe in. The biggest and most important thing that we have accomplished in Guatemala is to bring the violent conflict to an end: a conflict of thirty-seven years that created all kinds of separate interests—a war in which many people made their life from it, earned their daily income and made a lot of money as well. So it's a very good thing that their war is over!

But we have not all won in that war. And those who are most affected by that war are the victims of the war: the internal refugees, that are probably 95 percent indigenous peoples; the former combatants on both sides, on the side of the government, the military, and of the guerrilla. Those combatants have not really obtained or gotten anything. They are no longer mobilized or no longer members of groups, but we find that they don't have anything! They don't have land or a way to earn their income, and we find that they're always beginning to look for something.

Since Jody Williams knows El Salvador and we make comparisons, we often feel that more has been accomplished in El Salvador than in Guatemala. And what has been obtained, what we've managed to get in El Salvador really is quite minimal. We [in Guatemala] are still struggling to streamline the judicial system. And if I were to tell you just one case of trying to get a legal, judicial process going against the military, you would recognize how very, very difficult and complex that is. There are still judges being bought. There are threats, blackmail drives—I don't know what it's called, but we've got it!

I have said that the peace accords are political agreements. And political agreements have to become judicial agreements. And to go from the law to the actual practice is a very, very long process. We are changing the entire police system. We're trying to change the army from a repressive to a not-repressive army. All of this will take a very, very long period of time.

And we, the indigenous peoples, it appears that we are absent from all of this. We're absent in the sense that we're absent among the elite, among those who are making the decisions. But we are very, very active in all other regards. There are many changes taking place. There are more indigenous people who are local mayors, and we are participating all the time in this broader peace process. That has been our struggle, that *it's not enough to simply sign the peace accords, but what really matters is what happens after those peace accords have been signed.* What is oftentimes worse than the war is the period after the war, and all the legacies that it has left in the country we find ourselves suddenly in, as we're able to see it.

FROM THE POINT of view of the indigenous communities on the landmass often called the Americas, the experiences that the Guatemalan Maya have suffered at the hands of a European-descended elite over the past forty years are nothing new. Harvard anthropologist David Maybury-Lewis has written that the demographic consequences of the invasion of the Americas by Europeans

> are the most drastic that the world has ever known. They were heightened by the unique circumstances of the encounter, which was among the most extraordinary meetings in the history of humankind. It brought together two large portions of the human race that had virtually lost touch with each other and been separated for at least forty thousand years . . .
>
> A century [after 1492], the indigenous population of the entire hemisphere had been cut in half. Initially they were massacred; later

they were worked to death in the mines or on the plantations; but the greatest killer was disease and the famine and dislocation that went with it. . . .

What happened to the native peoples of the Americas is on a vast scale that which has been happening and continues to happen to indigenous peoples the world over.[14]

Describing the situation of indigenous peoples in the present era, Maybury-Lewis and a colleague wrote, "Since the states that claim jurisdiction over indigenous peoples consider them aliens and inferiors, they are among the world's most underprivileged minorities, facing a constant threat of physical extermination and cultural annihilation. This is no small matter, for indigenous peoples make up approximately five percent of the world's population."[15]

In her presentation at the University of Virginia conference, Menchú told the audience that throughout the world, indigenous peoples were "running the risk of becoming reduced to indigenous ghettos. I struggle to break that silence! I struggle to call out to you so that you will know that the indigenous peoples have an intercultural experience, a multiethnic experience. I also struggle so that together we can erase the stereotypes that there are about indigenous peoples.

IF THE GUATEMALAN military really committed as many atrocities as were reported by both the United Nations and Bishop Gerardi's team, then how, as Guatemalans from all the country's different communities struggle to build a lasting peace in their land, are the military to be dealt with? In chapter 7, a very similar set of issues regarding South Africa is examined: how members of the different communities there have sought, during the few years of democracy, to come to terms with atrocities committed—by both sides, though also, as in Guatemala, highly asymmetrically—during the long decades of apartheid. But when thinking about how to transform a deep-rooted system of violence like that in Guatemala it is also useful to probe a little deeper into what the military leaders themselves were thinking of as they planned, authorized, and executed those atrocities.

Menchú answered one part of this question when she said that the military had aimed at "the elimination of all witnesses to their [earlier] crimes." From that point of view, the military's campaign of terror had its own, inbuilt mechanism of escalation, regardless of anything anyone else might have done. For if they considered it necessary to kill fifty people to eliminate witnesses to ten earlier killings, then later it would be necessary to kill 250 to eliminate witnesses to those fifty, and so on.

And what have leaders of the military establishment themselves said about the reasons for their own actions? (This question echoes what the Dalai Lama said about focusing on the *motivation* of the party against whom one struggles for one's rights, and what Aung San Suu Kyi once said: "It is more important to try to understand the mentality of torturers than just to concentrate on what kind of torture goes on, if you want to improve the situation."[16]) In 1993, Oscar Arias and some colleagues from Canada made a significant attempt to probe the Guatemalan military's views, when they invited Defense Minister Mario René Enríquez Morales and other Central American defense ministers to take part in a forum on demilitarization and democratization in their region. Enríquez and his counterparts were each invited to lay out a fairly detailed description of the nature of the threats they saw their respective countries confronting.[17]

In the description that Enríquez gave of the Guatemalan military establishment's "threat perception," he listed five types of external threats faced by his country. These threats were drug trafficking, foreign support of the subversive movement, immigration, economic effects of the establishment of NAFTA, and ecological degradation. Regarding foreign support of the subversive movement, he wrote, "Groups persist today which, professing the communist ideology, insist in the use of arms to take power. . . . The persistence of this support suggests the permanence of the external threat; it provides the armed radical groups with a means of continuing their struggle." He also listed six "internal threats": political instability, the socioeconomic situation, ethnic problems, common organized crime, radical terrorism, and internal immigration. Regarding ethnic problems, he warned, "The absence of a national conscience [consciousness] and the deepening contradictions among different ethnic groups suggests the peril of a centrifugal force that could threaten national unity."[18]

Rigoberta Menchú said at the University of Virginia conference that, in the case of Guatemala,

if the agents in the war . . . had decided twenty years ago to speak with each other, then we would have prevented thousands and thousands of deaths, we would have avoided a great deal of destruction. It is important that *those who are participating in war* must decide to seek peace: this is important throughout the world, not just in our own case. Right now we are reconstructing our country also in the midst of great difficulties, especially when there has been so much distrust, so much social fragmentation. And especially when the system of justice has always favored certain groups, it has been a great struggle to create a just legal system. . . .

We want to contribute to intercultural education, to education in peace, in which peace does not just come as a result of war but rather as a conviction: peace as *mutual* conviction. We must also understand that today's world is a multicultural world, a multilinguistic world, a multiethnic world. If we don't understand that, then we will also always be playing to the dominant groups.

When I'm in an indigenous community in Bolivia, in Ecuador, in Mexico, I understand that misery and poverty are not the sole property of indigenous people, but of many, many people. When I see street children, I notice that there aren't very many who are indigenous. Why? Because the children are in the community, they're in the family, or because they have found a new family. The same thing has happened in the areas of conflict with indigenous children. All [the children of] of indigenous peoples were absorbed by the community. . . . But in other communities, in other conflicts not involving indigenous peoples, I find that the orphan children were left out on the street.

This is to say that indigenous peoples have a lesson to teach in the prevention of conflicts and the resolution of conflicts. And we also have a message for the reconciliation of our peoples. In order to do so, we have to create a very different climate, a climate of mutual respect. So each time we see that we have common problems, and we must find common solutions.

This is why I'm here with my colleagues, my fellow Nobel laureates. I believe that each of us has a specialty in our own areas, in our own convictions that work in favor of peace. When we struggle individually, we sometimes give it an accent—more Maya, more woman, more radical, less radical, but we're all working toward the same goal.

A few hours earlier, East Timor's José Ramos-Horta spoke about the need for education for a multicultural world. He recalled that, from a young age, he had always been fascinated by stories about the Jews. And later, he had come to learn that he had some Jewish heritage in his family, too, "going back to the Inquisition."

"But why the Jews?" he asked.

> [They were] almost literally destroyed in the thirties. What wrong have they done? A powerless group of people, no power behind them. It was prejudice, ignorance, for centuries, that led to the hatred toward the Jews, but if those who are so hateful of the Jews were to read and to study their extraordinary culture, the wealth, the richness of their history and their culture, their music, maybe that would not have happened. . . .
>
> What I want to drive at is my conviction, my belief, that it's ignorance of each other that feeds into prejudice. Prejudice leads to suspicion and then conflict. I do not wish to oversimplify. There are other reasons for wars, such as the fight to control natural resources, or territory. But a lot of the wars in the past and today are caused by prejudices, because of ignorance. And then, mistrust and fear of the other side.

ONE OF THE most pervasive of the stereotypes that indigenous people in particular suffer from centers on allegations of their "backwardness." When "nonindigenous" people explore what is meant by this quality, they (we) can learn quite a lot about their (our) own values, too!

Historically, there have been three main types of context in which "nonindigenous" people have come into contact with people "indigenous to" any particular piece of land. One of these has been as good neighbors, engaged in trade and perhaps a little politics with each other, over a period of generations. The other two contexts have been far less benign, from the viewpoint of the indigenous peoples involved. One was war or interimperial rivalry, a context in which soldiers and explorers representing a society based elsewhere have pushed onto new continents, or deep into the interior of lands they previously knew only from the sea, in an effort either to gain strategic advantage for their own forces, or—equally importantly—to deny it to their rivals. The other was a desire for clean-cut commercial advantage: control over the land and its resources; domination over a captive market—even, in West Africa and elsewhere, domination over a market in enslaved persons. Quite often in this process, as American Quaker John Woolman noted back in the 1760s, the demands of war and of commercial advantage proceeded hand-in-hand.[19]

Viewing other human groups as *secondary features*, whether of a landscape whose primary importance was the topographical requirements of war, or of a landscape and economic system where the outsiders' goal is profit and monopolistic control, requires that the outsiders view these people quite differently from the "good neighbors" with whom they may, elsewhere, have sustained stable relationships over generations. It requires that the indigenous people be viewed, at a deep level, as *substantially less than human*. Their "function" in the view of the dominating outsider is either to get out of the way and leave the advantages of the land to the arriving outsider, or if they remain, to be used by the outsider as cheap or forced labor.

Bishop Tutu noted in a 1986 sermon, "We Africans speak about a concept difficult to render in English. We speak of *ubuntu* or *botho*. . . . It has to do with what it means to be truly human, it refers to gentleness, to compassion, to hospitality, to openness to others, to vulnerability, to be available for others and to know that you are bound up with them in the bundle of life, for a person is only a person through other persons. And so we search for this ultimate attribute and reject ethnicity and other such qualities as irrelevancies. *A person is a person because he recognizes others as persons.*"[20]

But that was definitely not the view that dominated most of the discourse inside the Europe-based empires, regarding the indigenous peoples encountered in distant continents. Indeed, the highly individualistic cast of most traditional Western views of personhood may have made it easier for the proponents of these views to adopt very instrumental views of other humans. Among the rulers of most European empires, the discourse of the "backwardness" of indigenous peoples, and of their essentially subhuman status, was all too pervasive. Many of the distant lands "discovered" by European explorers were described in their chronicles as *terra nullius*—nobody's land—despite the evident presence of indigenous communities there. In our own century, Robert Frost wrote about North America prior to colonization by the Europeans as having been "unstoried lands," as though either the native Americans had never existed—or, if they did exist, still, the stories they told on and about these lands counted for nothing.[21] In Tasmania, British settlers even used to hunt the indigenous peoples for sport, until finally, like numerous other Tasmanian and Australian "species," they were nearly totally exterminated.

Maybury-Lewis noted one recurring aspect of the European colonizers' concept of "backwardness." Despite all the political and doctrinal differences among the European empires that invaded the Americas, they were all "uniformly outraged by those indigenous societies that did not recognize private property, particularly the private ownership of land. The invaders felt vaguely (but quite correctly) that this was the basis of *civilization as they knew it*, and they expended enormous effort in trying to stamp out the communitarian beliefs and practices of indigenous peoples, whom they deemed backward for subscribing to them. At the present time indigenous societies that believe it is immoral not to share with one's kin or with those less fortunate than oneself are also considered backward, for this surely hampers capital accumulation and therefore 'progress' as the modern world sees it."[22]

In the United States, the federal government tried to force native Americans to overcome this communitarian aspect of their "backwardness" more than a century ago. Under the 1887 General Allotment Act, the lands of many Indian reservations, which different Indian communities had until then held in common, were broken up: individual community members were "allotted" 80 to 160 acres of land apiece. But then, the federal government turned around and claimed that these same Indians were incapable of managing their own land, so it set itself up as "trustee" for many of the new landowners. Acting for the federal government, the Interior Department leased out to various (white-dominated) commercial interests the rights to extract various resources, including oil, from the trust lands. A century later, the situation had become chaotic, to say the least. The government supposedly held more than ten million acres in trust for up to half a million individual Indians, but tens of thousands of the relevant records had been completely lost. A March 1999 news report noted that even the basic numbers about the system were unknown: the Interior Department claimed to manage about 300,000 trust accounts, with roughly $500 million passing through them each year, but even they admitted that they could not account for 50,000 of the active trusts. What was evident was that over the preceding century, hundreds of thousands of native Americans had been denied, first, the ability to continue managing their lands in common, and then, many of their rights as individual trust beneficiaries.[23]

Regarding the supposed backwardness of indigenous peoples, Maybury-Lewis wrote that the colonists who came in from outside and dominated indigenous societies traditionally used two parallel arguments to justify their destruction of indigenous peoples' ways of life: "Such societies are said to be doomed to extinction anyway because they cannot survive in the modern world. They also stand in the way of development." As a longtime specialist on indigenous cultures, Maybury-Lewis challenged the first of these arguments head-on:

> It is quite clear that the stereotype of indigenous cultures being bound to disappear because they cannot deal with the modern world is quite wrong. Indigenous societies have shown themselves to be extraordinarily resilient in maintaining the spirit of their cultures through dramatic changes. Indigenous cultures only disappear if the bearers of the culture are scattered or annihilated by external force, or when drastic changes are forcibly and rapidly imposed on indigenous societies, rendering them unable to cope. The point to remember is that indigenous cultures are not extinguished by natural laws but by political processes which are susceptible to human control. To argue otherwise is to obscure the fact that they are victims of the convenient use of power against the relatively powerless.[24]

For her part, Menchú has written that

> many people want to return to the old Inca and Mayan ways of five hundred years ago. It is impossible to do that! How can we go back and be the same? Indigenous tradition itself says that time is long and wide, and it has its own signs. Each sign has a different meaning, it may mean the time has come for a generation of great leaders or great achievements. . . .
>
> Many people believe that indigenous peoples have been no more than spectators over the past five hundred years, that we are the conquered people. . . . People should remember that indigenous peoples built great cities with our own hands, we created the most wonderful works of art with the sweat of our brows. All were carefully designed and built in our own distinctive way. We have contributed so much to

the richness of our peoples in America that it is impossible to say where indigenous culture begins and ends.

Culture isn't pure, it is dynamic, it is a kind of dialectic, it is something that progresses and evolves. As for purity, who can determine what that means? I don't think our peoples were ever passive bystanders. The advances made have just as much been ours, for we contributed to them, just as we have contributed to the enormous ethnic diversity.[25]

At the conference, the Mayan laureate said that over the years many people have asked her, "What happens if we give indigenous peoples technology? Will they lose their culture?" Her reply:

Don't worry so much about what we will gain and what we will lose. Just give it to us! If those technologies are *imposed* on us, and they do not serve our interests, our communities will reject them. But if our peoples incorporate those technologies into their own cultures with their own knowledge, with their own local technologies, then certainly those things that are offered to us and given to us will have many positive results. So that if there are some rich people here and some big corporations, they too can work with indigenous peoples — as long as it is in a relationship of trust and understanding!

WHEN DEFENSE MINISTER Enríquez wrote about "the peril of a centrifugal force that could threaten national unity," he was expressing fears that numerous central governments have entertained concerning the aims of many geographically compact ethnic "minorities," including indigenous groups. At the conference, Julian Bond asked Menchú how a state can balance the needs of emerging ethnic or religious minorities with "its desire for stability and homogeneity among its people?"

She replied that this issue needed to be tackled at several levels:

I think that there's a legal question that has to be addressed, a question of laws and a change in a constitution in a country. All of the national constitutions recognize a homogenous people and do not speak of the multiple ethnic groups that exist within one nation. Maybe there was a point in time in history where dominant cultures had the right or the ability to dominate others, but that is no longer the case today. Because today everybody is multilingual, multicultural, and multiethnic.

And if there's a form of education that exists that goes *against* a culture, it means that it's not an education at all. So I think there are formal and legal changes that must be made—but what is most difficult is the change in the *attitude* that people have. Because we also have countries and constitutions with wonderful laws, but these are never enforced! In Guatemala, in the peace process we have managed to produce a series of wonderful laws that recognize the different ethnic groups and indigenous groups of the country. But those accords will take a long, long time—many, many years—before they can be implemented.

People thought that peace had simply arrived and that everything was fine, and nothing much more had to be done in order to accomplish the peace. [But] I think that much has to be done educationally from a perspective of multicultural identities. . . . In the last two decades, I have to say that many governments have simply refused to take a positive attitude and to begin to discuss questions about native peoples and indigenous cultures in their own countries—or ethnic minorities, or religious peoples.

One of the big fears that immediately emerges is that people say, Well, if we give these people more rights, they'll suddenly want to become independent. Then it appears that independence, our independence, within nations is what people worry the most about. But I think that in our day and age, there are very, very serious problems with the lack of comprehension, the lack of understanding amongst people of different ethnic and religious orientations. This is a very, very serious problem that has to be on our agenda, and we have to engage it.

THE CLASH BETWEEN state sovereignty and the rights of indigenous and other minority communities thus seems almost as hard to resolve as that between state sovereignty and individual rights![26] While the existing boundaries between states seldom coincide satisfactorily with the lines between compact and culturally homogenous peoples, still, these boundaries cannot be redrawn willy-nilly, and can never be redrawn "perfectly." In addition, a powerful state's claim of "concern" for the rights for some minority group allegedly oppressed by a rival government has throughout history sparked several major wars.

In Guatemala, members of the military establishment may feel they have particular reason to worry that too strong a concern for minority or other indigenous rights could lead to the break-up of their country. Many in the Guatemalan ruling establishment have a folk memory of how, in the middle of the nineteenth century, most of the lands of the former captaincy-general of Guatemala were pulled away from rule by Guatemala City—and often by force. Canadian researcher Hal Klepak has written that since then, "Guatemala has seen itself as having security problems of significance on three of its four borders. In two of those three cases, issues arose with powers much greater than itself [Spain/Mexico, and Britain, in present-day Belize]."[27] The fear of the emergence of new centrifugal forces seems quite genuinely held.

However, Guatemala's rulers are by no means the first rulers of a multi-cultural country to face such a fear. And elsewhere, robust solutions to these problems that do not rely on the use of force have been found in various countries. In Spain, for example, the central government had frequently repressed the language and customs of the people of the region of Catalunya (Catalonia). This repression happened under the historic Spanish monarchy and under the profascist president General Francisco Franco, who ruled from 1939 through 1975. But after Franco died in 1975, Spain saw a bloodless and effective transition to democracy that paralleled the democratic transition in neighboring Portugal. In 1977, Spanish citizens took part in their first free and fair elections in over forty years, and in 1978, their parliament introduced a new constitution that devolved many of the central government's powers down to seventeen "autonomous regions." Of these, three—Catalunya, the Basque region, and Galicia—were defined as "historic nationalities." Through this simple procedure, these nationalities achieved broad cultural and administrative autonomy within the wider structure of the Spanish state.

By the early 1990s, the new administration of Catalunya was running regular advertisements in American papers, urging people to visit "Catalunya, a country in Spain." The region's capital, Barcelona, was a bustling, polyglot mixture of different European nationalities—but most public signs were at least bilingual, in Catalan and Spanish.[28] (In 1986, democratic Spain had joined the European Union, a development that provided an important broader dimension to the country's devolution-of-powers story.)

Could these same elements—democratization, devolution of many powers to local regions, active multiculturalism, and inclusion in a broader regional economic and political order—come together in a country like Guatemala? Perhaps. But at least in Spain and some other countries at the end of the twentieth century, old problems of cultural domination and multiculturalism that previously seemed quite intractable were succumbing to solutions that left everybody's heritage affirmed and respected.

Harn Yawnghwe—himself a member of an ethnic minority—asked Menchú if it would be legally possible for someone like her to be active in national politics. "For example, could you run for president?"

The audience laughed appreciatively. "Sí," she replied cautiously.

> Yes, indigenous peoples can participate in the political institutions of the country, but they cannot do so *as indigenous peoples.* If someone who's an indigenous person would like to be president of Guatemala, he or she would have to work with an established political system, or political party. That political party would have to support him or her, and maybe they will not support, they will not work for, someone who is indigenous. Maybe I'm not completely correct here. Maybe there will be a change in the new millennium? So maybe then the question is, Why don't indigenous peoples themselves make a political party?

She switched to English to make her point totally clear: "Because we don't have money!" Amid more laughter (and some confusion for the translator), she returned to Spanish. "Because we indigenous peoples are the poorest people of this earth. We have not had our own businesses, our own companies. We have not been able to make our own money.[29] In addition, we are not very experienced in the world. We don't have a lot of experience in politics. We don't know what the intrigue of politics is. We haven't learned what it's like to *trip up another political candidate.*"

She broke into a broad smile as she looked around the room—and one suspected that she may have considerably more political skill than she was admitting. "And in terms of whether I would like to be president of Guatemala," she added, "what I can say is that it is the main worry of a lot of people that I do want to be that!"

5

Resisting the Domination of Stronger

Neighbors: José Ramos-Horta on

East Timor and the Dalai Lama on Tibet

José Ramos-Horta grips the podium as he recalls the events of 1975 when Indonesia invaded his country:

East Timor, a country of 700,000 then, 95 percent of them subsistence farmers, peasants . . . experienced in the following years one of the worst massacres amounting to genocide since the end of World War II. The tens of thousands of people who died in East Timor in the following days, weeks and months and years, were, in fact, just a footnote to the cold war, a casualty of *realpolitik* and the pragmatism of states.

We the East Timorese joined the Tibetans, the Kurdish, the Armenians, in the past—the Palestinians, the Gypsies, the Jews for centuries—*as expendable people*, as casualties of the grand scheme of the larger powers. Some of us managed to survive and get out of oblivion, or at least, cease to be ignored—like the Palestinians. But if we were to try to understand why all of this happened, what happened to the Jews for centuries, to the Tibetans for the past fifty years, to the Kurdish in endless wars, to the East Timorese, I would say we are all sacrificed on the altar of *realpolitik* and the pragmatism of states.

Much of this must have seemed familiar to Rigoberta Menchú. When Ramos-Horta or other East Timorese leaders talk about the difficulties they have met in trying to hang on to their people's cultures and traditions in the face of assaults from the Indonesians, the issues they raise are the same as those that dominate Menchú's words and writings. The same is true when the Dalai Lama or other Tibetans talk about the pressures their people have come under to "assimilate" to the culture of their current Chinese rulers.

There is, however, one significant distinction in international law between the situation in East Timor or Tibet, and that in Guatemala. In Guatemala, the assault against the indigenous cultures is carried out by a government that is accepted by all other governments as the "legitimate" authority over all of Guatemala's territory, including its Maya-majority regions. That means that under international (that is, intergovernmental) law, relations between the *ladino*-dominated government and the indigenous peoples of Guatemala are considered a matter of purely "internal" politics. In East Timor and Tibet, by contrast, the oppressing government was by no means universally recognized by other governments as being the "legitimate" authority over the territory concerned.

That distinction alters the dynamics of the encounter between oppressors and the oppressed in a number of ways. For example, the primary goal of East Timorese and Tibetan leaders is to win control over the fate of their own communities rather than to expand their presence and influence within the politics of, respectively, Indonesia or China. In the case of Menchú and other Guatemala Maya, by contrast, they have placed a high value in their political work on expanding their influence within Guatemalan national politics. Externally, meanwhile, the situation that the East Timorese and Tibetans enjoy under international law should mean that they can win more effective support than the Guatemalan Maya from sympathetic governments and peoples elsewhere, since the governments that have ruled so brutally over the East Timorese and Tibetans cannot wrap their actions in the flag (or shroud) of international legitimacy and "state sovereignty."

But how much difference does this make at the end of the day? Not as much as it used to. In the era of modern communications, an atrocity is much more easily seen by outsiders and recognized for what it is—regardless of whether the military or paramilitary organization that commits it does so in the name of a legitimate, sovereign authority, or not. And from the early 1990s on, some Western governments have shown themselves ready to intervene militarily in an attempt to protect besieged peoples, even in cases like those of the Iraqi Kurds or the ethnic Albanian Kosovars where the intervening governments did not directly challenge the "right" under international law of the central governments concerned to exercise sovereignty over the areas inhabited by these peoples.

In the era of modern communications, too, smart leaders in small nations like Tibet or East Timor realize that they can help to win the national goals they seek by appealing to forces inside the society currently dominating them. Thus, though they still do not aim to win control *over* national decision making within China or Indonesia, they do actively seek to *influence public attitudes within* Chinese or Indonesian society. These leaders realize, too, that even after they win a substantial degree of independence from the rulers who currently oppress them, they will still face a longer-term future in which their vastly bigger and more powerful neighbors will still be there, right next to them, dominating the strategic environment in which they live. Thus, a "decolonization" in these cases will be very different from the decolonizations that sent most of the European imperial rulers back to their homelands in the quarter century after 1945: in the present cases, the former colonial power will still be a close and powerful neighbor.

So the issue of the "sovereign rights" of states is no longer, at the dawn of the twenty-first century, as clear-cut as it was over the preceding two or three centuries. What are the implications of this for a small country like East Timor or Tibet, chafing under the yoke of a powerful neighbor? The 1998 gathering at the University of Virginia both opened and closed with a consideration of this issue. At the beginning of the gathering, José Ramos-Horta described the situation of his people in some detail. And just before the conference ended—after he had given his main presentation on the need for internal and external disarmament—the Dalai Lama responded to a request from Jody Williams for more information on the situation in Tibet. ("Yes, in fact, that was supposed to be the theme of my talk!" he exclaimed, to much laughter from the audience. "I have forgotten! Now actually, I really feel about the Tibet situation, [that] more or less now, many people know it. And if I repeat, then of course, only painful information and experiences.")

JOSÉ RAMOS-HORTA'S MOTHER was Timorean, a member of one of the two dozen indigenous communities that have lived on that rugged, mountainous island three hundred miles from the coast of Australia for centuries. His father was Portuguese and had been exiled to Timor for trying to protest the policies of Portugal's long-lived dictator, the Franco-era fascist António Salazar. When the future laureate was born in 1949, Portugal still held the eastern half of Timor under a tight imperial administration that would continue until 1975. The western half of the island, however, had been grabbed by the Dutch during the earlier contests in this region among the rival European powers: in 1949, along with the rest of the extensive Dutch empire in the East Indies, West Timor was handed over to the "post-colonial" regime of Indonesia, to be governed from Jakarta, thirteen hundred miles away.

So long as Salazar and his comrades ruled in Portugal, that country slipped ever further behind other European countries economically. The Portuguese never invested much in developing their overseas possessions, including East Timor. East Timor had one government secondary school: the young Ramos-Horta graduated from it then started work in the capital, Dili, as a journalist. Soon enough, he too was getting into trouble with the Portuguese administrators. In 1970, when he was twenty, he was heard making some pro-independence comments: the colonial authorities sentenced him to a year-long exile in another of Portugal's overseas possessions— Mozambique, in southeast Africa. Four years later, he was only saved from a second period of exile from his East Timor home by the eruption of the Carnation Revolution, a peaceful mass movement within Portugal that overthrew the fascists' forty-year rule and brought the country rapidly into line with the democratic norms of most of the rest of Western Europe.

The leadership of the Carnation Revolution consisted almost totally of midlevel army officers, many of whom were disgusted with the burden the military service in the colonies had placed on their lives and freedoms. One of their first orders of business was, not surprisingly, a speedy withdrawal from the former colonies. But no one in the colonial administration had done anything—at the level of politics, education, or basic physical infrastructure—to prepare these infant "nations" for independence. In Mozambique and Angola, the rapidity of Portugal's withdrawal left punishing civil wars in its wake. In East Timor, Ramos-Horta and his fellow nationalist activists used their new-found freedoms to found a social-democratic party. That party later became the Timorese National Liberation Front, Fretilin. In November 1975, Ramos-Horta, only twenty-six years old, was named foreign minister of the independent government that was trying to establish its hold over East Timor.

Ramos-Horta and his friends may have been preparing for independence, but Indonesia's powerful dictator, President Suharto, had other ideas. In December 1975—just hours after a visit from U.S. President Gerald Ford and Secretary of State Henry Kissinger—Suharto sent his army across the border to seize control of East Timor. In July 1976, he signed the Bill of Integration, which incorporated East Timor into Indonesia as its twenty-seventh province. No major government outside Indonesia (with the notable exception of Australia) ever recognized the legitimacy of that act of annexation. In the United Nations, the formal status of East Timor remained that of a Portuguese colonial possession. But after Indonesia's occupation of East Timor in 1975–76, no outside government ever proposed using force to oust Indonesia from there.[1] (Contrast this to the reaction of NATO to Saddam Hussein's 1990 attempt to incorporate Kuwait into his country as "just one more province.")

In his presentation at the conference, Ramos-Horta painted a vivid picture of the geopolitical context in which the events of 1975 unfolded:

You might recall a picture that made headlines in 1975. It was a picture of an American helicopter trying to land on the rooftop of the U.S. Embassy in Saigon to rescue American diplomats, CIA officials, South Vietnamese collaborators. Soon after: the collapse of the U.S. presence in South Vietnam, followed [by] Cambodia, Laos. Better than a thousand words, that picture illustrates the humiliating retreat of one of the two superpowers from a peasant war in Asia.

In another country the same year, the Portuguese empire had collapsed. Cuban and Soviet forces entered the battleground for influence in Angola. Mozambique became independent under a Marxist movement. The battle between East and West for influence in southern Africa rages on. In the Horn of Africa, Haile Selassie of Ethiopia had been overthrown again, shifting the balance of power to the Soviet side. The Soviet Union was already in control, so to speak, in Somalia. With the collapse of Haile Selassie, a Marxist regime took over. It seemed as if the "domino theory" first articulated by Lyndon Johnson, which served as the strategic rationale for U.S. intervention in Indochina, was being confirmed.

It was against this background that then-President Gerald Ford and Secretary of State Kissinger visited Indonesia, December 6th, 1975.

Within twelve hours of their departure, East Timor was invaded by Indonesia.

The Timorean laureate's years of exile from his homeland must have been difficult to bear. A report published by the prestigious, London-based Minority Rights Group (MRG) has estimated that "between 1975 and 1979, an estimated 200,000 East Timorese—a third of the population— lost their lives due to massacres, war-related starvation and disease."[2] Among those lost were three of Ramos-Horta's siblings. He has written that "in the summer of 1978, the war in East Timor came close to my own home. My young sister, Maria Ortencia, was killed by a Bronco aircraft, the prime counterinsurgency aircraft at the time, and the pride of the American Rockwell Corporation. The same year I lost two brothers, Nunu and Guillherme, the first killed by M-16 fire, and the second by a Bell helicopter assault on a village."[3]

During his time in exile, the laureate had the opportunity to reflect more deeply on who should take responsibility for what happened in and after 1975. Toward the end of his presentation, he admitted,

> You know, no one is clean in this conflict in East Timor! We, the East Timorese, fought each other too, in 1975, and many people were killed unnecessarily. Indonesia invaded East Timor. It should not have done so. No reason whatsoever for a country invading another! But at the same time, looking back, it was 1975, post-Vietnam, cold war: maybe we understand Indonesia's fears at the time, that an independent East Timor could turn into "another Cuba." That was the argument at the time. Rightly or wrongly, that was their fear.
>
> And the U.S., post-Vietnam, having just come out of Indochina, I also understand why would they bother about East Timor. So, they turned [their backs] and allowed Indonesia to resolve a potential communist problem. The reality is in the end we were the ones who were victims, remain victims today. And I just hope that we all seize on this [present] opportunity to redress the wrongs done to the people of East Timor.
>
> And first, yes, we have to be courageous enough and humble enough—and both go hand in hand, courage and humility—to say that, "Well, it is not [only] Indonesia that is at fault, not only the U.S.,

or Australia." First, we, the East Timorese, must ask ourselves, and address *our* responsibility in this conflict.

Ramos-Horta did not speak at length about the woes his people have suffered during their decades of repression. (Nor did any of the laureates dwell much on their people's sufferings: it was not that kind of discussion.) The MRG report judged that the original 1975 invasion was "a disaster. Indonesia underestimated the size of the task. It expected a quick victory, but misjudged the skill of its own forces and the determination of the East Timorese to resist invasion. In terms of population, the war had one of the highest casualty rates in the world since 1945. Eighty-five per cent of the original leadership of Fretilin were among the 200,000 East Timorese killed. It was an extremely brutal invasion, with rape, torture and physical abuse in addition to the murders."[4]

A semi-official East Timorean source has recorded that in the months after the fighting died down, 80 percent of the East Timorese who survived were forcibly relocated to new, army-guarded "guided villages," most of which were located on the plains, far from their original mountain homes. "Here they had to adjust to new crops and farming techniques, and to the prevalence of mosquitoes and malaria; socially they had to adjust to new village members, and psychologically, to the loss of their traditional lands to which they were legally and, as animists, spiritually attached. Meanwhile they were guarded and politically educated by an army whose intention it was to completely annihilate Timorese social and cultural structures and practices."[5]

In 1989, the territory was opened up to migrants coming from Indonesia's many overpopulated regions. (Since Indonesia's population is two hundred million, there were potentially huge numbers of such migrants.) By 1999, the migrants were thought to constitute 20 percent of the territory's population. There were other effects of Indonesia's efforts to assimilate East Timor's people into their (already very multiethnic) "nation":

It is hard to imagine having one's country invaded—as was East Timor. It is a profound shock. . . . A foreign flag flutters on flagposts, and there is a foreign national anthem to learn, a state creed (Pancasila) to memorize word for word, as well as indoctrination classes to attend, which tell about Indonesian nationhood and the responsibilities of the "new Indonesian man." More disturbing is the sudden demand to learn a new foreign language, which is essential for daily survival; the children must use it at school, adults must pick it up as they go. With all this physical and cultural change, it is hard to continue the old animistic ceremonies and, in the new villages where transformation of the total Timorese social structure has been engineered, hard to maintain the old songs, dances, marriage obligations, and ceremonies. In addition to all of this is the memory of slaughtered family members and neighbors, together with indelible pictures and stories of atrocities embedded in the mind. This is culture shock at its most damaging. Ironically Colonel Kalangie, the military commander for East Timor in 1982, explained the process like this: that he and his armed forces were in fact bringing "the new Indonesian civilization to Timor," but he regretted that it was not as easy as he had wished "to civilize this backward people."[6]

The colonel's use of the discourse of "backwardness" (as well as its supposed opposite, "civilization") was a classic of the genre. And the many parallels between this description of the situation of the East Timorese and descriptions of the situations faced in their ancient homelands by the Tibetans, the Guatemalan Maya, or other marginalized communities throughout history, seem very clear.

During his presentation, Ramos-Horta expressed the hope that, in more recent years, his country's situation had started to improve:

Twenty-three years ago, no one thought the East Timorese could survive the onslaught. Every major country in the world provided weapons to Indonesia. *Countries that preached democracy and human rights were the ones that provided most weapons,* not only to Indonesia but [to] many dictators around the world. All kinds of weapons were unleashed on the people of East Timor.

Twenty-three years later, we are there kicking, surviving—and it is the Indonesian empire that is collapsing around us! The Suharto dictatorship is gone. There is a dynamic, lively democracy movement taking shape in Indonesia, and Indonesian people are beginning to ask, "What have we done to this small nation of East Timor?" Who is going to explain to the Indonesian people the loss of their own people? Thousands of Indonesian soldiers, young people, lost their lives in the fields in East Timor. *Who is going to explain to the Indonesian*

*people the hundreds of millions of dollars wasted in weapons purchases
instead of channeling them to education, health care, clean water, housing for their people?*

BACK IN 1975, during those tumultuous weeks of aborted hopes for independence, Ramos-Horta never did get to present his credentials as foreign minister and East Timor's ambassador to the United Nations. There
followed many years of living out of suitcases, shuttling between Australia, Portugal, New York, and elsewhere, in an attempt to keep his
country's cause alive. He had already, as he explained in Cabell Hall,
been a longtime admirer of President John Kennedy, and Robert Kennedy: "It is remarkable, interesting, how far away in Timor we had no
television, only some very bad shortwave radio, and [yet] we heard a lot
about John Kennedy and Robert Kennedy. I think they influenced me
a lot." During his time in exile, Ramos-Horta found some additional
heroes:

> Then came . . . Martin Luther King, and then the living ones, you
> know, this gentlemen sitting opposite: His Holiness the Dalai Lama.
> The first I heard about the Dalai Lama was simply curiosity. The
> name was exotic, the country was exotic! So, everybody spoke so
> much about the Dalai Lama that once I went to listen to His Holi-
> ness. I was among the first to line up, because I want to see him up
> close. After a half hour, I left. I was bored! Because he kept talking
> about peace, and peace, and I wanted to hear more about his trip
> from Tibet to exile.
>
> But then when I left the meeting, and I kept thinking about how
> this man whom the Chinese authorities have done so much harm, to
> him and to his people, he is so compassionate— And then I start
> thinking more seriously about his words, and began reading more, *In
> Exile from the Land of Snows.*[7] And it made me very embarrassed,
> you know, when at that time I would hate the Indonesians, and would
> love to see someone bombing Jakarta! And then I was embarrassed,
> and I learned tremendously from His Holiness.
>
> But the list of people I admire is enormous, you know. I get tre-
> mendous inspiration, lessons, from Oscar Arias, Desmond Tutu . . .
> Aung San Suu Kyi. So I could not say, you know, one particular per-

son, because fortunately there are so many. But the very first that affect me probably . . . was the Kennedys.

In 1983, Xanana Gusmão, the veteran resistance hero who continued to lead Fretilin's armed liberation movement from deep inside East Timor's mountain forests, launched the movement's first preliminary peace talks with the Indonesian military. Though that first overture reached a dead end, Gusmão and Fretilin kept on trying. In 1986, Gusmão named Ramos-Horta as his special representative. Two years later, Fretilin was reorganized into a body called the National Council of Maubere (Timorean) Resistance, CNRM: Ramos-Horta was named its cochair.

In 1992, a law professor from Tufts University drafted a new peace plan for the CNRM. It proposed a multiyear, multiphase transition from Indonesian rule to the hoped-for independence. Gusmão gave his approval to this plan shortly before he was captured in November 1992 by the Indonesian forces and given a twenty-year sentence—to be served far away from Timor, in Jakarta.

Ramos-Horta carried on with the peace initiative and presented the peace plan to various international bodies, including the European Parliament and the United Nations. The plan proposed a multiphase peace process that would stretch over between five and eight years. Throughout the interim periods, Indonesia's heavy troop presence in the territory would be thinned and then replaced by a local police force under UN command; basic human rights—including free use of the Portuguese and (native) Tetum languages—would be restored; and rapid social and economic development programs would be undertaken. At the end of the interim, residents would vote in a referendum between three options: full independence, free association with Portugal, or integration into Indonesia. If the voters chose independence, they would then elect a constituent assembly and government, which would apply for UN membership and would declare East Timor to be a nonmilitarized Zone of Peace and of Neutrality, under international guarantees.[8]

Ramos-Horta described UN Secretary-General Kofi Annan as "the best secretary-general in at least thirty years." He said that Annan had put "enormous effort" into bringing Portugal, Indonesia, and the East Timorese to the negotiating table. Those efforts received new momentum after May 1998, when the anti-Suharto riots in Indonesia forced the aging dictator to declare a rapid retirement after thirty-two years in office. Ramos-Horta said that he now saw "a real, genuine move in Indonesia" toward resolving the East Timor question, "in spite of—and we understand this—their extraordinary problems. They also realize that it is one of the most costly problems to them. But as you know in a situation of transition, like in any place, there is lack of cohesiveness, lack of direction, lack of a central authority, to make the necessary move. And we have to wait a few more months for clarification in Indonesia."

He also disclosed that he had asked Oscar Arias to lead a team of advisors to the East Timorese negotiating team. "And he agreed! When I informed my colleagues, we are all thrilled that Oscar Arias has accepted to be our advisor: someone who brought about peace in Central America. When the two superpowers were fighting each other, it was that little country, Costa Rica, and Oscar Arias, that brought about peace there. That's why I thought, if he can pull it off in Central America, he can help us in East Timor."

(Later, Julian Bond asked Arias what advice he would give the Timorese. Arias replied, "It seems to me that the international community should support the East Timorese, and what you need is political will. . . . What you need for negotiations is patience, humility, political will, and the knowledge that you need to compromise. And certainly, the Indonesians should understand and should know that the international community is with the East Timorese. . . . They deserve to become a nation, an independent nation, and the international community should support them.")

RAMOS-HORTA, LIKE THE rest of the CNRM leadership, had always been strongly in favor of the East Timoreans choosing, during the referendum proposed in their peace plan, the route of complete national independence. But he understood that some of his countrymen might, even in a free and fair referendum, prefer to support a continued link with Indonesia, under some long-term form of autonomy. And anyway, he realized the need that even a fully independent East Timor would have, for healthy long-term relations with its huge neighbor. "I still believe," he said in his presentation at the conference "that in the long run, beyond the Band-Aid type of diplomacy which is peacemaking and signing treaties, you actually need to go for community dialogue."

He said he had been surprised to learn, during a recent visit to Greece, that on the divided Mediterranean island of Cyprus, there was still not much intercommunal dialogue between Greek-Cypriots and Turkish-Cypriots. If that situation is allowed to continue, he surmised, then intercommunal divisions that might have seemed artificial a few years earlier can start to take on the appearance of "part of history, part of culture." But he warned that such dialogue can take a long time before it builds up lasting ties of trust. "It does not produce the [quick] result that we all like in a peace treaty signed between two parties, like you have done in Bosnia and Kosovo, with the threat of force behind it. But it's the only way, I think."

In the case of East Timor, he said that, in the preceding months,

> we have been making appeals and appeals to our people on the ground: Please! We don't want to see one single Indonesian migrant touched. We don't want to see one single house burned. Because with the collapse of the [Suharto] regime, and because we have so many migrants in Timor, the temptation to exact revenge on them is great. Even before the collapse of Suharto back in May, we began a massive, active campaign of telling our people not to use violence on the innocent migrants. And so far, beyond some occasional verbal abuse, not one single Indonesian migrant has been harmed and not one single house has been torched. But this process [of building intercommunal trust] will take months and years.

Regarding the dialogue on East Timor that Suharto's successor, President B. J. Habibie, had launched, Harn Yawnghwe asked Ramos-Horta whether the Indonesians still had some fears that a withdrawal from East Timor "might lead other islands, within the Indonesian nation, to ask for more autonomy."

Ramos-Horta replied,

> Yes, there is some genuine fear—unfounded but genuine fear—on the part of some Indonesians. Because Indonesia is a huge archipelago: there are thousands of islands, 250 to 300 ethnic groups speaking five hundred languages. They fear that letting go East Timor will set a precedent, and the ex–Soviet Union and ex-Yugoslavia scenario is not very much a good inducement to them to let go Timor.
>
> But the fact of the matter is that East Timor was never part of Indonesia! East Timor is predominantly Catholic, 95 percent colo-

nized by Portugal for almost five hundred years: culturally, ethnically, historically different [from Indonesia]. So it does not fit into Indonesian historical boundaries.

Whether their fears are founded or not, the reality is that there are some people who fear that. But at the same time we say, "But the longer you stay on in East Timor, the more costly it is for you, and *that* is when it could cause the unraveling of the Indonesian republic!"

I personally do not believe that Indonesia could disintegrate . . . because it's still becoming independent, you know. It doesn't work like that. You have to have a real movement on the ground in Indonesia of people wanting to separate from Indonesia for this to happen. And so far, there are some protests in other parts of Indonesia, but by and large, it's not over the question of independence or sovereignty. They just want more autonomy to deal with their cultural and economic matters.

East Timor therefore is very unique in this regard. But increasingly, there are many people in Indonesia, including very important Muslim leaders such as Dr. Amien Rais, who are calling for a referendum on self-determination in East Timor.[9] There are people in the military—top in the military!—who are also calling for a referendum in East Timor. So I believe if we, on our side, the Timorese side, are also responsible enough to be flexible and creative, to enable Indonesians to get disengaged from East Timor gradually without loss of face, with honor, with dignity, and if we look into a long-term strategy, not seeking independence a year from now, or two years from now, who knows? In five, ten years from now, the new Indonesia would see an independent East Timor as very normal. That's our belief, and that's the strategy we are pursuing.

While working toward a healthy long-term relationship with Indonesia, the East Timorese leaders have also attended to the need to improve relations among their own people. (In India, in an earlier era, that task was an important part of Mahatma Gandhi's program of *swaraj*, or self-rule.) For the East Timoreans, the work of reconciliation has been a priority both inside their country and among its far-flung community of political exiles. Inside the country, it has been mainly Ramos-Horta's colaureate, Bishop Carlos Filipe Ximenes Belo, who has led the effort.

Belo was named as the Vatican's representative in Dili back in 1983. Soon after his inauguration, he used Dili's main cathedral to preach a sermon that strongly protested the brutality of some recent massacres and the Indonesian military's subsequent campaign of arrests. Since the authorities found it far harder to crack down on the church than on most other nongovernmental organizations working in East Timor, Belo's ability to communicate with the outside world—and to receive and distribute help for the many suffering East Timoreans—made a vital difference to the life of the people over the years that followed.[10] In 1991, after Indonesian troops fired on a crowd attending a memorial mass in Dili's Santa Cruz center, killing "anywhere between 100 and 400 participants," Belo protested strongly. He attempted to gather and disseminate as much information as he could about the massacre. The authorities retaliated by keeping his residence under tight surveillance. His phone lines were tapped, and there were several reported attempts to assassinate him.[11] The parallels with Daw Suu Kyi's situation in Rangoon are evident.

In October 1996, when the Norwegian Nobel Committee announced it was awarding the peace prize jointly to Ramos-Horta and Bishop Belo, it noted of Belo, "At the risk of his own life, he has tried to protect his people from infringements by those in power. In his efforts to create a just settlement based on his people's right to self-determination, he has been a constant spokesman for non-violence and dialogue with the Indonesian authorities."[12] Belo was holding negotiations in Jakarta when the Nobel award was announced. But the Indonesian government, with whom he was negotiating at that very time, refused to express even token congratulations to him! When he flew back to Dili, by contrast, about two hundred thousand people—one third of the territory's entire indigenous population—flooded to the airport to greet him.[13]

Ramos-Horta discussed Belo and his attempts at internal reconciliation:

Bishop Belo is a remarkable, extraordinary individual. He's in Timor, and he has been particularly, in the last few months, busy engaging the East Timorese society itself in approaches of reconciliation. A bit like in South Africa, and other places stormed by conflict, you have divisions within our community: [for example,] people who collaborated with occupation, and there is tremendous resentment toward those who collaborated. And so we are all engaged in this process of reconciliation.

Because although there is an ample opportunity now, a golden opportunity, to resolve the problem of East Timor— But if we don't at the same time embark on a process of reconciliation, then we could lose this opportunity.

If the Timorese begin to fight each other over [issues connected with] the past twenty-three years of collaboration with the Indonesian army— Because there are a lot of people that collaborate for different reasons: for fear, or for money. . . . Our collaborators, we view them largely as victims of the whole war itself. And I do not think that in our case a society, a country, can heal itself if soon after victory you embark on persecuting those who are on the other side.

He noted, however, that this attempt to reconcile with those who formerly collaborated with the Indonesian authorities presented nationalist leaders with a tough dilemma: how can you bring about internal reconciliation while also honoring the feelings of the many thousands tortured and bereaved because of the actions of those former collaborators? (This is the same dilemma Bishop Tutu discussed in depth during his main presentation; see chapter 7.)

Ramos-Horta also explored this dilemma—with respect to aging Chilean dictator Augusto Pinochet. Shortly before the Charlottesville gathering, British authorities had arrested Pinochet on charges arising from some of the "crimes against humanity" he was accused of committing when he ruled Chile between 1973 and 1990. "I was in Chile a year ago," Ramos-Horta said. "I met victims of torture, women who were raped, and I was angry—angry that the culprits were still there. But then, when I see the old man on the verge of going to jail, I say, 'Probably best to just send him home.'"

He shrugged his shoulders. "I'm not very good at dispensing justice, as you can see!"

Julian Bond asked more about the subject of internal reconciliation: "I think some of us in the United States look on the South African experience with envy, that we did not, at a time in our country, begin this process [a process similar to Tutu's Truth and Reconciliation Commission]. Perhaps it's not too late?" He turned to Ramos-Horta. "But *can* you embark on this process of reconciliation even before you've achieved your ultimate goal? Is it possible to begin now?"

Ramos-Horta replied, "Yes, it is possible for two reasons. One, a prag-matic reason on our part, that we must extend a hand to every Timorese in order to reduce the field of maneuver of our adversary. The less people on the other side, the better! So I'm not saying that our strategy is purely altru-istic, purely moral. It's also political. And then, the second [reason] is that . . . the country is small, too many people have died already. And I tell you frankly, you know, no one is clean in this conflict in East Timor."

IN MID-MARCH 1999, UN head Kofi Annan announced that Indonesia and Portugal had agreed to the holding of a direct referendum in East Timor, in which residents would express their preference for either independence or a continued link with Indonesia. Was this the breakthrough for which Ramos-Horta and his colleagues had been waiting?

A week after Annan made his announcement, Ramos-Horta told jour-nalists in Hong Kong that he was concerned that the UN chief had failed to mention any provision for Indonesia to withdraw its troops from East Timor before the vote. He warned that "if the U.N. simply relies on the will of the Indonesian side and pushes ahead with this vote, bloodshed is almost cer-tain, because the Indonesian army will be there, the [pro-Indonesian] para-military will be there, and their interest is to disrupt the vote, to intimidate the people."[14] In late August 1999, the vote did go ahead, under the super-vision of an (unarmed) UN vote-tallying body: nearly all the registered voters cast their ballots, and 78.5 percent of these were in favor of full independence. But over the days that followed, the military-backed, pro-Indonesian militias that Ramos-Horta had warned of rampaged throughout the territory. They attacked several UN workers and facilities, and ran-sacked the compound where Bishop Belo had been trying to shelter a thou-sand terrified civilians.[15] (Belo was just able to escape to safety.) The worst fears that Ramos-Horta had expressed the previous March thus seemed to have been realized. But finally, in mid-September, he and other backers of the East Timoreans' rights—including an activist foreign ministry in Portu-gal, and a concerned government in Australia—were able to persuade the Security Council to overrule Indonesia's previous objections and send an armed peacekeeping force to East Timor.

FOR RAMOS-HORTA, THE months that followed the University of Virginia conference brought some hopeful, and some very ominous, developments.

Regarding Tibet, meanwhile, those months brought what seemed like an unambiguous downturn in the political-diplomatic situation.

During all of the Dalai Lama's November 1998 visit to the United States, he was noticeably guarded in the references he made to the situation in his homeland. "When some recent Nobel laureates, and also the representative of Aung San Suu Kyi, explain about their nation's difficulties, then I have a sadness feeling coming in my mind," he said at the conference. "You can express very freely. [But] I have to look from various aspects, so sometimes it is a little difficult. So, while I am hearing some of the Nobel laureates expressing themselves freely, I felt, 'I wish!'"

The story of the long campaign the People's Republic of China has waged to wipe out the nationalist feelings and indigenous culture of the people of Tibet is numbingly similar to what happened to the people of East Timor. There are about six million Tibetans, of whom around 150,000 currently live in exile, mainly in India or Nepal. The rest have remained in their vast ancestral homeland, six times the size of California: 980,000 square miles of mountains, high plains, and rushing gorges, located in the lofty heart of the Himalayas.

The story of China's arrival in Tibet has several parallels with Indonesia's arrival in East Timor. By 1949–50, once Chairman Mao's armies had chased the noncommunist forces off the Chinese mainland and he was able to send motorized forces westward into Tibet, the British—whose presence in India previously served to check China's designs over Tibet—had left the subcontinent. Gandhi had been killed. And the man who was prime minister of India, Jawaharlal Nehru, was unwilling to force a confrontation with China over Tibet. So were Britain, the United States, and the other major powers. The Tibetans thus received no outside help, as vast numbers of Chinese troops poured into their country.

Under an agreement concluded between China and the British rulers of India in 1914, the British (and, by extension, international) recognition of a Chinese right to exercise some "suzerainty" over Tibet was explicitly tied to China's recognition of Tibet's right to local self-rule. Independent India, as successor to the British Raj, was obliged to stick to that formula. And when the Chinese poured into Tibet in 1950, they helped the Indians out by claiming a phony adherence to the principle of Tibetan "autonomy," which continues to this day.[16] But the "Autonomous Region" that the Chinese designated for the Tibetans included only half of the Tibetanpopulated homeland. Concentrations of Tibetans living outside that area were put under the administrative control of so-called Tibetan Autonomous Districts and Tibetan Autonomous Counties within provinces that China claimed were otherwise unambiguously Chinese.

Tibet's standing under international law and the status of China's rule over it, were therefore both quite murky. Under international law, Tibet has not been considered as lying unambiguously under Chinese sovereignty. But neither has China's rule there been deemed by most international lawyers to constitute a clear-cut example of a "belligerent military occupation," like the rule of Indonesia over East Timor, or Israel over Golan. It should be noted, however, that between 1959 and 1965, the UN General Assembly passed three resolutions calling for "the cessation of practices which deprive the Tibetan people of their fundamental human rights and freedoms, including their right to self-determination."[17]

In theory, if a people is ruled under belligerent military occupation, then their rights should receive special protection from any abuse at the hand of their military occupiers, under the terms of the 1949 Fourth Geneva Convention on the Protection of Civilian Persons in Time of War. Alternatively, if they are considered full citizens of the state that rules over them, then they should enjoy the range of human rights described in the Universal Declaration of Human Rights. But these protective codes have done little, in practice, to protect groups like the Guatemalan Maya or the East Timorese from the depredations of the governments that control them. The murky status of China's rule over Tibet has served the Tibetan people just as poorly.

For the first nine years of China's military rule over Tibet, the Dalai Lama and his advisors tried hard to make Tibet's relationship with Beijing work. But by 1959, Beijing was determined—as part of the disastrous Great Leap Forward policies it imposed on everyone under its control at the time—finally to stamp out all noncommunist thinking and culture among them. In Tibet, that translated into a broad new campaign to wipe out any capability the Tibetans might have had to defend or practice their ancient, predominantly Buddhist culture. As a vast, mechanized Chinese military force surrounded the Tibetan capital, Lhasa, in order to impose the new policy, the Dalai Lama and his followers tried to organize their followers to defend the city. But compared with the Chinese, the Tibetans were a ragged, ill-armed force. When it was clear that no military defense of the

holy places of Lhasa was possible, the Dalai Lama and thousands of followers fled over icy Himalaya passes to India. He was twenty-four years old. In
the blurred photos of those days, he appears a gangly, near-sighted youth ill
at ease with the sudden new hardships of his life in flight.

His Holiness and the rest of the exiled Tibetan leadership found a refuge
in the north Indian town of Dharamsala. It took them some time to recover
from the trauma of what they had been through, and to organize relief for
their many refugees. Along the way, some of the Tibetan exiles tried to sustain their resistance to China's rule of their homeland by mounting cross-
border guerrilla operations from Nepal and northern India.[18] But by the
early 1970s, the Dalai Lama had come to the conclusion that the only way
forward was through total reliance on a nonviolent strategy that would, he
hoped, open up a direct dialogue with the Chinese leadership. He has
described the Middle Way Approach he decided on then, as follows:

> I opted for a resolution of the Tibet issue, which does not call for the
> independence of Tibet or its separation from China. I firmly believe
> that it is possible to find a political solution that ensures the basic
> rights and freedoms of the Tibetan people within the framework of
> the People's Republic of China. My primary concern is the survival
> and preservation of Tibet's unique spiritual heritage, which is based
> on compassion and non-violence. And, I believe it is worthwhile and
> beneficial to preserve this heritage since it continues to remain rele-
> vant in our present-day world.
>
> With this spirit I responded immediately when [China's then-
> leader] Deng Xiaoping, in late 1978, signalled a willingness to resume
> dialogue with us. Since then our relation with the Chinese govern-
> ment has taken many twists and turns.[19]

Between 1978 and 1993, the two sides had intermittent contact. The
Chinese allowed the Dalai Lama to send four fact-finding delegations to
Tibet: on each occasion, the delegation was mobbed by local Tibetans
eager to have any contact they could with representatives of someone
they consider a living Buddha. In 1987, in a speech to the United States
Congress, he unveiled a Five-Point Peace Plan for resolving the Tibetan-
Chinese relationship. The plan called for a real autonomy for the Tibetans,
with the establishment of a Tibetan administration that would run every
aspect of daily life in the country; only defense and foreign affairs, the plan

said, would continue to be run by Beijing. Under the plan, however, the area of Tibet itself should be demilitarized and turned into a "zone of *ahimsa* (nonviolence)."[20]

Still, the Chinese stalled. They refused to engage in any substantive talks about the handover of everyday powers to the Tibetans. They continued to pour ethnic-Chinese settlers into Tibet, and ruthlessly to suppress any expression of pro–Dalai Lama feeling inside the country. Finally, in 1993, they broke off contact with the Dalai Lama's India-based exile government altogether.

At the conference, the Dalai Lama was hopeful that he was about to win a new breakthrough in his campaign for direct talks with Beijing. He noted that after the previous talks broke down in 1993, he had maintained some informal contacts with Beijing, and that since the beginning of 1998, those contacts had become "more substantive." He also drew a significant contrast between the attitude of the Chinese administrators within Tibet itself and that of the national Chinese leadership in Beijing. The main concern of the former was, he said, merely to keep the lid on the security situation, with a continuing appearance of day-to-day stability and no pro-independence street demonstrations. But he judged that the national leaders in Beijing were looking at the situation from a broader viewpoint. He said, "It seems that some leaders are thinking, I think, in a more moderate or a more serious way. So therefore, I think, now is the time better to be low key? So, let us see what new developments arise within the next few months. This is my thinking. . . . In the Tibet situation, I think there is a possibility to develop some kind of mutual trust. I feel that's coming."

The Tibetan leader stressed that he considered the main obstacle that remained was the continuing suspicion between the two sides. "Right from the beginning, I tried to solve this problem through direct communication with the Chinese government," he said, adding that between 1979 and 1986, he continued to try to open direct, face-to-face talks. But,

> the Chinese government formally or officially did not even admit that there was a problem about *Tibet*! The only problem was my return! Then the Chinese government made a five-point proposal about my return. And I told the Chinese government this is not the real issue. The main issue is six million Tibetan people, *their* rights, *their* welfare, preservation of their culture, their spirituality. In the meantime, inside

Tibet things are getting worse and worse. Therefore, there is no other alternative except to appeal internationally. Since then, the response year by year is really increasing, and is very, very encouraging. So, I want to take this opportunity to express my deep appreciation.

And I want to make clear: the final solution must be found through direct communication with the Chinese government. And you know, I feel that there should not be any basis of suspicion, since I am not seeking independence. I am seeking genuine autonomy, self-rule, because my main concern is the preservation of Tibetan-Buddhist culture as well as Buddhist spirituality. This is something not only of interest for the six million Tibetan people, but also for the larger community . . . in that part of the world. And particularly, among the Chinese! You see, historically, there are quite a number of Chinese following Tibetan Buddhism. Therefore, the preservation of the Tibetan-Buddhist culture, Tibetan Buddhism, is the interest of the Chinese also, in the long run. Therefore, my aim or my goal is very clear.

He said that ever since the days of Chinese leader Mao Tse-tung, the Chinese government had treated Tibet as a "unique" case, different from that of any of China's large number of other national or religious minorities.

Also, the constitution of the People's Republic of China . . . has provided for self-rule or autonomy now in the Tibetan case: Tibetan autonomous region, Tibetan autonomous counties, and districts, like that. So now, the problem is that this autonomy [is] not a meaningful autonomy!

I am seeking genuine autonomy. That means foreign affairs and defense are handled by the Chinese central government. Then the rest of the things, which we can manage: [for] those, Tibetans should have the full authority.

Julian Bond noted that the Dalai Lama had spoken of suspicion "on both sides," and asked what the cause of it was. Regarding the Tibetans' suspicions of the Chinese, the Dalai Lama recalled one of his people's sayings, to the effect that "once you have been bitten by a snake, you will even fear the next time you see a rope!" He hastened to add, though, that he personally believed things were changing for the better inside China.

Then, trying to put himself into the shoes of the Chinese, he noted that the Chinese had an authoritarian system, but,

> right from the beginning, the Tibetan community, when we became refugees, we started to work for *democratization*. So we can't stop the expression of Tibetan individuals or groups of Tibetans. We can't control them! People in the Tibetan refugee community here and there sometimes express their grievances or their resentment. There is a historical right for these things. Then the Chinese government gets more suspicion. All these, are they created by me, [they ask]—or, the Dalai Lama does not control fully these things?
>
> I can't do it, control them! Of course, once things we are seeking become clear from the Chinese central government, genuine self-rule, then of course I *can* persuade the Tibetan community: "Ah! Now, you see, we are getting something. So, therefore, please don't carry these kinds of demonstrations, these things!"
>
> Until that situation develops, I also find it difficult convincing the Tibetan refugee community that it should [restrain] certain kinds of expressions. So I think that also is a basis of suspicion.

Bond laughed and said that getting into cycles of mutual suspicion was something that happened to professors, too.

Religious studies professor Jeffrey Hopkins worked as the Dalai Lama's English translator for ten years, 1979 through 1989 (and had built on that long link to help organize the Charlottesville gathering). He now asked a question sent up by an audience member: "Your Holiness, how do you deal with Tibetan youth who are frustrated with oppression from the Chinese Communist government and turn to violence?"

"I always explain," came the reply,

> as I mentioned before: violence is not the human way. I believe, fundamentally, human nature is positive, gentleness. Therefore, they [should act] in a nonviolent way, the human way.
>
> Also, through nonviolence, whatever we achieve, the result, there is no negative side effect. Through violence, negative side effects. Through violence, even though we may get some kind of satisfaction, but negative side effects also immense.
>
> And then, most important, whether we like it or not, we have to live

side by side! So, in long future, generation to generation, in order to live happily, peacefully, friendly, it is extremely important, while we are carrying on struggle, it must be according to the nonviolent principle.

Sometimes, some youth have a little more frustration. Sometimes, we had a heated argument!

And then also, I had another [argument in favor of nonviolence]. Now, we get more and more support from Chinese, as a community. Not only outside, but even in mainland China: some writers, some thinkers, some educators. Now, only a small number, but growing— expressing their solidarity, their sympathy, and their concern. And they are critical about the central government's policy.

So these are, I think, the result of our nonviolent method, or approach.

His Holiness was asked what Americans could do to help Tibet. His first response was to express appreciation for the support for Tibet that already exists in the United States. "When President Clinton visited China, he personally spoke about the Tibetan issue. Very congenial!" he said. He suggested that Americans could also help Tibet by helping to change the attitudes toward Tibet held by ethnic Chinese people, both in the United States and beyond.

Since there are many Chinese students here, and many, many American Chinese, I think it's very useful to make known about this Tibetan culture. The Tibetan-Buddhist spirituality. You know recently, last year, I visited Taiwan—mainly, of course, nonpolitical, and a spiritual nature. So there were many Chinese [there], of course, many Buddhists. And some of them have a negative understanding, or a suspicion, are doubtful, about Tibetan Buddhism. Then, as a result of our meeting, it is my explanation, then these sort of get clear: the understanding about Tibetan Buddhism. They clearly want to study, and to practice.

So similarly, I think, there are an amount of Chinese brothers and sisters who do not know what Tibetan-Buddhist culture is. So now, year by year, more books, more materials, on Tibetan culture, Tibetan Buddhism, are coming! So that's also useful, helpful, you see, to make known to the Chinese brothers and sisters about Tibetan culture and Tibetan Buddhism.

THERE WAS A sad coda—at least, for a while—to the hopes that the Dalai
Lama expressed at the conference for an imminent breakthrough with Beijing. The following March, he issued a lengthy public statement to mark
the fortieth anniversary of the nationalist uprising whose failure had sent
him and his colleagues into exile. In it he revealed, "Late last autumn,
without any obvious reason, there was a noticeable hardening of the Chinese position on dialogue, and their attitude towards me. This abrupt
change was accompanied by a new round of intensified repression in
Tibet. This is the current status of our relation with the Chinese government."

He added,

It is . . . clear that force can control human beings only physically. It is
through reason, fairness, and justice alone that the human mind and
heart can be won over. What is required is the political will, courage
and vision to tackle the root cause of the problem and resolve it once
and for all to the satisfaction and benefit of the concerned people.
Once we find a mutually acceptable solution to the Tibetan issue, I
will not hold any official position, as I have clearly stated for many
years.

He noted that support for the Tibetans' position continued to grow, both
internationally and—a point he returned to at some length—among many
sectors of Chinese society, in Taiwan and on the mainland. "Today, the
Tibetan freedom movement is in a much stronger and better position than
ever before," he concluded. "And I firmly believe that despite the present
intransigence of the Chinese government, the prospects for progress in
bringing about a meaningful dialogue and negotiations are better today
than ever. I, therefore, appeal to governments, parliaments and our friends
to continue their support and efforts with renewed dedication and vigor."[21]

6

Transforming Systems of Violence at the

Personal Level: Betty Williams and the

Rehabilitation of Survivors of Violence

"**T**he absence of violence is only the beginning of the work for peace." These words, spoken by Betty Williams, summed up an important theme that ran throughout many of the laureates' presentations. Indeed, by centering on the personal-level dynamics that lie at the heart of peacemaking, Williams's own presentation drew together many threads that wove through the whole of the University of Virginia conference. In addition, by focusing on universal human themes like the need to overcome anger and find a path to forgiveness, Williams was able to spark a rich discussion among the laureates that provided added context for the Dalai Lama's call for "internal disarmament."

Another of Williams's comments reverberated throughout the gathering: her simple observation that "tears without action are wasted sentiment."

Betty Williams is a tall, ebullient woman with a strong Northern Ireland accent. She has a gift for establishing quick rapport with a roomful of strangers. As soon as she reached the podium, she wished everyone a brisk good morning. The response from the audience was sparse. "Let's do it again!" she commanded. With a big breath, she yelled, "Good morning!"

This time, the response was much stronger. "That makes me feel a little better," she said, laughing. "It might not make you feel any better, but it makes *me* feel better! I'm always terribly nervous when I get to speak, because before I became a Nobel laureate I only ever spoke in public once before in my life, which was at my sister's wedding, when my daddy got a little tiddly, and I had to stand up and thank all the guests! And then, Father Tutu was not a great help. He said, coming out, 'Are you going to perform?' I'm not quite sure what that means," she explained, to general laughter.

Later, she recalled with amusement that when she was awarded the peace prize in 1976, many people still considered her "just an ordinary housewife." "Did you ever hear such a disgusting word as an 'ordinary' housewife?" she asked in mock outrage. "Have you ever met an 'ordinary' housewife? Hands up! See, there's no such thing as 'ordinary' in the world. Everybody is extraordinary, and everybody can do something!"

A big part of what Betty Williams—like the other laureates—was trying to convey to the students and citizens in Cabell Hall was a message of empowerment, a message that "anyone" can, and everyone should, make a difference for the better in the world. "You see, there are no famous people in the world, ladies and gentlemen—there are only people who think they are! And when they gave me a 'Nobel' label . . . I didn't know what God's plan was, because you know, God has a very strange sense of humor. . . . He stuck this 'Nobel' label on me and threw me out in the world, and I very quickly became an expert in the issues of children!"

It was that concern that catapulted Williams into peace activism in her native Belfast in the first place:

> People say to me, why did you start the peace movement in Northern Ireland? The truth is, I did it purely for selfish reasons. Their names are Deborah and Paul: my children. And I really didn't want my babies to be brought up in a society that was destroying children. And so the movement for peace in Northern Ireland was begun by women, and I believe that women have a huge role to play in creating a just, nonviolent, and peaceful world.
>
> Now, that doesn't mean that we ostracize men. Ladies, get real! We cannot do it without our partners walking beside us. But at the same time, when presidents and what have you—I mean, in the last political campaign in the United States of America for President Clinton, the catchphrase was "It's the economy, stupid!" So, to the men of the world, [I say,] "It's a womb thing, stupid! Stop taking my children. Stop destroying my creation!"

In the months before the conference, many of the grassroots reconciliation projects that Williams, her colaureate, Mairead Corrigan, and others had worked on in Northern Ireland in decades past seemed finally to be bearing fruit at the political level. In April 1998, U.S. presidential envoy George Mitchell helped the British and Irish governments, and representatives of political movements from both sides of Northern Ireland's long-sustained sectarian divide, to conclude the notable Good Friday Agreement, which laid out a roadmap for peaceful political change in the province. A month later, in a referendum on the agreement, the province's voters expressed strong support for it. Then in October 1998 (a couple of weeks before the conference), the Nobel committee in Oslo announced that the 1998 peace prize would be awarded to Northern Ireland party leaders John Hume and David Trimble. In his award lecture in December, Nobel committee chair Francis Sejersted would refer back to the seminal grassroots work done in the 1970s by Williams and Corrigan. He also lauded the contribution that Sinn Féin head Gerry Adams, and others, had made to the cause of peace.

"What you see today evolving," Williams said at the conference, "is not that Gerry Adams finished the war in Northern Ireland. That's a lie. Gerry didn't finish the war in Northern Ireland. There was a groundswell that became so strong and so huge in its justice that really the men of violence had nowhere else to go. They *had* to get around a table. They *had* to begin discussing!" She described new laureate John Hume as a great friend who had "worked ceaselessly and tirelessly for justice, freedom, and peace in my country."

She noted that the negotiating relationship that had grown up between Hume and Trimble was similar in many ways to that between Nelson Mandela and former President de Klerk in South Africa. But some of the male political leaders in Northern Ireland were still, she said, "posturing" for the sake of their own, supposedly hard-line public opinion. "I think right now they have to stop posturing. . . . I was home very recently, and one of the greatest things that we have in our Assembly in Northern Ireland now is there's a woman's group in there. And while all the men are posturing at each other, the women's coalition is actually doing the work! . . . *You know, the absence of violence is only the beginning of the work for peace.* We have come a long way in Northern Ireland, and we will go that other mile to sustain the justice and peace we so richly deserve."

She recalled some details of how the groundswell that finally pushed the politicians to the peace table had been developed through decades of painstaking work. One of the early projects she worked on in Belfast was the establishment of a groundbreaking, intentionally integrated (Catholic and Protestant) school. In the early planning stages, she recalled, we asked the children, Would they name it? Now, you know there's a great fondness in Ireland for saints. You know, it's Saint Dominick, Saint Patrick, Saint Theresa, Saint, Saint, Saint—so we asked the children to name the school, and out of the mouths of babes and sucklings come the most incredible words. One little boy, about ten years old, was sitting there, and he said, "Why do we have to call everything here after saints? There's a river in the Belfast. It's called the Lagan. The Lagan River. Why can't we call it Lagan College?"

And then, we asked the children to design the motto of the school, and they designed a bridge over the river with two little hands going across that bridge. Perhaps it's time that we as adults gave more credibility to what comes out of the mouths of babes and sucklings! . . . I often say to people when I'm talking, "*Tears without action are wasted sentiment.* You can cry all the tears you want and that's not going to change anything!"

In the 1980s, Williams moved to the United States, living first in Texas, later in Florida. Along the way, she remained true to her commitment to work for the good of the people she calls "the littlest of our citizens." That concern led her to serve on the Texas Commission for Children and Youth. It has also taken her to many war zones and crisis spots around the world, where her emphasis has stayed on seeing what can be done to save, and then rehabilitate, the youngest survivors of man-made disasters. She recalled that

one of the first journeys that I took was to Ethiopia, and we went in with convoys of trucks delivering food around the little villages. And when you go to an area like that, it doesn't take too long before you start to suffer from what the people there are forced to live with on a daily basis. You get head lice—and anywhere you have hair, you have lice, which is very uncomfortable. You also get terrible sick stomach and then you become, after three or four days, when you start to try and acclimatize, you become kind of emaciated.

We covered about thirty-two villages in that journey, and in the last village—I mean, they were all absolutely horrible, but I'll just tell you about one village that we visited. By then we were almost out of supplies, and we were all very tired. We were also emotionally destroyed. And this village had 368 children. Let me rephrase that—368 little pieces of human garbage, because that's what we had made of these children. In a world that can feed itself, it's crazy that any child should starve!

And we didn't know what to do for these children because we were so, I suppose, destroyed emotionally at the time. But I managed to get friendly with an Ethiopian guard. I really kissed the Blarney stone that morning, Father Tutu, because I had to talk—I actually had to physically say [to myself] "Don't hate this person, don't hate this person," because he was one of the people who would be responsible for terrible actions. But I managed to get friendly with him and he let me use his telephone equipment. And I called a friend of mine in Norway, a wonderful man called Gunnar Borrevik, who is head of a newspaper called *Faedrelandsvennen*, which is rather on the part of the *New York Times*. And they flew in a small aircraft [to us], and we started transporting children to a field hospital the Norwegians had set up.

It would have taken us probably about five days by road to get the children to the field hospital, but it only took twenty minutes by air. This was only a little six-seater plane and into that we put forty children. And on a journey of twenty minutes, we lost fourteen of those children. Fourteen children! Think about that.

Those priorities— They talk to me about military budgets, and I have to sit in rooms with men who justify military budgets by telling me it's for defense! Do you know what I say? "No doubt the dead and dying are very gratified that you're defending them so well!" The insanity of what's going on militarily in the world has got to be challenged—not by me, or Jody Williams, or His Holiness, or anybody else who's supposed to have a "famous name." The insanity of that has got to be challenged by every single one of you, *every one of you*!

I'm proud to have a friend by the name of Oscar Arias Sánchez, because this man is challenging that, and we must all support that challenge. To look forward to a demilitarized world is not for idealistic fools! They call us idealistic fools. I've been referred to by many names, but that's one I object to the most. It's *not* idealistic to say that the world must begin to live together without guns or bombs, or better and bigger ways to destroy each other. It's not idealistic!

Williams said that her experiences in the twenty-three years since she was named a laureate have convinced her that the children of the world "must be given a voice, because the adults are not doing a very good job of representing them." In 1996, she founded an organization called the World Centers of Compassion for Children (WCCC): its aim is to give children the same kind of political voice that was created for senior citizens in the United States by the American Association of Retired Persons. She recalled that before that latter organization was established, some people had laughed at the idea of older people having political power, but "they ain't laughing anymore in Washington at those little old ladies, because when they go to Washington with an agenda, they have a voice. And we will do the same for the children!" She noted that while there are many different organizations doing good work to help children in different parts of the world, still, they did not coordinate well enough among themselves. "And they're all fighting about their dollars. That's got to stop! We must umbrella every organization out there that is working for children, and bring them under one roof to do the job better."

In June 1997, the WCCC convened a worldwide summit, Mothers of the Earth for World Peace. When Williams came to the University of Virginia gathering, she brought with her a copy of the declaration adopted by the summit, and at the end of her presentation she read out its text:

> "We, the children of the world, assert our inalienable right to be heard, and to have a political voice at the United Nations and at the highest levels of government world-wide. We, the children of the world, must live with justice, with peace, and freedom, but above all, with the dignity we deserve. We the children of the world require a Marshall Plan, a Geneva Convention, and a World Children's Court of Human Rights which meets regularly to listen to our testimonies and know what is actually happening to us. We intend to provide our own testimonies.
>
> We, the children of the world, demand the right to be taken to safe shelters in situations of war. We, the children of the world, consider hunger, disease, forced labor, and all forms of abuse and exploitation perpetrated upon us to be acts of war, and we the children of the world until this day June 20th, 1997 . . . have had no voice. We demand such a voice. We, the children of the world, will develop our own leadership and set an example that will show governments how to live with peace and freedom. We, the children of the world, serve notice on our abusers and exploiters, whoever they may be,

that from this day forward we will begin holding you responsible for our suffering."[1]

WHEN THE DISCUSSION period got under way, Jody Williams of the International Campaign to Ban Landmines asked a question that spurred one of the many riveting, thought-provoking conversations the laureates had throughout the two-day-long conference. "This would be directed not just to Betty, but to Rigoberta, to Archbishop Tutu, to everybody whose children have grown up in a culture of violence," she said. She endorsed what Betty Williams had said about the need to give children a political voice, and recalled,

> I worked with Madame Graça Machel, former First Lady of Mozambique, currently the wife . . . of Nelson Mandela, when she was the expert at the UN to look at the impact of armed conflict on children. I worked in El Salvador in and out for many years, and if I remember my statistics correctly, 85 percent of all families were directly affected by the violence in El Salvador.
>
> How do you create havens, and this was a great question we had in the Machel Project —How *do* you create havens for children? But even worse than creating a haven in the midst of conflict, what is the legacy for a country when 85 percent of its families have directly felt violence, when children have grown up in a state of conflict where that is all they know, where they learn that violence is the quickest way, at least seems to be the quickest way, to resolve conflict?
>
> How do you undo that so you really can reestablish the values, reestablish citizenship and good governance? This is an ongoing question. . . . How do you do it?

"I can only speak for Northern Ireland," Betty Williams said, and noted that one important technique they had discovered during their work establishing Lagan College was to "educate children to educate their parents. The child became the teacher at home." She said that when they were opening the school, they could still only convince the parents of a dozen potential students to send their children to it. "And that school now has fourteen hundred pupils and a waiting list *in utero*! So, you start. It has to start somewhere, Jody, you know. You cannot go out to a child in the Northern Irish situation and take the gun out of his hand, and take the bomb out of his hand, without replacing it with something. It has to be replaced with something, and so we replaced that with education. We're now seeing the results of this all these years later. There's no quick solutions, love, you and I both know that. It has to be worked for on a daily basis."

Rigoberta Menchú jumped in, pointing to the plight of children who are virtually abandoned in situations of prolonged crisis:

> There's a huge problem throughout the world, which is the street children. Street children who have only one parent, or don't have a regular family life. They suffer not only from situations of actual violence, but from the total lack of sensitivity on the part of other people in their society toward them.
>
> In terms of the knowledge and the experience that we have, in the conflicts in Guatemala, and Central America, and Chiapas, and in other places—in all those areas none of the peace accords that have been fashioned have remembered in any way whatsoever that there are *children* that live in those places, and there has been no provision for [children in the] peace accords. When those wars came to an end, it was as though everything was going to come simply back to normal for those children.
>
> After the peace accords in Guatemala, we have had to begin to struggle to have a code for children so that we can begin to defend their interests. And much to our surprise, we found a tremendous amount of opposition on the part of those in our country who sell children. It almost seemed like we were confronting a new struggle, almost as though the old violent struggle that we had just overcome did not have anything to do with this new situation that we were in.
>
> I believe very much in local struggles and in national struggles, and I think that in each nation we have to create laws and conditions which will protect the interests of children. I don't think that this can be done in a global fashion. I, too, have spent many, many years going from one international conference to another and I find that in those international conferences, people do not really know what's going on at different national levels. So that we really have to go from the national to the global.

After Menchú spoke, Betty Williams returned to the idea of creating a model refuge for children. "I believe all the laureates should be involved in this, to create the safe havens," she said. And until that happens, and adults start to allow the children's voice to be stronger than theirs, "we will see no changes."

"What I understand," Menchú said, "is that all human beings have mothers, and if all of us who *are* the mothers of the world get together, we will create a better world!"

"Here, here!" Betty Williams said, to general applause. Then, she remembered a good story from the early days of Lagan College that she wanted to tell, in particular, to the Dalai Lama. She recalled that nearly all the children in Northern Ireland had been brought up to know the difference between Catholics and Protestants—but they were not really aware that there even *were* any other religions in the world.[2] "So we decided we would bring [representatives of] the other religions in to talk to our children. And one day this little boy said to me— Well, I had said, 'We're bringing in a Buddhist monk today to speak to you.' And he said, 'Is he a Catholic Buddhist or a Protestant Buddhist?'"

It took awhile for the mirth provoked by that story to die down. Archbishop Tutu noted up-front that he was *not* a Buddhist. Then he said he wanted to make two main points:

> One is to—and I'm not trying to be politically correct—to underscore what Betty was saying, and Rigoberta. Sitting for two-and-a-half years or so, listening to some gruesome accounts of the sorts of things that have taken place in our country from all sides, it struck me more forcibly than I had ever been able to realize, that in fact *we would have not got our liberation without the women.* They've been quite, quite extraordinary! And somebody looking at the statistics, as it were, of our Truth and Reconciliation Commission, one of the things that struck them was the fact that when men came to testify to the commission, almost always they were testifying about what happened to themselves, and when women came, almost equally they were telling stories about what happened to somebody else. There was this kind of *nurturingness* that women have, that nurtured our freedom. And I think that we need to give a very special place to them in our struggle, which we probably don't always do.
>
> The second point, perhaps, is in relation to conflict and children, to say that in a sense the impact of conflict on children is like what

happens with landmines: the effect continues long after the conflict has ceased.[3] Our children who are going to be the adults of tomorrow are brutalized. They have lost in many ways a reverence for life. And the violence that then erupts in the society in part is the consequence of children having known nothing better. They have gone through life seeing people say the way you resolve a quarrel, a disagreement, is dispatch your enemy. "The best kind of enemy is a dead enemy." And we are going to be dealing with that at home.

How do you rehabilitate youngsters who had to fight for the right to be human? And in the process have lost the compassion, and the gentleness, and the reverence for life that ought to be natural to children?

"May I tell a little story?" Jody Williams asked. She recalled that when she worked with Medical Aid of El Salvador, the organization used to bring wounded children to the United States for donated medical treatment. "I met a young woman. She was sixteen. She was a guerrilla, and it was very curious to watch her. The juxtaposition of this woman who felt she had no option but to take up arms and— I'll tell you why she had to. When she was eleven years old, she came home to her village and she heard the screams of her brother. She hid, but unfortunately she could see the death squad killing her brother, and they were doing it by skinning him alive—"

The audience gasped. She continued the story.

She did not take up arms yet. She finally decided she had no option and no voice in [her] country when the death squad came back and killed both of her parents. By then she was thirteen or fourteen. At that point, she decided that it was either pick up a gun, or die herself. And it was also pick up a gun so that no other people would have to watch their brother be skinned in front of them.

So what does it mean—you know, "childhood" in this kind of situation? But then, I also saw her flirting. I saw this young woman, when we brought her to the States because she had been rehabilitated, if you will, and she needed treatment. I watched her flirting and trying to figure how a young teenage girl experiences all the other things in life that she was seeing by being in the United States, that she had never experienced in El Salvador. It just profoundly affected me, wondering [about] all of her lost childhood, and here [was] the adolescent she was trying to recapture in her new experience in the United States, juxtaposed beside a young woman that had to take weapons to defend herself, her village, and her dead family. Rigoberta would certainly understand that.

How do you deal with that? How do you deal with that—and I totally agree with your analogy. It's a landmine that will affect them throughout—

"You deal with it by changing it," said Betty Williams.
"I know!"
"By giving the children their own voices: that's how you deal with that," Betty Williams added. "I mean, there are no answers from adults. We've screwed it up royally for the children of the world and we need to fix that, and the only way that we—"
She changed tack and contributed another powerful story to the discussion.

There's a young man in Canada. His name is Craig Kildenberger. I don't know whether any of you have heard of this young man or not, but he read an article about a Pakistani child who was used in slave labor, and it moved him so much that he persuaded his parents to take him to Pakistan, and he met with this young man, and he saw the slave labor that was going on. He came back to Canada and he challenged—now this young child at this stage, Father Tutu, was only eleven. He's fifteen, I believe, now—and he challenged his own government on bringing in goods from Pakistan that had been used in forced labor, and he challenged them so well and so articulately.

See, children have tremendous brains and we don't give them credit for that. I mean, when my children were nine, ten, and eleven, they could outsmart me, outwit me, outfox me, outrun me. They're clever! They're really smart, you know. And when Craig came back and did that challenge to his own prime minister, he did it very publicly, and he changed that situation for the children in Pakistan. The Canadians no longer import those rugs.

So children *can* do it, Jody! We just have to give them the way to do it.

Julian Bond asked, "Who else can answer this difficult question: how do you restore humanity to people who may have lost their humanity in the struggle to gain their humanity? How can this be done? Bishop Tutu, is this occurring in South Africa as a result of the work you've been doing?"

"I thought I was raising that problem!"

"And now, I'm going to ask you for the answer."

Tutu laughed. He said,

Sometimes, it is really distressing. It is distressing, and you've got to have the organs of civil society seeking to permeate society with the right kind of values. At home just now, they've had a . . . moral summit in which the leadership of the various communities, religious communities—Christian, Muslim, Jewish, et cetera—and political leaders, and leaders in other spheres of life, have come and said, "We've lost a lot of things in the struggle. We've lost the sense of worth of people. We've got to try to recover the art of being human."

The whole business [is] about morality: trying to remind people that, in fact, this is a moral universe, that right and wrong, in fact, matter, and that you might get away with many things, wrong things—you could succeed—but you will get your comeuppance: it's *that* kind of universe. But you know, it's not something that you proclaim just by word of mouth. It's got to be incarnated in people. You've got to have structures that assist people in realizing, actually, that [the world] is ultimately hospitable to gentleness, to compassion, to love, to caring, to sharing, and that there ought to be people who are willing to live for that. And then children will, I hope, catch on.

But a lot of things have gone wrong at home, just as some things have gone right. And so, while we celebrate, there are other things that we realize . . . have gone wrong. And as I grow more decrepit, I realize that there are extraordinary truths that people might usually have poo-pooed, which are for real. There's no reason whatsoever to assume that, because I was involved in a just struggle and I had my idealisms—that when I win the struggle I will necessarily maintain those idealisms. But there is actually something, and it's not a myth— there is something called original sin, and each one of us has constantly got to be saying, "There but for the grace of God go I."

"Original sin—" said Betty Williams, who was raised as a Catholic, "you know, mortal sin and venial sins: I used to get so confused as a child! I think

I commit mortal sins constantly, 'cause I'm constantly angry about what's happening to the children. Anger is an emotion that can be very destructive. I have to be very careful about my anger, and direct it correctly."

She recalled a trip she made to South Africa earlier in the year, when she had visited a school in a place called Mannenberg, which had, she said, "over a thousand students, about two books in the library, and no computers. I want to get the students here involved in helping me bring computers to the school in Mannenberg. Will you do that? Hands up who wants to get involved. I want your names!"

Everyone laughed good-naturedly at this appeal, and quite a number of hands went up. "Your name, your address, your date of birth, your telephone number: on a piece of paper please, because that's a project that we are now doing at World Centers of Compassion for Children. We're taking out tears without action, wasted sentiment. We're going to take out twenty computers to the Mannenberg school, and ten to the city of Cape Town!" (Later, she would proudly report that seventy potential donors handed in their names and addresses during the conference.)

Bobby Muller spoke next. He recounted a very personal story that wove together the themes of the potential for harmful action that can lurk in anyone's heart, the psychological wounds that ripple out from all systems of violence—and also, as he noted at the outset, the resilience and potential for rehabilitation that also reside in all human beings.

> I'm just going to share a little bit of a personal thing that happened. I really considered myself a very righteous guy, a very good guy, and when I went into the Marine Corps, you know, I was really sensitive to kids. And I went through the whole training thing, went to Vietnam, and—
>
> Vietnam was a very confusing war. You didn't have a frontline, and you didn't have a clear identification of who your enemy was. And I had a lot of situations—I was a platoon commander—where I had my guys out doing operations. And as they would often do, you know, they would have the kids come in and we'd give them C-rations, we'd give them stuff. And a couple of times actually, you know, that night we would get hit, we would get attacked. And our command position and our critical positions were obviously known to the attacking force, the Vietcong, and it turned out that it was the kids that we had

befriended and given the C-rats to, et cetera, that had gotten their brothers to come in and attack us that night.

I won't get carried away with it, but a lot of things happened in my interactions with the Vietnamese that I remember. At one point, you know, we used to have these heating tabs that we would light up, and they'd burn with an invisible flame to cook up the C-rats. And we were on a truck convoy going down the highway, and my guys were lighting up these heating tabs and throwing them off the truck. And they were a valued little commodity, so, you know, kids would be coming out of the villages, and they would pick up these heating tabs, and being that they had an invisible flame, the kids couldn't tell that it had been lit up, and it would stick to their hand, their fingers, and burn them.

And I remember laughing at that.

When I got shot, I was medevacked to a hospital ship and they had me in intensive care for several days, and they had a psychiatrist come and talk to me. He said, "Is there anything you want to talk about?" He was presumably inquiring about the fact that I was going to be a paraplegic. But my question to him was, two days before, I had sat down, chowed down, and had a big lunch amongst a whole bunch of dead bodies. And it meant nothing to me. And I said, "Is there something wrong with me?" And he said, "No, there's nothing wrong with you. You've been in an extraordinary circumstance, and your mind has its automatic defense mechanisms that come into play to allow you to get through these extraordinary circumstances." He said, "You go back to New York City, and next year, you see somebody get hit by a cab, and you're going to be as affected as anybody else."

Which is exactly what happened. What I'm saying to you is that *I think people are inherently good.* I think the power of love and the power of good is a very, very strong force, but we can be affected by the negative. We can be affected by the forces of, for lack of a better term, darkness. And in being on the ground, and getting involved in a situation of killing people and having my guys killed, I sometimes say that I think I took a little bit of a walk down that path of darkness, and I personally realized how a good guy could wind up doing unconscionable things, have a value structure so fundamentally altered.

And remember My Lai, okay? In My Lai, it was "the good guys," it

was an American infantry unit that went in and murdered 505 Vietnamese women and children and old people without one single shot
being fired in return. That was the good guys, okay?

So, what I'm saying may not be clear but, you know, when you get
exposed to evil and when you get into darkness, and the circumstances around you are of that nature, they can have an affect on all of
us. Those of you that may say that could never happen to me, let me
tell you something: you're kidding yourself. I didn't think it could
happen to me. I was shocked when I realized it did happen.

But the positive part of this story, to wrap it up, is that by coming
back, getting love, getting nurturing, getting out of where the forces
of darkness and the negative energy of, basically, *evil* can work on
you, [it] allows you the opportunity to rehabilitate, to rejuvenate. And
I've seen it with literally hundreds of veterans that were exposed to
the most horrific combat. I've seen it in kids. I've seen it with a lot of
people in war zones that I've gone to.

So we have a rejuvenative capability. You know, stop feeding the
negative. Take them out of those situations. Provide love, and get a
decent environment, and even with those that have been crushed,
you can so oftentimes bring them back to wholeness and good
health.

"Absolutely!" said Betty Williams, as he finished. "There's just one more
thing that I'd like to add to this. I'm a Catholic, and I challenge my church
on blessing men to go to war. I think we have to challenge the leadership
of whatever church we belong to, and remove the padres from armies."

THE CONFERENCE SAW a number of loose interactions in which the laureates referred back to themes mentioned earlier, or sometimes the same
theme would emerge in another discussion in a different context. One of
these themes, as initiated in the story Muller told of his experiences in and
after Vietnam, was the hopeful message that it is indeed possible—even for
those scarred by direct experiences of trauma—to pull themselves out of a
deeply bedded system of violence, and to start to transform both themselves
and the way they relate to, and actively transform, the system of violence
itself.

Harn Yawnghwe was asked, in a question from the floor, "How would *you* educate the children affected by oppression and war to grow up not to retaliate?"

"It's not an easy process," he said,

> because as everybody has been saying, when they see the suffering, when they experience it themselves, it's very hard not to want to have revenge. . . . And in the case of Burma, there's a lot of give and take, so since I mainly am speaking about Burma, I'm hopeful that it will be possible, as long as you start. You see, the whole reason we have this problem in Burma is that, in a sense, it's a political problem, and the military has been trying to solve it by using violence. And what we're saying is that that will not solve the problem, and you have to solve political problems through political means. And hopefully, that kind of thinking— Also, what José has been talking about in East Timor, *not to take revenge* on Indonesian migrant workers: I think that is the way we need to go.

The next day, he returned to a similar theme. He was asked, "Could you please share with us the source of your openness and compassion for the government that has caused your people such immense suffering?"

The response he gave was evocative of what Aung San Suu Kyi said in *The Voice of Hope.* Harn said, "I guess it comes from a belief that even the generals, even the people who are doing all these things, are human. They have families, they have children. Some of them may be doing it through ignorance. Some of them may be doing it because they've been wrongly told. Of course, you may feel that the ones responsible, the generals, should know better, but they don't. I mean, myself—I have also made mistakes. I have also had different convictions which I thought were very right [at the time]."

"Could I do an anecdote about that?" Jody Williams asked.

> One of my closest friends had an extremely unpleasant encounter with two men who I wish I could call gentlemen, who left her beaten and naked in the street. For many years, I had the greatest hope that I would run into them sometime and do the same to them or worse. And then I got involved trying to stop the violence in Central America and watched what happened to people over time who only sought violent revenge against people who have done things to them, or peo-

ple they love. *You become them.* Violence does breed violence. It changes one's own being. And it was only after many years of seeing that personally that I realized that if I were to meet the two gentlemen in question, I would really rather talk to them and ask them about their humanity than do them harm and be like them.

"I agree!" said Harn. "And really, if you can't forgive somebody or someone for doing something, I think it hurts you more than it hurts them. It eats away, and its eats away, and eventually you are nothing but bitterness."

At the end of the conference, Rigoberta Menchú summed up the many references to this topic: "I want to reiterate what the Dalai Lama has said: that all of our actions, all of our motivations, are *motivations for others to act*, in society, with institutions, and with others. And also, in the belief of the possibility that human beings can change. We human beings can change! We were not born bad. We become involved in one or another negative action, but we were not born that way. I thought it was very important to reiterate this, to believe in us as a human species. We are bad, we human beings—but we can change!"

The role of religion—both in helping people to endure otherwise dispiriting situations and in helping them to effect the personal transformation needed for healing and reconciliation—was another important theme that wove its way through the conference. A number of questions asked by audience members touched on this topic. One of the earliest was directed to the Dalai Lama. He was asked, "Can the religions worldwide, given their dissimilarities and their followers' different passions, act as a coherent force in the peace process?"

His reply came as a thought-provoking surprise to many in the audience:

My belief is, of course, various traditions have great potential to increase compassion, the sense of caring for one another, and I think also the spirit of reconciliation. However, I believe that in terms of humanity, the role of religious belief is *limited*. Also, I believe that a human being without religious faith can be a very good human being: sincere, a good heart, a sense of caring for others, but no belief in a religious faith.

So I usually say there are two types of spirituality. One, spirituality with faith and a philosophy. Like you see, according to Christianity, and Islam, and Judaism, and many other traditions, the concept of a

Creator is very powerful, very powerful. And then, some other religious traditions like Buddhism and Jainism: no Creator; oneself is almost like a creator, self-creation. That also is a very powerful method to change our mind. They both utilize different methods, different ways, but more or less have the same goal—I am not talking about heaven or other things, but simply a *good human being,* a warmhearted person. Now there, of course, all religious traditions have the potential, as I mentioned earlier. However, we also need some other sort of spirituality without any religious faith. Simply on the basis of *awareness.*

He turned toward Ramos-Horta. "You mentioned that the ultimate source of conflict is ignorance," he said, and continued:

I think for all troubles, there are a lot of causes and conditions. Some are very subtle causes. And ignorance, lack of awareness: that is, I think, the *ultimate root cause.* And then, other different factors or conditions also are there. So, I believe, through analyzing, through education, [we come to ask]: what use is violence? What benefit, ultimately, to yourself? Ah, more violence! Counterviolence. And eventually, mutual destruction.

On the other hand, a certain amount of disagreement or different views or contradictions is always there. Even if we are involved in war continuously, day by day, that contradiction will not be solved. It will always remain. Different ideas, different economy reasons, and some kinds of disagreement, sources of conflict, always remain there. Then we need to think about that reality. Even if I use violence intensively, the problem cannot be solved; it still remains. Instead, mutual destruction, mutual suffering.

So then, the problems we have to solve—but through other means: dialogue, compromise!

He turned to Archbishop Tutu. "You are the great preacher! So the spirit of reconciliation [is important]: fully respect others' views, and others' rights, and develop a sense of genuine concern about others' welfare and others' right. And then, compromise. Only compromise. That's the only way! So you see, with awareness, I think this can develop without any religious faith or religious belief. Therefore, I usually call them basic human values. *That means the good qualities of human nature.*"

He recalled what Bobby Muller said about the rejuvenative capacities of the human spirit. "What you mentioned, I fully encourage. There are a lot of 'bads' in our emotion, but ultimately our nature is, I believe, gentleness. If everyone had a sense of commitment, a sense of responsibility, a sense of caring for one another—so, I believe that with various traditions we also have a greater potential. So, let us try to utilize that potential, isn't it?"

Rigoberta Menchú was also asked about the role of religion in helping to achieve peace. Her response was,

> I think it is very important to pray for peace. But *just* to pray for peace really doesn't do very much. Prayer and action are both things that are important together. And also, an individual struggle for peace has many limits. It is a lot better to struggle together with others, especially to do so with people who have a great desire and a great need for peace—and especially, to work with those people who also have a *proposal* about what to do for the future. Because a lot of people struggle for peace just to get a title and an award. It may very well be that he or she will get the award and nothing changes. And it may very well be that he will be waiting, and waiting, for the award—and it never arrives.

She laughed, summing up her thoughts. "So, I think it is more than a struggle of individuals. It is a struggle of peoples, of societies, of young people, and of old people and of institutions. I sometimes pray for humanity. But it's the easiest thing that one can do."

Archbishop Tutu also (and not surprisingly) had something to say about the role of religion in the struggle for justice. "May I just have a last word?" he asked at the end of the session in which he gave his main presentation. He wanted to make sure his listeners clearly understood his deeply considered view of God's relationship with the world.

> The God that I worship is a strange God, because it is a God who is omnipotent, all powerful, but he's also a God who is weak. An extraordinary paradox, that it is God, a God of justice, who wants to see justice in the world, but because God has a such a deep reverence for our freedoms all over the place, God will not intervene like, I mean, sending a lightning bolt to dispatch all despots! *God waits for*

God's partners—we! And God has a dream: God has a dream of a world that is different, a world in which you and I care for one another, because we belong in one family.

And I want to make an appeal on behalf of God. God says, can you help me realize my dream—my dream of a world that is more caring, a world that is more compassionate, a world that says people matter more than things, people matter more than profit. That's my dream, says God. Will you please help me realize my dream?

The whole gathering was spellbound. This gifted preacher had made his r's roll like thunder and his x's explode like firecrackers. Now, he dropped his voice to a hoarse whisper, still heard at each seat in the hall. "And I have nobody except you."

"THERE ARE NO famous people," Betty Williams had told us, "only people who think they are!" Yet much in the structure of Western society seems to cry out for "celebrities," or "famous people," even in the tough, heartbreaking business of building world peace. And while Alfred Nobel's peace prize project has met with huge success over the past century in drawing attention to the efforts of those who strive quietly and behind the scenes for peace, its very success has brought with it a temptation to many to consider peace laureates as another class of celebrities, to fête them, "collect" them, or treat them as somehow different. The laureates who gathered at the conference worked hard to deflect such problematic projections, and to deflate unrealistic expectations of their "specialness."

Archbishop Tutu, whose aim seemed to be putting other people at ease, had an engaging way of dealing with this whole topic. He was asked at one point, "What impact did receiving the Nobel Peace Prize have on your ability to move toward your goal?"

"Well, it had the effect," he said, "of turning me into an oracle!" He rolled his eyes heavenward as the audience laughed. "Things you said before you got the Nobel Peace Prize and not too many people paid attention, you say the same things [afterward] and people think it's pearls from heaven!"

A few hours later, Jeffrey Hopkins asked him on behalf of an audience member, "What thought, what idea did you communicate to your country's leaders that finally compelled them to action?"

"What?" asked Tutu, as though to dispute the very idea that he might have had that much influence over the course of events.

Hopkins repeated the question.

"Which action?" Tutu insisted. "Quite seriously, I did nothing! There were many other people who were doing some superb work. I often say that I was a leader by default, because our real leaders were in jail or in exile, and perhaps it was part of God's sense of humor that God chose to have someone like me. It was probably because I had an easy name!"

Menchú also had a refreshingly down-to-earth way of referring to her own international stature. "I think peace is not the result of one person. In the first place, it is the conviction of everyone involved in conflict. And after, the building of peace is for the people themselves, the children, not for the Nobel laureates. We are a unique, privileged group, and we can push forward some processes. But the social actor is the [important] one, and I consider myself a social actor."

THE "ACTOR" CONCEPT was one referred to throughout the conference. Speaker after speaker echoed, each in her or his own way, Betty Williams's judgment that personal transformation on its own is not enough: "Tears without action are wasted sentiment."

At the end of the first morning, a self-identified African American woman in the audience sent up a question asking Williams whether she had any advice for "our often divided ethnic and religious conflicts in contemporary U.S. culture?"

"That's a huge question!" was Williams's first reaction. But she tackled it, anyway.

> There is great injustice in the United States. Anybody who denies that is blind or lying. I think that [regarding] racism in the United States right now—I liked it better when it was more out front, when you knew the enemy. It's more insidious now, and I agree that outside help is necessary.
>
> Perhaps I agree because I live now in the United States of America and I'm one who loves this country, but I also see the problems here. I mean, how dare we call a society democratic that has twelve million hungry children? There is no democracy where there's that kind of hunger. I agree that—you know, I sometimes get terribly confused

even within myself because I have trouble with my own bigotries: when I'm really pushed into a corner, the Catholic stands up, you know. So I totally understand how, as an African-American woman, whoever wrote that question must feel. *I think peace begins with me. . . .*

Whoever wrote that question, you have the power within yourself to change what's wrong in your society!

Jody Williams got a question about the role of the Internet in helping people disseminate information and organize effectively to achieve peace. She transformed this question, too, into an appeal for listeners to engage in action, not just talk.

I think there's a tremendous mythology about the role of the Internet in the landmine campaign. What was important in the landmine campaign, apart from many other things, was the desire to involve a huge array of groups and individuals immediately. We did that from the beginning through fax machines. When you're trying to bring together lots of people who have huge agendas of their own in their own organizations, you need them to believe that their immediate input in the growth of whatever you're doing is important. So we used the fax initially. But it's also more than that. It's the individual. It's sharing information—but it's making people believe they are part of the process, not just information.

Information by itself can be overwhelming. We got to the point with the speedy use of e-mail where colleagues in the campaign would say to me, stop sending so much information. Why don't you just send a summary? So, you can have too much information. It has to do, and with this I agree with Betty absolutely completely, with *individual responsibility to want to make change*, to take whatever the information is and decide how to use it to contribute to a process of change. Information by itself can't do anything. It's how you use it.

(She also expressed her concern regarding the Internet issue that a number of governments were seeking to restrict the freedom of communication on it.)

For her part, Betty Williams returned again and again to the need for individuals to become involved in social activism. Quite frequently, this was in response to questioners who had been deeply touched by her words about the uselessness of tears without action. "How can I, as a college student with very little money, move beyond being emotional about people, justice, and reconciliation, and act in such a way that will help to make a difference?" one audience member asked. Williams answered:

> I'd like to quote for you now one of my favorite people in the whole world, an anthropologist called Margaret Mead, and she said (and we have it in all of our literature), "Never doubt that a committed group of people, however small they may be, can change the world. In fact, it is the only thing that ever has." So, this being afraid of just being the one person that would take that step will keep you forever from taking the step.
>
> And I sometimes get out there, even when I get a [metaphorical] punch in the jaw, which happens quite frequently: I'll get knocked over. You know that song, "I Get Knocked Down But I Get Up Again"? Well, that happens to me at least forty times a week—boom, boom, boom! This work is really very like that. One of the things that we have to know too is that there are no quick fixes. Our world did not get into this condition overnight. We as human beings are not capable of pulling it out of this condition overnight. It's going to take hard work, dedication, and courage and commitment to do it.
>
> Over lunch today, I was asked a question about the peace movement. Mairead [Corrigan] and I thought it would take fifty years, at least, to deal with three hundred years of bad history. It took much less than that! But if you go out there and think that you're going to have an immediate solution, then you're absolutely crazy. The campaign that I'm running to create safe havens for children, I know that I may never see that in my lifetime. And that's okay, because if I do the job right, the job goes on when I'm not here, and I think each one of us at this table would feel that way. We would all love to see a nonviolent, beautiful, just, and peaceful world. But until we're willing to work for it as individuals—not just people around this table!—it's never going to happen. So don't be afraid, and don't think that your voice doesn't make a difference. Your voice makes a huge difference!

Even at the very end of the conference, as Julian Bond was trying to bring matters to a close, Williams was living up to her own advice. Somewhere along the way, she had donned a big orange pin saying "$8," which had been handed to her by a supporter of the university's Living Wage Campaign. "Now I'd just like to say something about acting locally," she said. "You see this little pin that we're wearing? It says '$8' on it. You've got people working on this campus for very, very low wages. It's time you changed that!" The audience applauded loudly.

BETTY WILLIAMS WAS quite candid about what she saw as some of her own shortcomings. She could find herself slipping into pro-Catholic "bigotries," she said. She confessed to sometimes feeling strong anger. Then, one of the questions that came to her through Jeffrey Hopkins was a tough one for anyone to answer: "How can one strike a balance in daily life between forgiveness and standing up for oneself?"

"Oh dear," she started, amid laughter from around the hall. "I'm not known to be very even-tempered, so I don't know. I can forgive very easily. It's the forgetting I have a problem with—much to my shame, Your Grace [speaking to Archbishop Tutu]. Because every now and again I think, well, that person did so-and-so, and that little devil gets on this shoulder, you know, and for a while forgiveness goes out the window! Standing up for oneself—I guess it depends on what oneself wants. What are you standing up for? I mean, I stand up for children."

Indeed, these are not easy issues—whether at the level of individuals trying to deal with their own emotions and find a way to get beyond cycles of interpersonal hatred, or for members of large groups trying to deal with the traumas of the past and escape long-sustained cycles of deep, systemic violence. It was an exactly similar question, that of striking a balance between forgiveness and standing up for one's own rights, that Archbishop Tutu had been dealing with, at the large-group level, in South Africa's Truth and Reconciliation Commission for the preceding three years. In his main talk at the conference he described the unique way the South Africans had tried to meet that challenge—as we shall now see.

7

Transforming Systems of Violence at
the Intergroup Level: Desmond Tutu
and Reconciliation in South Africa

The acclaim as he stepped up to the podium was tumultuous. "Thank you very much!" he called into the microphone. Then, louder: "Thank you very much!" As the clapping began to die down, Desmond Tutu set up an oratorical icebreaker with a classic act of understatement: "I am a preacher—I don't know that you will be exposed to quite the treatment that one particular preacher gave to his congregation. He started preaching, and he went on and on, and on and on. And he said at some point, 'What more can I say?' And somebody in the back said, 'Amen!'" His sense of how to deflect what otherwise threatened to become a tsunami of hero-worship was impeccable.

The man who is Archbishop Desmond Mpilo Tutu, former head of the Anglican church in South Africa, recently retired chair of his country's Truth and Reconciliation Commission, had won over another audience.

He let the laughter unleashed by his joke die down. Then he gave a more serious greeting:

I greet you, dear friends, as someone who comes from what is still described as the new South Africa, the free South Africa, the democratic South Africa, the nonracial South Africa, the nonsexist South Africa! And almost all of us have described what happened in April 1994, in that historic election, as a miracle. And I think, yes, that is probably the most adequate way of describing something that was almost ineffable. We scored a spectacular victory over the awfulness of apartheid! But you know what? That victory would have been totally impossible without the support that we got from the international community. That victory would have been impossible without the love, and the prayers, and the commitment of very, very, very many people right around the world.

And it is not given to too many people who go round the world and say, "We have an awful system: please help us to destroy it," and the people give you the help, and the system *is* destroyed — It is not given to too many to be able to *return* to those from whom you asked for the support, to say, "We've done it! Thank you!"

Thank you, all of you, who made the miracle possible. I would like to give you a clap, but it will look weird if I do it all on my own, isn't it? So how about joining me in giving you and others who have been part of our support a very, very warm hand?

Delighted audience members joined him and each other in laughter and applause. "Thank you! Thank you very, very much!" he called out. And he could not resist another quick joke: "I did that once with a group of young people in Australia, and I said, 'Part of our trouble is that we don't celebrate who we are.' And I said, 'Well, why don't give ourselves a warm hand?' And they gave a humdinger of an applause! And then I said, 'Let's give God a standing ovation!' And they all got up, and they gave God a standing ovation. And without thinking, I said, 'Thank you—'"

THE FUTURE ARCHBISHOP was born in 1931, in Klerksdorp, near Johannesburg, South Africa. His father was a teacher in a school run by the Anglicans, where his mother also worked, doing housekeeping. One of his strong boyhood memories was an occasion when, walking down the street with his mother, they met Father Trevor Huddleston, a white priest who was a strong beacon of witness against the evils of apartheid. What struck the young Desmond about Father Huddleston was something smaller and simpler: the esteemed white priest took off his cap to Mrs. Tutu in the street and greeted her, "Good morning, Mrs. Tutu!" The image of a white professional man who would treat a humble black housekeeper *with normal human respect* stayed with Tutu for decades. When he was twenty-seven and trying to work as a teacher, the government imposed tight restrictions on the scope of what it called Bantu Education and dashed Tutu's hopes that he could serve his people effectively through teaching in such a system. He thought about what Huddleston had done, and was continuing to do, to push forward the cause of equality in South Africa. He decided to enter the ministry.

He rose rapidly through the priestly ranks, and in 1975 was named the first black dean of St. Mary's Cathedral, in Johannesburg. He refused to apply for the special government "permit" that would enable him to live in the customary deanery, located in a leafy, whites-only area of the city. Instead, he took his family to live in the sprawling, black "township" (that is, dumping-ground) called Soweto, where he experienced firsthand the rage growing among that 87 percent of South Africa's population who were denied any political rights based solely on the color of their skin. The pain, the anger of his black compatriots was all around him.

Tutu tried every way he could think of to open up communication with the country's white rulers. In May 1976, he addressed a famous open letter to Prime Minister John Vorster in an appeal for greater understanding:

> I am writing to you, Sir, because I know you to be a loving and caring father and husband, a doting grandfather who has experienced the joys and anguish of family life, its laughter and gaiety, its sorrows and pangs. . . . You have flung out your arms to embrace and hug your children and your grandchildren, to smother them with your kisses, you have loved, you have wept, you have watched by the bed of a sick one whom you loved, you have watched by the deathbed of a sick relative, you have been a proud father at the wedding of your children, you have shed tears by the graveside of one for whom your heart has been broken. In short, I am writing to you as one human person to another human person, gloriously created in the image of the self-same God, redeemed by the self-same Son of God who for all our sakes died on the Cross and rose triumphant from the dead. . . . I am, therefore, writing to you, Sir, as one Christian to another, for through our common baptism we have been made members of and are united in the Body of our dear Lord and Saviour, Jesus Christ. This Jesus Christ, whatever we may have done, has broken down all that separates us irrelevantly—such as race, sex, culture, status, etc. In this Jesus Christ we are forever bound together as one redeemed humanity, black and white together.[1]

Tutu appealed as well to Vorster's sensibilities as a member of the originally Dutch Boer (that is, farmer) group of colonists that, throughout the first half of the twentieth century, was brutally oppressed by the British colonial administrators of South Africa. "I am writing to you, Sir," Tutu wrote, "as one who is a member of a race that has known what it has meant in frustrations and hurts, in agony and humiliation, to be a subject people." But the main thrust of the letter was a warning: "I am writing to you, Sir, because I have a growing nightmarish fear that unless something drastic is done very soon then bloodshed and violence are going to happen in South Africa almost inevitably. A people can take only so much and no more."[2] The letter then suggested—in the Boers' own Afrikaans—that the two men might meet to discuss these issues *onder vier oë* (face-to-face).

Vorster disdained that invitation. Within weeks, a vast antigovernment uprising had erupted in Soweto. The struggle for equality in South Africa had entered a new phase.

Throughout the years that followed, as Tutu continued his ascent up the church hierarchy, he maintained a constant and visible public witness against the horrors of apartheid while he continued ministering to those injured or bereaved by the growing levels of violence in his country. In 1984, when he was general secretary of the South African Council of Churches, he was awarded the Nobel Peace Prize. The chair of the Nor-wegian Nobel Committee paid tribute to his efforts "to solve South Africa's apartheid problem by peaceful means." Tutu's contribution, he added, "represents a hope for the future, for the country's white minority as well as the black majority."[3]

One Thursday evening in early September 1989, Tutu—who by now was archbishop of Cape Town—faced a new challenge. For days, paramilitary police riding in the dreaded Casspir armored cars had been running rampage through the black townships that ringed the city, and the number of black deaths was mounting. The next day, Tutu would be presiding over a memorial service for some of the victims of the violence: as he prayed long, hard, and tearfully in his private chapel into the wee hours of night, preparing himself for the service, he agonized over what he could do to help his countrymen break out of the mounting cycle of violence and counterviolence. Finally, he decided. At the memorial service the next day, he announced that he planned to lead a *peaceful protest march* through the city center the following Wednesday.

To many, this seemed like a crazy idea: all such public gatherings had been banned for decades. In the climate of violence then stalking the country, there was a very real chance that the government forces might simply mow down all the marchers—priests, archbishops, and all. A new South African president, Frederik de Klerk, had been sworn in only weeks before, and was still an unknown quantity. No one could guess how many people would dare to take part in the march that Tutu proposed.

In the event, a totally unexpected throng of thirty thousand people joined him in walking in a vast, multiethnic, and peaceful multitude to city hall. As Tutu's collaborator and editor, John Allen, has explained, "After the Cape Town march, the government was compelled to relax its prohibition on public protest, and huge marches swept the country, with church leaders in the front ranks."[4]

De Klerk's assumption of power turned out to be a welcome breath of fresh air, after the stultifying decades in which first Vorster, then P. W. Botha, had run the country. In December 1989, the new president held a first, totally clandestine "summit" meeting with imprisoned ANC leader Nelson Mandela, who was then in his twenty-eighth year of life imprisonment on political charges. On February 2, 1990, de Klerk announced a sweeping series of reforms, including the legalization of the long-banned ANC and other pro-democratic parties. Seven days later, he held a second meeting with Mandela, in which he informed the very surprised prisoner that he intended to release him *the next day*. The tumultuous welcome that greeted Mandela as he walked to freedom the next afternoon reverberated around the globe, delighting the hearts of democrats everywhere.[5]

It took de Klerk, Mandela, and their respective supporters four more years of hard work to complete their negotiations over the dismantling of the deeply bedded system of interracial violence that, between "simple" European colonialism and institutionalized apartheid, had dominated their country for nearly three hundred years. (Along the way, in 1993, those two leaders were awarded their own Nobel Peace Prizes.) In April 1994, Tutu, Mandela, and millions of other black South Africans were able, for the first time in their lives, to exercise their new-won right to vote. The ANC won a strong victory in that election, though there was still enough support for other parties to ensure that the country's infant democracy would remain a lively one.

On May 9, 1994, the new National Assembly held its first meeting. But the hundreds of thousands of South Africans who wanted to see their elected leaders on that historic day could not dream of all fitting into the assembly's chamber! Instead, they gathered around the city hall in Cape Town's Grand Parade, where (as he had done back in 1989) Archbishop Tutu once again emceed a huge political event. On this occasion, he introduced to the crowd, first, one new executive deputy president, Frederik de Klerk, then another, the veteran ANC activist Thabo Mbeki. Finally, to wild applause and dancing, he introduced the country's new president— Nelson Mandela.

TUTU HAS SPOKEN often about hoping to return to a life of quiet priesthood, but his political role was by no means over with the advent of democracy in South Africa. A significant strand of the negotiations that the ANC had conducted with de Klerk's National Party between 1990 and 1994 dealt with the issue of how, exactly, those who had—from both sides—perpetrated politically motivated acts of violence could be held accountable in post-transition South Africa. The negotiations over that aspect of the transition came to fruition in an act passed by the new National Assembly in July 1995, which stipulated that the government would establish a Truth and Reconciliation Commission (TRC), with the following objectives:

> To promote national unity and reconciliation in a spirit of understanding which transcends the conflicts and divisions of the past by . . .
>
> (a) establishing as complete a picture as possible of the causes, nature and extent of the gross violations of human rights which were committed during the period from 1 March 1960 to the cut-off date [April 1994], including the antecedents, circumstances, factors and context of such violations, *as well as the perspectives of the victims and the motives and perspectives of the persons responsible for the commission of the violations,* by conducting investigations and holding hearings;
>
> (b) facilitating the granting of amnesty to persons who make full disclosure of all the relevant facts relating to acts associated with a political objective and comply with the requirements of this Act;
>
> (c) establishing and making known the fate or whereabouts of victims and by restoring the human and civil dignity of such victims by granting them an opportunity to relate their own accounts of the violations of which they are the victims, and by recommending reparation measures in respect of them;

(d) compiling a report providing as comprehensive an account as possible of the activities and findings of the Commission, . . . and which contains recommendations of measures to prevent the future violations of human rights.[6]

In a move that surprised no one, Tutu was named chairman of the commission. Over the years that followed, the TRC heard wrenching testimony from twenty-one thousand victims of crimes committed during the relevant period. Its work was always controversial to some degree: some black South Africans claimed it did not do enough to punish those who had orchestrated and administered the violence of the apartheid regime and that it placed abuses committed by the antiapartheid forces on the same level as those of their oppressors; some whites claimed that it was running an anti-white witch-hunt. Clearly, even after Tutu delivered the commission's thirty-five-hundred-page final report to President Mandela in October 1998, the work of reconciliation would still continue.

Throughout his engagement with his country's pro-democracy movement, Tutu's work had been informed by a number of important principles. First among these was the deep root of Christian faith from which his engagement sprang. Second was a determination—shared by President Mandela and other ANC leaders—that their opposition to white-minority rule would not lead them into the counterproductive folly of dehumanizing white South Africans. As the excerpts from his 1976 letter to Vorster show, Tutu went out of his way to try to connect personally not only with the family and religious concerns of the apartheid rulers—concerns that, after all, he felt he shared with them—but also with their distinctive status as members of the country's small Boer minority. In a 1985 address to a group of supporters, he was at pains to remind them, "White South Africans are not demons. White South Africans are human beings. Most of them are very scared human beings, and I ask the audience, 'Wouldn't you be scared if you were outnumbered five to one?'"[7] And during the glorious victory address he delivered in 1994 from the balcony of Cape Town's city hall, he revealed that the day before he had sung the Boer national anthem, "Die Stem," for the first time in his life. "And I loved it!"[8]

A third Tutu principle was a determination to hold to high standards of accountability even those who were struggling for an evidently just cause. "Ultimately we must turn the spotlight on ourselves," he preached when interblack violence was on the upswing in 1991. "We can't go on forever blaming apartheid. . . . What has gone wrong, that we seemed to have lost our reverence for life, when children dance round someone dying the gruesome death of necklacing?"9

A fourth principle, which he displayed throughout the conference, is always to try to keep alive his strong sense of humor.

DESPITE THE LEVITY of his opening remarks, the main subject Tutu had come to the conference to talk about was an extremely serious one. Just one week earlier, he had presented the TRC's weighty final report to President Mandela. The TRC's mandate had been designed to try out a completely new approach to the thorny issue of how emerging democracies can deal with, and get beyond, the grievances engendered by long, preceding periods of authoritarianism. Tutu said he believed strongly that the TRC's approach was one that should be considered by leaders in countries like Bosnia, Kosovo, Burundi, Rwanda, Sri Lanka, Burma, or East Timor. In all such places, he noted, there is both a present conflict to be dealt with and a postconflict period to be planned for. The central question he asked was therefore, *"How do you deal with a postconflict, postrepression period, as most of these countries are going to have to do?"*

He outlined four possible responses to this question. The first, which he described as "almost atavistic," is revenge: "You clobbered me, I am waiting for my chance to clobber you back. That's exactly what happened in Rwanda. The Hutu did something to the Tutsi. The Tutsi disappeared for thirty years. They came back, and we had genocide. Kosovo, Bosnia—what happened? Why? Now, that's one way."

The second type of response is a war-crimes trial, along the lines of those held by the victorious Allies at the end of World War II, both in Nuremberg, for leading German war criminals, and in Tokyo, for Japanese war criminals. "Nuremberg—" said Tutu, "now most people say, 'Yeah, that's probably not a bad option.' But Nuremberg happened where there were clear victors on one side and clear losers on the other side, and the winners could enforce, as they say, victors' justice. And have you noticed, in Nuremberg, the prosecutors and the judges when the case finished—they could pack their cases and leave! In most of the situations we're talking about"—he gave a chuckle whose dry tones spoke of decades of wrestling with this conundrum—

the judges, the prosecutors, the perpetrators, the victims, can't up and leave! They have to share the same geographic space. They're going to have to work out a way, really. *How do we, in fact, live together?*

A third option is do nothing. You say, "Let bygones be bygones. Let's forget the past: for goodness' sake, let's forget the past! Why, why, *why* do you want to rake up the past? Forget the past, and let's get on with the business of living in the present."

And so you can give yourselves, as they did in Chile, blanket amnesty: blanket amnesty which is really amnesia. "We forget. Let's try to forget—"

But, he argued, this approach would not work for countries like those mentioned, or for South Africa, either: "Mercifully, mercifully, God has created us in a particular kind of way. The past, dealt with in a cavalier fashion, does not remain the past. It refuses to lie down quietly. Bygones don't become bygones just by your say-so. You don't have a fiat, and you say, 'Now, bygones, you are gone.' They don't go. They return inexorably. They will return to haunt you. And you remember those quite haunting words in Dachau, the concentration camp museum, at the entrance there: 'Those who forget the past are doomed to repeat it.'"

None of those approaches provided the resolution that Tutu and other South Africans sought for their country, so they pioneered a fourth way:

Yes, but there is the best way, the South African way, which didn't happen because South Africans were particularly smart: it was *forced on them* because of the realities of our situation. No one won. The government didn't win. The apartheid government didn't win. The liberation movements didn't win. Stalemate.

Hey, how are we going to deal with this? And they struck on this compromise. Compromise tends to have a bad press, but it's not always a bad thing. Because they said, "Okay, in exchange for truth, you'll get amnesty. In exchange for telling us everything you know about what you want to ask amnesty for, you'll get freedom. Of course, if you don't, the judicial process we hope will take its course."

You see, to say "let's forget about it" was unsatisfactory also for other reasons. One of them is that you revictimize the victim. You say to the victims, "What happened in your case either didn't happen, or it doesn't matter."

And you remember in Dorfman's *Death and the Maiden,* the woman recognizes the voice of the man who tortured and raped her. And she manages to tie him up, and she's got a gun, and he still denies it. And she's on the verge of killing him! And then, he turns around, and yes, he admits he did it. And she lets him go, because the lie subverted her identity, her integrity. And we found, you know, that just in the telling of the story, people have experienced a catharsis, a healing. And it has been an incredible *privilege* sitting there, and listening to people who by right should be consumed by anger, and bitterness, and revenge, and you experience their magnanimity, their willingness to forgive.

Of course, you know Nelson Mandela. He's our spectacular example of this sort of thing that has happened in that crazy country. It *is* a crazy country: it's an extraordinary country! But it has been made extraordinary by all of you upholding us, praying for us, sustaining us, supporting us. You might not believe it, but *you are a real part of us.* I would not be standing here today had it not been for some extraordinary people like yourselves.

He gave some examples of the magnanimity and healing he had witnessed during his service on the TRC:

A white woman is a victim of hand-grenade attack by one of the liberation movements. A lot of her friends are killed, and she ends up having to have open-heart surgery, and she goes into ICU. She comes to the Truth and Reconciliation Commission to tell her story. And she tells her story, and she says, "You know, when I came out of hospital, my children had to bathe me, had to clothe me, had to feed me. And I can't walk through the security checkpoints at an airport. I've still got shrapnel inside me, so all kinds of alarms go off when I walk through."

Do you know what she said? She said of *this* experience, that left her in *this* condition, "It has—" Can you credit it? She said: "It has enriched my life." And she says, "I'd like to meet the perpetrator. I'd like to meet him in a spirit of forgiveness. I'd like to forgive him."

Which is extraordinary. But then, she goes on to say, she goes on to say—I can't believe it, she goes on to say, *"I hope he forgives me."*

A second example: one of the former homelands, the Ciskei,

banned the ANC from its territory and said it was a "no-go" area. And the ANC said they were not going to accept this, and so we went on a march, a demonstration, to Bisho. Bisho was the capital of this Bantustan homeland. A number of people were killed because the Ciskeian Defence Force came out: they shot and killed a number of people, and injured others.[10]

We had a hearing on the so-called Bisho massacre. The first person who came—and the hearing was in a hall packed to the roof by people who'd either been injured there or people who'd lost loved ones—and the first person who comes to testify is the former head of this Ciskeian Defence Force. And I have to say, even I was riled, not so much by what he said as by how he said what he said.

So the tension, you could cut with a knife! And then, the next set of witnesses was four officers: three black, one white. And the white was the spokesperson, and he says, "Yes, we gave the orders to the troops to open fire." Oh, the temperature just shot up! Then he turned to the audience and said, "Please forgive us. Please receive these three of my colleagues back into the community."

You know what that audience did? That audience broke out into deafening applause.

The Archbishop's voice dropped to a whisper, and he cradled the words that followed in long pauses. "When the noise had subsided, I said, 'Let's keep quiet, because we are in the presence of something holy. Really, we ought to take off our shoes, because we are standing on holy ground.'"

He let that story sink in. He noted simply that it had been "an incredible privilege to have been asked to preside over such a process." Then he moved on.

The very last example. The ANC had exploded a bomb in Pretoria in one of its main streets, called Church Street: they were attacking the headquarters of the South African Air Force. One of the officers was blinded in that attack, a white man.

When the ANC operative applied for amnesty—and amnesty is applied for in an open hearing—the ANC operative, Abubakr Ishmail, turned to Neville Clarence and asked for forgiveness. And the two, the one white blind man and the Indian, shook hands. And that picture became a kind of icon. It was emblazoned on the front pages of our newspapers and on television. And Neville Clarence said, as he shook hands, "It was as if both of us didn't want to let go of the other."

God has been very good to us, and maybe there is something for the world to learn from both our mistakes and some of our achievements —and I believe that we *are* going to succeed in this experiment that is happening in that crazy country. We're going to succeed because God wants us to succeed. And that's not because I have a hotline that I know this. . . . God is wanting us to succeed for the sake of God's world: because God wants to be able to point Bosnia, Northern Ireland, Middle East, Rwanda: "Just look at them [in South Africa]!"

Who could ever have imagined that South Africa could be an example of anything but the most ghastly situation? But now God wants to say, I think, "Just look at them! Utterly unlikely! But they are the symbol of hope." South Africa, a symbol of hope! [He laughed in delight.] God's sense of humor! Just look at it. Look at it. I mean, they . . . are not even too bright, you know, because if they had been bright, smart, they wouldn't have held on to apartheid for so long!

You know that story of— We were talking [earlier] about astronauts, and the South African was upset that America and the Soviet Union were getting all of the kudos for the space program, and so he announced that we in South Africa were going to launch a spacecraft to the sun. And then people said, "No, no, man, you can't be serious. Long before it reaches the sun, it will burn to cinders." He says, "Oh, you can't think that. You think we South Africans are stupid? No, no, man: we will launch it at night!"

But . . . God is going to be saying, "They had a nightmare called apartheid. It has ended. Your nightmare will end, too. They had a problem that the world had described as being intractable. They're solving it—"

Once again, the whisper, which felt like a holy utterance: "Bosnia, Kosovo, Sierra Leone, Angola, Burundi, Rwanda, you name them: your problem can't ever again be described as intractable."

DURING THOSE CRUCIAL years in the early 1990s in which Mandela, Tutu, and their colleagues were searching for the best way to transcend the wounds of the past—and *negotiating* this issue, meanwhile, with the head of the outgoing regime—they had good access to a corpus of lessons drawn from the ways this same question had been dealt with in other, earlier transitions to democracy in the modern age. Between 1990 and 1995, the U.S. Institute of Peace, in Washington, D.C., ran a large project to pull together the facts about, and assess, how emerging democracies around the world had dealt with issues in this field of "transitional justice." This project culminated in a thorough, three-volume report, which looked at the experiences of twenty-one countries, including post-Nazi Germany, postdictatorship South Korea, Greece, Portugal, Spain, several countries in South America, Uganda, Russia, and several countries in Eastern Europe. The introduction to this report was written by President Mandela. "As all these countries recover from the trauma and wounds of the past," he wrote, "they have had to devise mechanisms not only for handling past human rights violations but also to ensure that the dignity of victims, survivors, and relatives is restored. In the context of this relentless search for appropriate equilibria, profound issues of policy and law have emerged."[11]

Many of the contributions to this project had particular relevance for the South Africans. Regarding the value of giving publicity to the truth about previous abuses, legal scholar Lawrence Weschler wrote, "Fragile, tentative democracies time and again hurl themselves toward an abyss, struggling over this issue of truth. It's a mysteriously powerful, almost magical notion, because often everyone already knows the truth—everyone knows who the torturers were and what they did, the torturers know that everyone knows, and everyone knows that they know. Why then this need to risk everything to render that knowledge explicit?" One answer offered during a 1988 discussion of that question came from American philosopher Thomas Nagel: "It's the difference . . . between knowledge and acknowledgment. It's what happens and can only happen to knowledge when it becomes officially sanctioned, *when it is made part of the public cognitive scene.*"[12]

A team of mental health specialists who had worked with survivors of torture in Chile provided numerous insights, including this one:

> The term *reparation* has a double meaning. First, it is a psychoanalytic concept, developed by Melanie Klein, that is used to explain the intrapsychic process of repair. But it is also a legal term used, for example, in connection with economic compensation after a war.

This double meaning is significant because repair in the psychoanalytic sense must occur at both the individual and social levels, but it can only take place fully if it is linked to reparation in the legal sense—that is, with truth and justice for the victim and compensation when it is helpful."[13]

In this volume, too, veteran Chilean human rights activist José Zalaquett wrote eloquently about the dilemmas faced in situations when—unlike what happened during the Allies' post-1945 occupation of Europe—the institutions and military power of the "old" authoritarian regime will continue to be very much a part of the local political equation. "The implications of the dilemmas involved in transitional political situations have become fully apparent," he wrote. "In ambiguous transitional situations, dealing with past human rights violations is indeed a wrenching ethical and political problem. But there are no hard and fast rules on how to proceed. Ethical principles can provide guidance but no definite answer. Political leaders cannot afford to be moved only by their convictions, oblivious to real-life constraints, lest in the end the very ethical principles they wish to uphold suffer because of a political or military backlash."[14]

Throughout all his work with TRC, Tutu was keenly aware of these constraints and dilemmas. In June 1998, he spoke to a group of foreign diplomats in Pretoria about the attitude of the security forces of the apartheid regime. "It is certain that they would not have agreed to a peaceful transition from repression to democracy if they had known that we were going to have Nuremberg-type trials," he was reported as saying. He noted that the amnesty process had been a necessary compromise, given that there had been no clear-cut military victory. "Compromise has had a bad press, but it is not necessarily a bad thing," he explained, on that occasion also.[15]

In October 1998, as the TRC wrapped up the work mandated to it three years earlier, it did so amid lingering controversy. Many ANC leaders were still upset that abuses committed by forces under their command seemed to have been placed on too equal a footing with the considerably more numerous and graver crimes committed by the apartheid regime. There was a sense of grievance among many antiapartheid activists that aging former President P. W. Botha seemed to have "gotten away with" resisting all the notices the TRC had issued, summoning him to appear before it. Nevertheless, the commission had registered many achievements in charting a new course for the application of transitional justice. In his introduction to the TRC's final report, Archbishop Tutu wrote,

> We believe we have provided enough of the truth about our past for there to be a consensus about it. There is consensus that atrocious things were done on all sides. We know that the State used its considerable resources to wage a war against some of its citizens. We know that torture and deception and murder and death squads came to be the order of the day. We know that the liberation movements were not paragons of virtue and were often responsible for egging people on to behave in ways that were uncontrollable. We know that we may, in the present crime rate, be reaping the harvest of the campaigns [previously waged by many antiapartheid groups] to make the country ungovernable. We know that the immorality of apartheid has helped to create the climate where moral standards have fallen disastrously.[16]

Pumla Gobodo-Madikizela, who had served on the TRC's Committee on Human Rights Violations, commented that the report "should be seen as part of dealing with the past and seeking reconciliation, even if such reconciliation will not come in this generation." She added,

> The commission allowed some victims and survivors an encounter with their perpetrators in ways that would not have been possible in a court of law. And here lies one of the successes of the commission: The requests for forgiveness made by some perpetrators, and the granting of forgiveness by victims and survivors who are the primary generation of sufferers of atrocities, is unprecedented in the history of atrocities in the 20th century. *The commission's final success is that South Africa did not plunge into a spiral of violence and revenge.*[17]

When he handed the report over to President Mandela that day, Tutu acknowledged that many people would be upset by it, and that some had already sought to discredit it preemptively. "Fellow South Africans," he implored, "accept this report as a way, an indispensable way of healing, where we have looked the beast in the eye."[18]

ONE WEEK LATER, Tutu was giving his impassioned evaluation of the TRC's work to the gathering at the University of Virginia conference. Was that a hard act to follow? That difficulty did not stop Bobby Muller, who is not only a former Marine but also someone who has thought long and hard about how people should try to deal with the kinds of justice issues that get tangled up in long-lasting systems of violence.

There ensued, between Muller and the archbishop, an exchange that plumbed some of the hardest-to-resolve aspects of this question.

"I really respect what you've done with this effort," Muller started,

> and I understand a lot of the emotions that you describe, having had the opportunity myself to go back to my war zone, meet my former enemy, and really come to terms with a tremendous amount of emotions based on the commonality of our experience. . . .
>
> But there is an aspect of this which I'm totally confused about, and it's got to do with personal accountability, and when you draw the line and you hold people accountable for, let's say minimally, crimes against humanity, for which I don't think there should be any statute of limitations. And I don't think the fact that Pinochet is an eighty-two-year-old guy should exonerate him, or let him off the hook, for the torture and the murder of as many innocent people as he's responsible for!

He referred to the way the principle of personal accountability had been addressed in the Nuremberg judgments, which explicitly disallowed the defense that people were "only following orders" when they committed atrocities, and to the 1949 Geneva Conventions, which codified many preceding limitations on actions performable in war.[19] But despite the general agreement that these "laws of war" had met with, Muller noted that during the twentieth century the balance between military and civilian casualties in warfare had shifted badly, to the detriment of civilians. "All of this body of agreement known as the 'laws of war,' as codified in those various mechanisms, apparently seems to mean nothing! And one could easily say that they're not laws, they're sort of like 'recommendations,' because if you break the law you're punished—

"South Africa's got a lot which makes it unique," he concluded, "but you know, I'm sure you support the idea of an International Criminal Court to try those guilty of crimes against humanity, and the concept of personal accountability. . . . Can you sort of help clarify that a little bit?"

"Yes," said the archbishop.

What we did at home, in fact, is to take very seriously the whole question of impunity. Because, you see, before we had our own Truth and Reconciliation Commission, almost everywhere else they had granted themselves, and the *military* before moving out, granted themselves amnesty: a blanket amnesty. And our case, which is unique, is that we said amnesty's going to be granted on the basis of an individual application. That's one. Two, the conditions for granting amnesty are not that you get amnesty just because you come along and you say I have done such and such, you know. That is, amnesty is not automatic.

We received 7,000 applications for amnesty. . . . At the time of the printing of our report, only 154 had been granted, with another 2,000 still to be considered. But the other condition is you *acknowledge*, you *accept*, you *say* you are guilty. That's accountability! There's no point in giving amnesty to someone who is innocent or who claims to be innocent. And there are people who came applying for amnesty and saying they were really innocent, and the committee said, "We can't give you amnesty if you're innocent. We can give you amnesty only if you are guilty."[20] And so people have to accept their responsibility for the atrocity that they have committed, and so your worry about accountability and law, the significance of law, the autonomy of the law, that is taken account of.

But, you see, the other thing is that I think lurking behind your question is concepts of justice. Now you said everybody has got to be punished. So your concept of what constitutes justice is retributive justice. Now that's not the only kind of justice. We believe that there is restorative justice. Because, you see, the application is heard in an open hearing, not behind closed doors. Television lights are panned on the applicant, and in fact for quite a number, this probably was the first time that their wives knew that this apparently decent man was actually a member of a death squad. And that public appearance constitutes a public humiliation which is, I think—if you're looking for punitiveness—that *is* a punishment. But we didn't think that is the way we wanted it to end. We were looking for feeling, for— And it's probably an African concept of our understanding of penology: what is the purpose? The purpose is ultimately *the restoration of a harmony*.[21]

And now we are able actually to have the luxury of discussing all of these wonderful things at home *because the compromise was, in fact, made.* Had the security forces known that they were going to be for the high jump, we wouldn't be sitting here! The victims accepted that there was a price that was being paid, a price that was being paid for ensuring that the transition happens, but it isn't a price that is out of proportion to the realities of our situation.

Let me just give you an example. I didn't speak about Rwanda. I went to Rwanda very soon after the genocide and I went to Kigali, to the main prison there. It was choc-a-bloc full, and some people had actually died of suffocation. And I said to the president of that country, that jail is a disaster waiting to happen. I said your history in this country is this kind of thing. You have a top dog and an underdog. Maybe the top dog is Hutu, the underdog is Tutsi. And your history is: underdog seeks to become top dog, and underdog *becomes* top dog, and there is hell to pay for the erstwhile top dog for the things that they did to the new top dog when he was underdog. And so the things turned around. Tutsi now become top dog, and Hutu as is happening now, are the underdog. And the game, you play that game—

And I said to them, I was preaching in Kigali, and I said to them, "If retributive justice is your last word in this country, you've had it. You can write off the possibility of ever having a stable Rwanda because even as we speak now, the Hutu have mostly been the ones who've been arrested, mostly Hutu have been found guilty, and Hutu have been executed. They're not going to say, 'We were found guilty because the evidence indicated that we're guilty. We were found guilty because we were Hutu. We were found guilty sometimes by Tutsi judges. We are waiting for our chance.'"

And I said to them, "My own understanding is, for what it is worth, your history of the spiral of reprisal, provoking a counter-reprisal, provoking a counter-reprisal, will remain this way. You need something to go beyond that spiral, to break through, and you need forgiveness."

Muller wanted to push the discussion further. The purpose of law, he said, should certainly go beyond retribution. It should also, clearly, include a measure of deterrence—

to set an example of those that are guilty of these crimes, so that those that may be contemplating whether or not they want to try and get away with that will have in their mind that if they do that, they will pay a price similarly to that. And it's the deterrent aspect of the accountability factor more than . . . retribution that I think is an issue.

I've spent a lot of time working with Cambodia, a lot of years. And Cambodia changed my life more than the war in Vietnam did, because Cambodia was a case of genocide. The war in Vietnam was brutal, but the genocide of Cambodia dismantled the society and it was a chill to my soul. And it completely changed my life to have some exposure to the degree of horror that was involved there. The guy that really drove the show there was Pol Pot, and shortly before Pol Pot died, he was in a public court, and given a chance to explain himself. And he said, yes, in fact, "No, no, I'm sorry. I made mistakes." He may have said that very sincerely. He may feel, "Well, I made mistakes, but I tried."

So, I don't know. Where something like that fits in the equation, I think, is open for some discussion.

One of the things we talked about earlier today was evil, and how vulnerable we are . . . to being seduced by the negative force. We are. We're shockingly vulnerable to being affected. Not that it's quite the same thing, but there was a movie about the Marines that Stanley Kubrick put out, called *Full Metal Jacket* that illustrates extraordinarily well how eighteen-year-old kids, coming in to the Marine Corps as basic nummies, can be processed through indoctrination to wind up charging enemy machine-gun positions—which is not a natural act!

The point of this is that there are people—Milosevic, Kabila—that foster the negative, and have blood on their hands in a way that is something that demands accountability. I don't know, it's a—

"It's perhaps fairly straightforward," Tutu said. "What we are seeking to do at home is to cultivate a culture of respect for law." What the TRC had done was, he suggested, to tell South Africans

that you have to take responsibility for what you did: the fact that you have to stand up in an open forum and say "I have done so, and so, and so." Remember, the amnesty provision isn't something that is going to stay on forever. It's a provision for a transition, you see? There is a limitation to when you can apply for amnesty. In our case, it's long over. That is why part of our recommendation is that those who did not apply for amnesty, and where there is evidence that they were guilty of violations, gross violations, of human rights, then, the judicial process should take its course.

But I think, I mean, that even with the amnesty process, it incorporates your deterrence element. I mean, no one wants to stand up in public and say, "I abducted this young man. I gave him spiked coffee, and I shot him in the head, and I burned his body. And while we were burning his body we had a barbecue." Which is something that was part of the testimony. . . . I mean, nobody likes being known in public in that kind of way. So that there *is* a deterrent. The very fact that not everybody applies shows, I mean, that there is a reluctance to appear.

But with regard to Pol Pot, the fact that he stands up and says, "I am sorry, I made mistakes"— Unless the country says, well, we are willing to have amnesty, an amnesty provision, I don't think that that is actually a very relevant example for the kind of thing that I'm trying to talk about.

I'm talking about a specific [situation]—and we are going to get many such situations!—of the transition. What is going to happen in East Timor? They are going to be trying to work out, "We had collaborators with the Indonesians. How are we going to deal with them?" And they can't just say, well, that is okay, we will forget about it. Because they won't forget about it! They've got to find a mechanism. And what one is saying is that, "We're not claiming that this is an infallible blueprint. It is an option that people ought to be considering as a serious option."

Other laureates had questions. The first was Rigoberta Menchú. "I think that this topic is of greatest importance," she said,

and I think that the Nobel laureates, and perhaps other institutions, should put together a program of study, a program of work, to try to figure out the line for truth and justice, and for amnesty. I as a victim would like to know who are those responsible for the torture of my mother! And if I were to find them, I would like to bring them before justice. And I would at least like that they demonstrate their innocence of all these things. On behalf of the victims, there can be decrees, but making restitution for the damage that has been done is not a matter of a decree.

But how can we hope that they at least ask for forgiveness? I can't forget that forgiveness comes with truth and with justice. And while I recognize Bob's concern, I ask, "What can we do to perfect the process by which we address this in the future?" Because the past is something that we have lived, that we have acted in. And normally, [in Latin America] the processes of peace have ended in a climate of impunity.

How in the future can impunity not have a place in the countries that have suffered these conflicts?

"I'm very interested," Harn Yawnghwe said, "because we have a very brutal regime in Burma, and will have to come to terms with it very soon." He noted that in South Africa, East Timor, and Guatemala, peacemakers were able to work on the basis of the Christian concept of forgiveness, and he asked Tutu whether an approach like South Africa's could be applied in a country like Burma where, he argued, the cultures did not really include a strong concept of forgiveness. "We have compassion," he said, "you may excuse people. But the concept of forgiveness is something quite different. I know there's not enough time but that's something that really I would like to explore."

Betty Williams took a different tack: "Dear, dear, dear Father Tutu," she said, "I love you so much! Because the only way forward for the world is in forgiveness, and I think that South Africa has created a model that should be copied by other places. Burma could learn a lot from His Grace's work in South Africa." She said that one of the references Tutu made in his presentation that particularly interested her was his reference to the need to build a culture of respect for the law, since,

> when the law, as we know, has no respect for the people, then the people will have no respect for the law. And I taught in Texas for four years at a university, and while I was there, then-Governor Ann Richards appointed me to the Texas Commission for Children and Youth. The answer to everything in Texas was to build bigger and better prisons. And to me, "Duh!" Don't you know that if you work in the ghetto, you won't need the prison to be as big? We spend billions and billions of dollars here in the United States of America incarcerating people instead of spending that same billions of dollars in the ghettos, in better housing and jobs for people, and all of that. It just doesn't make sense!

With this part of the session nearing its end, Julian Bond asked Tutu to sum up.

"Well!" His Grace exclaimed, to much general laughter. "Betty was making a comment, and we said we concur with her. I don't know about Buddhists not knowing anything about forgiveness." He turned to Harn. "What happens when you quarrel with your wife?"

"You don't," came the reply. The audience laughed.

"Because, I think . . . that in every language, every culture, the most difficult words you have to say are, 'I'm sorry. Forgive me.' Otherwise, actually, there is no future in that relationship. Basically, I'm saying that even in the world, forgiveness is not just a spiritual [thing], you know, something that is nebulous. It's, in fact, *realpolitik*: that there will be no future without forgiveness. That is for real. And I think, I mean, looking at a military junta that is scared of a woman of about that size" — he held his hands inches apart, in reference to Aung San Suu Kyi's small stature — "I mean, speaking about authority, moral authority! Let's guard our sister laureate, who is remarkable in her gentleness and her willingness to say, 'Let's talk, let's talk!' And that is what . . . is maybe the paradigm that the world wants to be looking at."

DURING HIS PRESENTATION, Tutu described the other laureates sitting around the table as "quite, quite exceptional persons." He added:

> And I'm always intrigued by His Holiness, particularly, because, you know, he's suffered a great deal. He's in exile from his country for I don't know how many — donkey's! — years, and yet he has this incredible serenity and bubbliness. He's actually — I was going to say "naughty" —
>
> And the world recognizes that! You know, we speak of a world that is often dismissed as cynical, hard-nosed. And yet actually, it has an instinct for goodness. You *admire* a Nelson Mandela. You *admire* a Mother Theresa. You *admire* a Dalai Lama. Because inside you there is, there is something that *tells* you — It homes in to goodness. . . .
>
> This world which we condemn so frequently, and perhaps quite rightly, for all the awfulnesses there are in it. Awfulnesses caused by *us* [humans], and you know, sitting and listening to horrendous stories as we have done, you can't have any illusions about our capacity for evil:

we, all of us, without exception, have the capacity for the most incredible levels of evil.

Ah, that is just one side of the story, because do you know, we also have an incredible capacity for goodness, and we shouldn't forget that. We shouldn't forget that we have had young people go away from *this* country as part of the Peace Corps, go and work in remote places where they needn't do so, and they don't get banner headlines. [Instead, young people] get banner headlines because they are substance abusers. . . . We forget that actually, it was young people largely, when we were asking, "Please, we want sanctions against South Africa," it was young people at universities and colleges who were striving for disinvestment. And I take my hat off to them!

Yes, this world has got many awful things, but it has also got some very beautiful things.

Jody Williams responding to Oscar Arias Sánchez's reading
(Photo by Lynne Brubaker)

Harn Yawnghwe and Julian Bond (Photo by Jim Carpenter)

Bobby Muller presenting comments (Photo by Bill Sublette)

*Rigoberta Menchú Tum
during a classroom visit
(Photo by Tom Cogill)*

Harn Yawnghwe conversing with a student at lunch
(Photo by Jim Carpenter)

Betty Williams in a seminar (Photo by Jim Carpenter)

Rigoberta Menchú Tum and her son, Mash, at dinner (Photo by Lynne Brubaker)

Desmond Tutu on the University of Virginia Lawn (Photo by Lynne Brubaker)

Julian Bond with Desmond Tutu and Bobby Muller
(Photo by Jim Carpenter)

Dean Melvyn Leffler conversing with Betty Williams on the University of
Virginia's Lawn (Photo by Lynne Brubaker)

The laureates, Julian Bond, and others posing for a group photo, as the Dalai Lama helps Desmond Tutu with his hat (Photo by Lynne Brubaker)

His Holiness the Dalai Lama on the University of Virginia's Lawn (Photo by Bill Sublette)

8

Oscar Arias Sánchez and Structural Aspects
of the Struggle for Human Security

Former Costa Rican President Oscar Arias Sánchez is a shy man with a powerful message: "Those working today can decide whether the age of globalization will be remembered as a time of profit and plunder, or as a time of diversity and enlightenment. All of you *here* will decide, with your activism or your complacency, whether the new world order will be governed by a corporate ethics of selfishness, or by an ethical character of equality and human rights."

He is engaged here, as he has been for many years, in a strong campaign of moral suasion. The Dalai Lama may be right to argue that the transformation of human motivation—of everyone connected, in whatever way, to the global system—is the key to escaping from its broad systems of violence and counterviolence. And indeed, in his presentation, Arias joined the other laureates in trying to urge such a transformation of motivation. But he reminded us vividly that there are also considerable structural factors at work in the world—at the level of globe-circling economic relations, military-power relations, and arms-transfer relations—that further feed the violence within it. In his presentation, he sought to lay out the facts regarding the economic and arms-transfer underpinnings of global violence, and to urge commitment to transformation at those structural levels, too.

Trained as an academic economist, with a doctorate from Britain's University of Essex, he was appointed minister of planning and economic policy in Costa Rica in 1972, when he was only thirty-two. Six years later, he was elected to Parliament; in 1986, he was elected president of his country.

It was a tough time to assume office. Costa Rica had abolished its standing army nearly forty years earlier (at the initiative of Arias's mentor, President José Figueres Ferrer). But in 1986, the other four states of Central America—Nicaragua, El Salvador, Guatemala, and Honduras—were all being torn apart by an interlocking system of civil wars, which were fueled and stoked from outside in one of the last acts of the global cold war.

Arias stepped in where most angels feared to tread. In August 1987, he brought the four other Central American presidents together at a regional summit held in Esquipulas, Guatemala. At the end of that meeting, the leaders all signed on to a peace plan known as Esquipulas-II, that envisaged cease-fires, national reconciliation, and progress toward democratization *within* each of their countries, and a ban by each on the use of its territory by groups seeking to destabilize any *other* signatory government.[1]

Arias won that agreement in the teeth of fierce opposition from the United States, which strongly opposed the inclusion in the peace process of Nicaraguan president Daniel Ortega Saavedra. At the time, the Reagan administration was giving covert military aid to Ortega's opponents, the Nicaraguan contras. But the Esquipulas-II agreement won valuable diplomatic backing from the West European governments, from Pope John Paul II—and from the Norwegian Nobel Committee, which that year named Arias its peace laureate. In its nomination, the committee cited his "outstanding contribution to the possible return of stability and peace to a region long torn by strife and civil war."[2]

Throughout the remaining years of his presidency, Arias continued to try to push the regionwide peace effort forward. He used his peace prize money to establish the Arias Foundation for Peace and Human Progress, which promotes efforts at peace-building, democratization, and human development throughout Central America, as well as globally.

At the global level, as the cold war wound down in the early 1990s, he became increasingly concerned that its end was *not* being accompanied by any real attempt by the rich weapons-producing nations to stanch the flow of arms into the poor, underdeveloped regions of the world. Quite the reverse. Arms transfers from the rich countries to the "developing" world continued, and in many cases grew. And too frequently, governments or other groups in recipient countries ended up using these weapons in hideous internal and regionwide wars. In 1995, Arias launched a new initiative: to institute an International Code of Conduct on Arms Transfers. Any country supporting this code would undertake to transfer arms—that is, sell, give, or otherwise deliver control of them—*only* to recipient countries or parties that complied with a fairly extensive list of democratic and human rights standards.[3]

By May 1997, Arias and his colleagues in the Code of Conduct project considered they had drafted good language for it. At an event in New York that month, Arias, the Dalai Lama, José Ramos-Horta, and Betty Williams joined with four other Nobel peace laureates to present the code to the world. The declaration the laureates made that day called on all governments to support the code and urged the citizens of the world to demand that their governments do so. "Only through solidarity, compassion, and courageous leadership can we make violence and its vestiges a distant memory of the past," the declaration stated.[4]

At the University of Virginia conference, Arias's main presentation was listed in the program as dealing primarily with the Code of Conduct. But, like the Dalai Lama, he did not entirely follow the script. Instead, he devoted the first half of his presentation to describing "the larger context of the struggle for human security," within which he had launched the Code of Conduct campaign. "I am sure," he told an attentive audience,

> that you have seen many times the images of the Berlin Wall coming down, watched commentators pronounce the end of the cold war, and heard that a new era has begun. Indeed, few terms are as important today as "globalization." Though only a small number of individuals take time to closely examine this concept, many feel entitled to invoke it regularly. Not only does "globalization" portend to characterize our present age, but it also seems to carry the weight of destiny. Certainly, technological advances and the emergence of sophisticated markets have increased the affinity between different global societies, allowing for rapid transportation of people and information.
>
> But globalization points to several other distinctive phenomena as well. Traditional understandings of economics are changing. For some, the new economic system means being able to make investments with a worldly perspective, minimizing labor costs and maximizing profits. For many others, it means facing the end of job security, and at the same time witnessing the reappearance of sweatshops. Structures of government must also adapt to a "new world order." Conventional states find themselves weakened in the face of trans-

national agreements and fluid capital. The $1.5 trillion that race around the planet daily are largely unaccountable to any accepted form of public oversight.

This globalization is a Janus-faced beast, offering *unimaginable* prosperity to the most well-educated and well-born, while doling out only misery and despair to the world's poor. The system encourages insatiable consumption for some, but denies many others the basic necessities of life. Who would not question the priorities of a system in which Americans spend $8 billion a year on cosmetics—$2 billion more than it would cost to provide basic education for everyone in the world if these funds were redirected? Europeans spend $11 billion a year purchasing ice cream, yet we know that only $9 billion a year would be adequate to assure water and sanitation for all people![5]

This argument provided considerable food for thought. If a person in the United States makes one small purchase of cosmetics, does that constitute participation in a "system" that somehow also comprises the lack of human services in a community halfway around the globe? Arias was arguing that in one sense, it does, that the stark facts of economic interconnectedness draw everyone into a single global economic system. And he was urging each individual to take a Copernican leap away from considering only one small part of the system, toward understanding the working of the system as a whole, and starting to evaluate his or her own role in it.

In past years, he continued, dissenting views on the merits of economic globalization had been muted. But

today things have changed. Undoubtedly, you are all aware that we are in the midst of a global financial crisis. Now, we can watch even the high priests of the unregulated market, powerless in preventing panic, coming down from their pulpits. Rather than sanctifying the capricious benevolence of the invisible hand, many are falling to their knees and hoping that total collapse will be averted. Jeffrey Sachs, a Harvard economist who supervised the program of "shock therapy" for Russia and much of Eastern Europe, now tells us that the "dream of quick economic liberalization lies in ruins."

But what is not stressed in the talk of Wall Street analysts, who seem preoccupied with the profitability of their investment houses, is the true human dimension of this crisis. Imagine if half of the people you know, people earning a modest but adequate living, were suddenly thrown into desperate poverty. This is the situation that our brothers and sisters in Indonesia are now confronting as one hundred million people are made to feel the crushing blow of financial panic. The economies of Thailand and South Korea have shrunk by 45 percent in the past two years; indeed the currency of South Korea lost half of its value in the past year, witnessing substantial declines in a matter of days. And as the shockwaves from these devaluations extend through society, it is the most vulnerable and economically insecure populations who often bear the miserable brunt of the impact. These people do not need a market observer to tell them of the shortcomings of an economic system based on greed and speculation, rather than on human need.

Moreover, compassionate people can only shudder when they consider the combined horrors of military insecurity and human desperation in Russia. Every day we receive word that the safeguards protecting the country's twenty-two thousand nuclear weapons are growing less secure. Even before the turmoil of the past few months, life expectancy for males declined from a pre-reform 65.6 years to 57 years today, a decline unheard of in times without war or massive natural disaster. And as winter begins, there are indications that millions of people may die, lacking food to strengthen their bodies and fuel to warm their homes, unless the international community undertakes a massive humanitarian intervention, and not merely a bail-out for wealthy investors.

Thus, while the age of the cold war has ended, it has not been followed by the promised era of peace and prosperity. For how can we say that there is peace when thousands are made to work under dehumanizing conditions? How can we say that there is peace when the United States builds more prisons and fewer schools? How can we say that there is peace when so many go hungry?

The Costa Rican laureate drew on his long involvement in peace-building in Central America and elsewhere, when he presented the heart of his argument about "human security," which is also, centrally, an argument about the nature of peace itself.

This historical moment requires that we think about peace in a new way. Traditionally, peace has been discussed with reference to the demands of national security. The United Nations Development Program, however, stresses the need for us instead to think of peace in terms of human security. This distinction bears frequent repetition. *Human security goes beyond concern with weapons—it is a concern with human life and dignity.* When we demand peace, it must be not only a peace which halts bombing and gunfire. It must also be a peace concerned with the welfare and health of all people. For truly, when poverty and inequality remain at such terrible levels, armed conflict will be inevitable.

This concept of peace as encompassing elements of basic human well-being beyond the condition of a simple absence of war is one that also comes to us from the Semitic concept of *shalom* or *salaam*. Arias expanded on it in a more mainstream U.S. context:

During the Great Depression of the 1930s, Franklin D. Roosevelt looked out on forty million people "ill-housed, ill-clad, ill-fed." *Now, with our global vision, we must face over thirty times as many fellow citizens living in desperate circumstances.* Each person must face the fact that of the 4.4 billion people living in the developing world, nearly three-fifths lack access to adequate sewers, a third have no access to clean water, a quarter live in woefully substandard housing, and a fifth have no access to modern health services of any kind. As a result forty thousand children die each day from malnutrition and disease, and nearly one-third of the people in the least developed countries are not expected to survive to the age of forty. While the world as a whole consumes $24 trillion worth of goods and services each year, the planet holds 1.3 billion people who live on incomes of less than one dollar a day.

In human history, our societies have always known poverty and suffering. But what makes the poverty of today so sinister is that this terrible suffering exists alongside tremendous wealth. Today, the three richest people in the world have assets that exceed the combined gross domestic product of the poorest forty-eight countries. In the United States, the richest 20 percent earn nine times more than the poorest 20 percent; this country has one of the worst distributions of wealth in a world full of stark inequalities. Indeed, my friends, our global society cannot sustain these inequalities. Decent people, concerned with peace and justice, cannot allow them to persist.

He decried the lack of leaders willing to confront the evils of poverty and inequality:

> Despite the huge potentials for moral progress in the current age, the ethics of greed and militarism remain. Beneath all the talk of presidential embarrassment and cover-up lies an even deeper and more disgraceful scandal, one which few leaders have the courage to address. *The true scandal is that rather than proudly pronouncing the end of world poverty, so many policymakers and businesspeople are solidifying a global economic order based on cynicism and individual profit.* The true scandal is that rather than promoting the noble values of compassion and solidarity, leaders quietly allow the most wealthy to prosper at the expense of poor and working people throughout the world. The true scandal is that politicians tell the people what they want to hear, instead of what they need to know.
>
> Sadly, these same politicians underestimate the impact that suffering in the inner cities and tragic poverty in the wider world have on the democratic consciousness, disheartening all those who dream of a more just human society. Thus, those here may have little trouble relating to the words of Robert Kennedy, a graduate of this great university, who told us that while each of us may not be poor, "poverty affects *all* of us . . . The facts of poverty and injustice penetrate to every corner, every suburb, and every farm in this nation. Our ideal of America is a nation in which justice is done; and therefore, the continued existence of injustice—of unnecessary inexcusable poverty in this most favored of nations—this knowledge erodes our ideal of America, our basic sense of who and what we are. It is," he said, "in the deepest sense of the word, de-moralizing to all of us."

For his part, Arias saw the remedy to these woes as lying with the emergence, and the real engagement in efforts at reform, of a body of "global citizens":

> The lack of moral leadership will only be rectified if global citizens demand a new ethics for the new millennium. When Voltaire wrote *Candide* over two hundred years ago, he was acutely aware of the

moral obligations created by an integrating world. In this book, Candide meets a slave from the Americas who is missing both a hand and a leg. The slave's hand was cut off by dangerous machinery in a sugarcane mill; his leg was cut off by cruel masters to prevent him from escaping. As Candide looks on, the miserable slave tells him: "this is the true price of the sugar you eat in Europe."

If ethics required global thinking in Voltaire's time, think of how relevant this powerful anecdote is in the age of globalization. As Americans today, you have only to look at the label on your clothes and wonder if foreign garment workers labored for a just wage, to see that you already participate in the global system that brings great wealth to some and great misery to many others. The question is not whether you will be involved in the ethical challenges of globalization, but what your contribution will be. Will you, in your apathy, be complicit in the injustices I have described? Or will you, with your action and your example, bolster the ranks of those fighting for human security?

The age of narrow-minded nationalism has ended. Today, we must accept the fact that the evils of environmental destruction and human deprivation, of disease and malnutrition, of conspicuous consumption and military build-up are global problems—problems which affect us all.

Each of you must reconsider the privileges you enjoy as well-educated citizens in a wealthy country. And you must embrace the responsibility that comes with this privilege. The point is not to feel guilty about the gifts you have received, but to feel always committed to the struggle to guarantee that all people may live such dignified lives.

Pausing only to turn the page of the text he had prepared for the occasion, he urged his listeners not to be overwhelmed by the problems ahead:

Instead, be determined to make your mark against poverty and inequality! For it is this determination that builds hope. And it is hope that allows people to join together in the movements that change the world.

Do not doubt that such movements have accomplished much. The United Nations Development Program reports that, in the past fifty years, poverty has fallen more than in the previous five hundred.

Infant mortality in the developing world is one-third what it was in 1960. And during this same period of time, life expectancy in the poorest countries has been extended more than fifteen years, owing largely to a revolution in women's health.

I share these facts with you not so that we may grow complacent and stop working, but to convey a sense of the momentous possibilities for progress. Did it not take a movement of scorned but persistent abolitionists to end the scourge of slavery? Let us similarly join together today to end the scourge of poverty. Did not relentless advocates for independence succeed in ending colonialism? Let us now join in solidarity with the oppressed people of the world so that all may know freedom and liberty!

LATER IN HIS address, Arias argued that "in order to understand the true human cost of militarism, as well as the true impact of unregulated arms sales in the world today, we must understand that war is not just an evil act of destruction, it is *a missed opportunity for humanitarian investment.* It is a crime against every child who calls out for food rather than for guns, and against every mother who demands simple vaccinations rather than million-dollar fighters." These opportunity costs involved in arms procurement (and in decisions to use arms) are clearly indicated in a biannual publication that has been painstakingly researched and compiled for a quarter of a century now by Washington, D.C.–based researcher Ruth Leger Sivard.

Sivard noted in her 1996 edition that the twentieth century stands out as both the most economically productive and the most destructive century in human history. In the data tables appended to her book, she divided the world into three broad categories: twenty-four countries were described as "industrial" (these included Israel and Japan, but no other Asian country); twenty-seven were described as "transitional"—these were the east European countries, and all the successor states to the former Soviet Union; and the remaining 109 states as "developing countries." Using these broad global aggregations, her figures showed that between 1960 and 1994, the total Gross National Product (GNP) in the industrial countries rose 220 percent, from $4.7 trillion to $15.0 trillion, while that in the developing countries rose 343 percent, from $0.7 trillion to $3.1 trillion—all in constant 1987 dollars.

In the industrial countries, military expenditures increased by just over

50 percent in that same period—from $274 billion to $416 billion. But the level of economic growth in those countries was so high that, despite that increase, the level of military spending as a proportion of GNP fell from 5.8 percent to 2.8 percent over those years. In the developing countries, meanwhile, military expenditures more than *quadrupled* between those years: from $25 billion to $110 billion. That high rate of growth meant that the increase in military spending in those countries almost kept pace with the increase in GNP: military spending as a proportion of GNP fell only from 3.7 percent to 3.0 percent. And this in countries which could barely afford such extravagance. In 1993, the latest year for which she provided comparative figures, *per-capita* public spending on military items in the developing countries came to $25 (in constant 1987 dollars), while the comparable figure for health was only $17, and for education, $31. The corresponding figures in the industrial countries were $529 (military), $1,082 (health), and $946 (education).[6]

"Without a doubt," Oscar Arias said,

military spending represents the single most significant perversion of global priorities known today, claiming $780 billion in 1997. If we channeled just 5 percent of that figure over the next ten years into antipoverty programs, all of the world's population would enjoy basic social services. Another 5 percent, or $40 billion, over ten years would provide all people on this planet with an income above the poverty line for their country.[7]

Unfortunately, half of the world's governments dedicate more resources to defense than to health programs. Such distortions in national budgets contribute to poverty and retard human development. War, and the preparation for war, is one of the greatest obstacles to human progress, fostering a vicious cycle of arms build-ups, violence, and poverty.

Examples abound throughout the world of instances where arms purchases have resulted in suffering and injustice. Perhaps one of the most relevant comes from South Asia, where an arms race rages between India and Pakistan, fueled by the dispute over the Kashmir territory. India spent more than $12 billion on arms purchases from 1988 to 1992 alone—more than either Saudi Arabia or Iraq during that same period. From 1978 to 1991, Pakistan increased its defense

Social Indicators for Some Relevant Countries

	Human Development Index, 1997 (premier indicator from UNDP)	Real Gross Domestic Product per capita, 1997 (PPP$)	Defense spending per capita 1997 ($)	Public expenditure on education as % of Gross National Product, 1996	Percentage of population without access to safe water, mid-1990s	Infant mortality per 1,000 live births, 1997	Index of (denial of) political rights, 1999 (scale of 1–7)
Costa Rica	0.801	6,650	8.1	5.3	4	12	1
China	0.701	3,130	7.9	2.3	33	38	7 (Tibet: 7)
South Africa	0.695	7,380	5.7	7.9	13	49	1
Indonesia	0.681	3,490	16.4	1.4	25	45	6 (East Timor: 7)
Guatemala	0.624	4,100	8.0	1.7	23	43	3
Burma	0.580	1,199	30.3	1.2	40	81	7
Norway	0.927	24,450	75.5	7.5	n.a.	4	1
United States	0.927	29,010	94.0	5.4	n.a.	7	1
United Kingdom	0.918	20,730	105.8	5.4	n.a.	6	1 (Northern Ireland: 3)

Sources: Data in columns 1 and 2 from *Human Development Report (HDR) 1999* (New York: UN Development Program and Oxford University Press, 1999), pp. 134–36, table 1; in column 3 calculated from *The Military Balance* (London: International Institute of Strategic Studies, 1997/98 and 1998/99 editions), in column 4 from *HDR 1999* (New York: UN Development Program and Oxford University Press, 1999), pp. 189–90, table 13; in column 5 from *HDR 1999* (New York: UN Development Program and Oxford University Press, 1999), pp. 146–47, table 4; in column 6 from *HDR 1999* (New York: UN Development Program and Oxford University Press, 1999), pp. 168–70, table 8; and in column 7 from *Freedom House Report, 1999* (see <www.freedomhouse.org/survey99/tables>).

budget seven-fold, so that defense now accounts for nearly 40 percent of all government spending. More recently, these countries have raised the horrible specter of nuclear war with highly publicized atomic testing. We can only hope that courageous and dissenting voices in these countries will further propel Pakistan and India's leaders toward endorsing the Comprehensive Test Ban Treaty—an agreement that has yet to be ratified by the U.S. Congress.

He argued forcefully that the United States too often failed to take responsibility for its role in sustaining the kinds of injustice associated with excessive global militarization:

In his recent address to the Russian people, President Clinton argued that the countries of the world should "harness the genius of our citizens not for making weapons but for building better communications, curing disease, combating hunger and exploring the heavens." Unfortunately, one can only wonder if these optimistic words do not themselves express a certain cynicism. President Clinton speaks to the benefits of disarmament while U.S. missiles fly over Sudan, and while the U.S. government assures the Pentagon billions of dollars more than it asks for. Many people in the U.S. government, and even many people within the Clinton administration, have spoken in theory to the benefits of demilitarization, but commit themselves in practice to the sale of deadly armaments.

Since the end of the cold war, many industrialized nations have reduced their defense budgets. As a result, those countries' arms merchants have turned to new clients in the developing world, where the majority of today's conflicts take place. The United States stands out as an extreme case. Currently, the U.S. is responsible for 44 percent of all weapons sales in the world. And, in the past four years, 85 percent of U.S. arms sales have gone to nondemocratic governments in the developing world.

At the end of 1997, weapons manufactured in the United States were being used in thirty-nine of the world's forty-two ethnic and territorial conflicts. It is unconscionable for a country that believes in democracy and justice to continue allowing arms merchants to reap profits stained in blood. But ironically, vast amounts of taxpayer money goes to support this immoral trade. In 1995, the arms industry received $7.6 billion in federal subsidies—this amounts to a huge welfare payment to wealthy profiteers.

He also referred to the "boomerang effect," whereby arms exported to the developing countries can end up (as José Ramos-Horta later noted) being used against the country that exported them. "When will lawmakers learn?" Arias asked, "that when we allow arms merchants to profit in death, no one is safe?"

SUCH, THEN, WAS Arias's introduction to his topic. Now, he turned to the topic listed on the program, the International Code of Conduct on Arms Transfers. He explained that under the code, any arms-transfer decision should take into account some important political characteristics of the country of final destination. The recipient country should "endorse democracy, defined in terms of free and fair elections, the rule of law, and civilian control over the military and security forces. Its government must not engage in gross violations of internationally recognized human rights." And the code would not permit arms sales to any country engaged in armed aggression in violation of international law.

Many people, he noted, had said that such an effort was "impractical." He did *not* sound happy with that accusation!

Impractical because it puts concern for human life before a free market drive for profits! Impractical because it listens to the poor who are crying out for schools and doctors, rather than the dictators who demand guns and fighters! Yes, in an age of cynicism and greed, all just ideas are considered impractical. You are discouraged if you say that we can live in peace. You are mocked for insisting that we can be more humane!

But I am proud to say that I am not alone in denouncing this cowardly status quo, and in supporting an International Code of Conduct on Arms Transfers. Indeed, today I am in good company to promote this ambitious agreement. For Nobel peace laureates Elie Wiesel, Betty Williams, and the Dalai Lama stood with me in presenting the code last year. So did José Ramos-Horta, Amnesty International, the American Friends Service Committee, and the International Physicians for the Prevention of Nuclear War. Since then, Archbishop Desmond Tutu and Rigoberta Menchú have joined this "impractical" group. As have Lech Walesa, Adolfo Pérez Esquival, Mairead Maguire [Corrigan], Norman Borlaug, Joseph Rotblat, and Jody Williams. In all, seventeen winners of the Nobel Peace Prize, as well as former President Jimmy Carter, have endorsed the code.

But more importantly, thousands of individuals, groups, and community leaders have expressed their belief that a Code of Conduct is not only a morally sound idea, but also a politically necessary agreement. It is these people, and the force of their convictions, that turn possibility into progress, and turn impractical ideas into reality.

He judged that, although much work remained, still, the campaign for the code had already made valuable progress. In the spring of 1998, European Union foreign ministers had reached agreement on the European Union's first-ever Code of Conduct to govern arms exports. Arias said the European code still required strengthening in some areas, but it was a good first step. In the United States, meanwhile, a similar move to establish a Code of Conduct on Arms Transfers had failed to pass a joint House-Senate Conference Committee, "owing to back-room dealings." But advocates of a code were, he said, continuing their campaign.

Arias brought in another pro-code argument, too: "If the president, and indeed all national leaders, are serious about stemming international terror, they must look first at their own policy of arms sales to undemocratic governments worldwide. Moreover, they must actively support the International Code of Conduct as a means of reducing the global availability of deadly weapons."

He noted that some "courageous representatives" in the U.S. federal government had stepped forward to champion the code. But, "unfortunately, we cannot expect all national lawmakers, many of whom have received large campaign donations from arms merchants, to stand up to the weapons industry on their own. Congress as a whole will not respond to the moral demands of the code unless those here today, and many others like you, generate the kind of popular pressure that forces immediate action."

He—like most of the other laureates—concluded his address with an appeal to audience members to commit themselves to the ongoing struggle for peace:

Friends, you will remember that at the beginning of my remarks, I addressed the unique challenges to human security that our complex and changing world presents. Truly, no one can deny that a new era of globalization has begun. But I can say with equal certainty that this new era has not ended—its final force and significance have yet to be determined. Globalization, if it is skillfully managed, can be indeed a great opportunity. It can be a promising chance for progress in the developing world. But we must remember that unregulated markets are not divine or uncontrollable creatures; they are human creations, subject to moral oversight and intervention. Those working today can decide whether the age of globalization will be remembered as a time of profit and plunder, or as a time of diversity and enlightenment. All of you *here* will decide, with your activism or your complacency, whether the new world order will be governed by a corporate ethics of selfishness, or by an ethical character of equality and human rights.

In conclusion, I want to stress that although the International Code of Conduct on Arms Transfers would be a significant step in promoting global security and protecting human rights, it is not an end in itself. For the struggle for human security will not end until the world undertakes a comprehensive and humanitarian demilitarization. It will not end until all people enjoy fundamental liberties. And it will not end until all public policy embodies a thoroughgoing affirmation of human dignity.

I am but one person in a larger movement. It is a movement of many people in many walks of life, all working to see that these just ends are realized. Together we gather our courage and our determination, for when we do not lack these we will embark on a great journey. Our path will be perilous, but our eminent destination will be a new, more humane planet Earth. Many of my fellow laureates, and many of the scholars and activists in this audience, have already helped to lead us on our odyssey. To all of the rest of you, I say that the moral journey to a better world is a trip worth taking, and I *invite you to join us*. Thank you!

ARIAS'S PRESENTATION DEALT with two distinct, though linked, dimensions of the present global system: an economic dimension that has often been inimical to the advancement of true human security, and the damaging and expensive system of worldwide arms transfers. The first question that came his way—from Julian Bond—dealt with economics. The

NAACP chair picked up on a remark Arias made during the conference's first session, when he described himself as "a strong believer in . . . the market economy, as well as in political pluralism." Bond questioned the effects of this belief. "Indeed, the market system in the great struggle of the cold war has triumphed. Yet it is as unforgiving quite often as the corporate ethics you spoke about just a moment ago. How are we to balance the unforgiving nature of the market system with the very real demands of the poor?"

Arias replied,

> I believe, Professor Bond, that everybody agrees now that with globalization of the market system, of communications, of capital flow, et cetera, some people will become losers and some winners. Certainly, those who have no education or little education will be losers. Those who have a good education will be the winners. So it's very simple: how can we spend, like in many countries in Africa, and the Middle East, and in Asia, three times more of GDP [Gross Domestic Product] on defense, on huge armies which are not needed, on forces which very often are used simply to oppress the people, or other people—like Indonesia, or Turkey, or Iraq—instead of educating our children?
>
> To govern is to educate! A statesman is a person who tells people what people need to know. A politician is a person who tells people what people want to hear. We need to educate the leaders of today so that they have the courage and determination to tell people what people need to know. And what the children in Latin America, in Asia, in Africa . . . need are schools and health clinics, and not F-16s and tanks.

Harn Yawnghwe recalled that Arias had said that the three richest people in the world have more wealth than the poorest forty-eight nations, and he noted that many corporations, too, were bigger than smaller nations. "Do you think we are wasting our time working with governments?" he asked. "We work with the United Nations, we work with governments trying to control things, but the actual power base has shifted to the corporations —and in the name of free trade and globalization, there are almost no restrictions on corporations. How can we deal with that?"

"Yes, I agree with you," Arias said.

We all know that, as I pointed out, capital flows amount to $1.5 trillion a day. . . . Let's take foreign direct investment from corporations: it amounts to more than $300 billion per year. Two-thirds of those investments go to industrialized nations. One-third goes to developing nations. Of the one-third that goes to developing nations, about 85 percent goes to twelve countries—China being the most important one.

So that most poor countries get very little! As a matter of fact, sub-Saharan African gets no more than 2 percent of foreign direct investment. A country like Nicaragua, a country like Honduras, a country like Haiti, gets peanuts. A country like Bangladesh gets just a few million dollars. So we are competing with Russia, we are competing with Eastern Europe, we are competing with Southeast Asia, we are competing with, you know, China in order to attract foreign direct investment—corporations, to invest in our country. And in order to be able to compete, we need to provide them with some basic infrastructure. How can we build that infrastructure if we are spending 3, 4, 5 percent of GDP on arms? It's as simple as that.

I mean, demilitarization is not an end in itself. In our discussions of yesterday, the word *poverty* was not mentioned. I have mentioned poverty and inequality about ten times today! My main concern, because this is the real danger for peace, is poverty. Poverty needs no passport to travel. And I don't want this great nation to keep building walls to prevent the poor Latin American from entering this country. I've seen the nine-feet-high wall in San Diego. It's humiliating—for you, as well as for Latin Americans who would like to come here.

Some thoughtful applause greeted that last comment. A little later, Rigoberta Menchú came back to the topic of economic and educational inequities. "I have a doubt," she said,

when you state that the educated people will come out ahead. What is your concept of education and to whom are you referring? I also want to comment that when we talk about global economies, political globalization, we talk about material globalization—but we don't talk about the globalization of problems. And for me today, I no longer can see the borders between what was called the third world and what was called the first world. I have seen street children in Los Angeles, I have seen poor people in Europe. I can't find at the end of this millennium the difference between the first world, the second world, and the third world.

But there are other, more serious problems. The privatization of the state resources: this benefits people who have already been rich, and it lowers the ability for the country's poorest people and the ability to defend the country. This is a very political concept. The phantom of privatization is a threat, a very deep threat against the beginning democracies. Because for me there is no democracy that has been fully built in any Latin American country. It is a goal to build democracies. It's not something we have yet reached.

We have to have a *global* view of the problems that the world has now. You said that some people would win, and some would lose. And to me, the ones who will lose are the millions of people who have always lost!

Arias replied that in his view there is still a huge difference between the poor people of the developing world and those of industrialized countries. "The definition of a poor person in the industrialized world is that person earning less than $8,000 to $10,000 per year, instead of $1.00 a day in the developing world," he said. Then, he looked at the impact of population growth on economic prospects:

The population in this century has quadrupled. It is a fact that by the year 2050, there will be nine billion people on this planet. Ninety percent of them will be living in the developing world. Sub-Saharan Africa will have a population of two billion people, and sub-Saharan African countries' population doubles every twenty years. And sub-Saharan Africa is spending on defense, on the military, five times more now in 1998, than thirty years ago. Isn't that immoral, for the leaders of that continent to prefer to make armed forces the priority over housing, health, education, basic nutrition, for their children?

Isn't it immoral for the industrialized nations to keep sending arms to sub-Saharan Africa to profit with the sale of weapons, instead of helping them? President Clinton just discovered that there is a lot of poverty in sub-Saharan Africa when he was in that country. There are 700 million people in sub-Saharan Africa, and U.S. aid to that region is $700 million dollars—one dollar per person per year—while you provide Israel, a tiny country of five, six million people $3 billion in foreign aid, both economic and military, ODA [Overseas Development Assistance].

How can we deal with . . . countries that double their populations every twenty years? The only way is to cut military spending in order to educate our children. Knowledge is power. Knowledge is wealth. This is obvious for all of you who are well educated. Every day, every twenty-four hours, 400,000 children are born, 90 percent of them in the developing world. For a high percentage of these children, their destiny is ignorance. Fifty percent of them in many Latin America countries—Guatemala is one of them—are born from single mothers. What is their destiny? Not to go to school, but to work at the age of twelve, thirteen, fourteen years of age.

I want to tell you that even in my own country, which sometimes is represented as some sort of Switzerland of Central America—I would prefer it to be the Denmark of Central America, and not necessarily the Switzerland of Central America—but anyway, even in my own country, which does very well in the human development index, 40 percent of our children from thirteen to sixteen years of age do not attend high school. In Guatemala, perhaps, it's 80 percent, as well as in Peru, as well as in Nicaragua, as well as in Honduras, as well as in Haiti. In sub-Saharan Africa, in many countries, only 5 percent of the children between thirteen and sixteen years of age attend high school.

So, again, *to govern is to choose*. If you are uneducated, you will certainly be a loser in a globalized economy, in a globalized world.

Later that morning, Menchú and Arias once again indicated some of the differences between their views on the role that free markets should play in the world economy. An audience member asked Menchú how the United States should respond to the devastation caused in Central America, just days earlier, by Hurricane Mitch. In her reply, she noted that there were various communities throughout Central America in which her foundation, the Rigoberta Menchú Tum Foundation, had projects—"but unfortunately we have not been able to establish contact with our companions in those communities." What was clear, she said, was that the communities of Central America, were not prepared to receive this devastation because people are poor, just they are so very, very poor. So I really can't say what the repercussions are going to be, until we're able to find out more clearly and more systematically what has actually happened.

There have been many, many people who have been killed. It is very, very sad that the Mayor of Tegucigalpa, the capital city of Honduras, has also died. . . . Any help that people can give will be very, very important in our endeavor to reconstruct these countries. And I would like to say that we all find we have the obligation to help in this sense, because we have all contributed toward the destruction of nature. And one of the repercussions of this destruction of Mother Earth is this unbalancing.

Arias, however, proposed a more free-market prescription for dealing with the storm's effects:

The best way you can help Central America is by opening up the U.S. market for our goods, industrialized goods and agricultural goods. Ironically, the U.S. Congress is in favor of the expansion of NATO, so that U.S. weapons can be sold to the Czech Republic, to Hungary and Poland, and not of the expansion of NAFTA—even though everybody is talking in this country about free trade and how important free trade is for developing nations. In other words, what is preached is not practiced.

He noted that foreign aid was a "very unpopular concept" in the United States—even though it had proven very successful in the case of the post–World War II Marshall Plan for aid to Europe.

The Marshall Plan implied [sending], I believe, at that time 3 to 4 percent of [U.S.] GDP to the destroyed nations of Europe. Now, fifty years later, among the industrialized nations, you are channeling to the developing countries much less than any other industrialized nation. As a matter of fact, it's only one-tenth of what the Dutch, the Norwegians, the Swedes, the Danish, spend on official development assistance to poor nations—just one-tenth! . . . The American people believe it is a huge percentage . . . of your gross national product, and of the federal budget. This is not true. Even in *absolute* terms, France, Germany, Japan, allocate more funds to foreign aid to the developing world than the U.S.[8]

And finally, it is very ironic, and sad, that only ten years ago, when there was the bloody conflict in Central America, you were channeling huge amounts of foreign aid to those countries through the years of the cold war. Now that the Central American countries have the courage and vision to silence the guns at the negotiation table, now that we have been able to bring peace to thirty million Central Americans who did not deserve to live in conflict, instead of rewarding the peace we have achieved, we have been punished by cutting all foreign aid to the five Central American countries! This indeed cannot be understood, I believe, by anybody.

ACCORDING TO THE London-based research organization the International Institute of Strategic Studies, between 1995 and 1997 the international arms trade grew by some 36 percent. The 1998/99 edition of the institute's annual global evaluation, *The Military Balance*, reported that, as of the end of 1997, "arms deliveries to East Asia have doubled in value since 1994, reaching a peak in 1997 as a result of delivery to Taiwan of large numbers of combat aircraft from the US and France. *Similar levels of growth are evident in the smaller regional markets of southern Asia, Latin America and Sub Saharan Africa.*"[9]

Within the ever lucrative international market for military items, the institute reported that "the US delivered arms and military services worth almost $21bn in 1997, raising its share of the international market to 45%. Foreign Military Sales (FMS), which are administered by the Department of Defense, were valued at some $18bn, compared to $12.5bn in 1996. US deliveries to developing countries were worth $11.7bn during the year."[10] While the United States had captured 45 percent of the international market in 1997, West European countries managed, between them, to win 39.9 percent; Russia and other formerly Soviet states won 5.4 percent; and Israel, 3.3 percent.[11]

During the discussion period that followed Arias's presentation, José Ramos-Horta homed in on the topic of international arms transfers. "Beyond the question of morality and ethics in weapons . . . sales to developing countries," he said,

Western countries usually argue that weapons provisions to some of their client states in developing countries have to do with strategic and security interests, [and that] they enhance the security interests of the United States, and stability in a given region. And so regardless of whether they like the regime or not, beyond human rights consider-ations, they say, "We have these issues at the stake, such as security and stability, that can be enhanced through our military-security rela-tionship with certain countries or regimes, as much as we might not like the way they behave." That's the kind of discourse. But what always amazes me is that even the security and the strategic argument often falls flat!

He gave two examples. The first was the 1982 war between Britain and Argentina over the Falklands/Malvinas, where weapons previously supplied to Argentina by France and Britain ended up being used against British forces in the South Atlantic: "The famous French 'Etendard' planes carry-ing Exocet missiles sunk British supply aircraft and ships that were used by the British in the Falkland War. So we saw that the weapons in the hands of the dictatorship turned in the end onto at least one of the NATO allies in the Falklands War."

Ramos-Horta then directed his considerable capacity for irony against the record of Western policymakers in another instance of "boomerang-ing" that he described as a dramatic case "which threw into question the wisdom or the intelligence of those people, seemingly the 'most intelligent people' in Washington, Quai d'Orsay, Paris, London. . . . Look at the case of the Gulf War!"[12] He recalled that in September 1980,

> Iraq unleashed a war, one of the most vicious wars since World War I, on Iran. At the time Iran was going through an Islamic revolution, and you might like it or not, Iran was having some serious and gen-uine grievances toward the United States. . . . And the post-Shah regime in Iran was seen as a center of exporting Islamic fundamen-talism, so Iran was seen as the threat to Western interests.
>
> As a result, Saddam Hussein was seen as the ally, the moderating influence in the Gulf region that would stop the spread of Islamic fundamentalism. So all the Western countries supported Saddam Hussein, including transferring technology for biological weapons — even when Iranian-Kurdish children and women were assaulted, were *killed by gas*, in the first time poison gas was used since World War I. We saw thousands of them killed. The West still turned a blind eye! Even after the Iraqi Air Force by mistake fired on a U.S.

war ship, killing fourteen Marines, they still found excuses for Saddam Hussein.

When the two countries, after ten years of war, exhausted, signed a treaty, and ended the war, Saddam Hussein turned his guns on Kuwait. The same guns that were provided by the West, and Russia, and so on! It was only then Saddam Hussein became the evil.

I am saying these things not as a criticism of those very "intelligent" people in Washington, the Quai d'Orsay, and the [British] Foreign Office, but only because, as a commoner with necessarily low I.Q. . . . I fail to understand those brilliant and strategic [calculations] that resulted in these fiascoes.

And my question to Oscar Arias is, as a former head of state: when heads of state or policymakers, foreign ministers, look into a given region of the world, look into the map, and then issue a statement about strategic and security considerations, *what does it really mean?* Because I'm totally at a loss, when they say it was in their strategic interests to support Saddam Hussein. Was it really? How did they come to this conclusion?

Arias sounded tired. "I don't know, José. I don't know." The audience laughed sympathetically. "I wonder myself," he continued,

but again, it is ironic that U.S. weapons have killed American soldiers in Iraq, in Panama, in Somalia—you remember Somalia—and in many other parts of the world. As long as you keep sending arms to nondemocratic countries, and I mentioned the figure—85 percent of the weapons you sell to governments in the developing world, goes to dictatorships, authoritarian regimes, nondemocratic governments— [you can get] the boomerang effect.

And then, at the end, it's a moral issue. It was Gandhi who mentioned the seven social sins—two of them were commerce without morality, and politics without principles. Politics should go always hand in hand with morality, and with responsibility. It is irresponsible to keep sending arms to dictators, but the U.S. has always considered that there are good and bad dictators. That it was acceptable in the cold war era. Somosa was a "good" dictator, Trujillo was a "good" dictator, President Marcos was a "good" dictator, the Shah of Iran was a "good" dictator. And the bad dictators were Saddam Hussein,

Pol Pot—Fidel Castro, for sure. But *all* of them are murderers! All of them are murderers. I mean, there is a need for the State Department indeed to learn that all dictators are bad, and for the United States government to put morality and principles before profits.

Throughout the conference, these two laureates gave thought-provoking examples of ways to address the problem of excessive militarization—through action at both the "supply" end of the arms-transfer process and the "demand" end. Regarding supply, one of the questions that came to Arias from an audience member asked how concerned citizens in the West could start to counter the influence of the arms dealers, which she described as "big companies with big lobbying budgets pushing government defense and foreign aid budgets."

He said he thought it was very unfortunate that there had not yet been enough political will in the United States to approve the Code of Conduct:

> This is the only way to restrict the sale of arms to dictatorships, to violators of human rights, to governments which are aggressors involved in armed aggression against other nations, to governments which have sponsored terrorism, to governments which do not comply with the UN register of conventional arms, et cetera.
>
> I think the treaty is very well known. As I said, it's a matter of principles or profits. It's a matter of values. It's a matter of morality.
>
> These people [the arms manufacturers] are very powerful. They make huge contributions, huge donations to congressmen. These are well known. Very few Americans, as I mentioned, are aware that the Americas taxpayer is subsidizing arms for exports. The arms manufacturers need to be exporters, because the Pentagon does not really need them.
>
> I usually make a parallel between the sale of arms and the sale of drugs. The sale of drugs is illegal; the sale of arms is legal. In Washington, they look at the supply side in the case of drugs: to the countries which are producing drugs and exporting them to wealthy nations. In the case of arms, they look at the demand side. And they tell me if there is a country willing to buy arms from us, we will sell them, "Because otherwise any other country will sell them." The fact that the sale of drugs is illegal and the sale of arms is legal doesn't

make the sale of arms morally right. Both kill people. Both kill innocent young children.

What would the Burmese tell you, or a Colombian or a Bolivian tell you, if you ask him, "Don't send drugs to America"? I believe the Burmese would tell you, "If I don't sell drugs to you, Bolivia will, Peru will." That's the answer I get from the United States: "If I don't sell arms to you, France will, Russia will, China will."

A little earlier, Ramos-Horta had described a couple of more focused efforts at blocking the plans of would-be arms exporters. One of these involved political organizing, and the other, action that was more "direct." But both succeeded—and both, in his view, were very cost-effective. Regarding the first of these campaigns, he recalled having successfully urged the Timorese freedom fighters to let him lobby politically in Washington, in order to decrease the flow of American arms to Indonesia:

> I said, well, getting some action at the U.S. Congress to end the delivery of an F-16 aircraft to Indonesia was far, far cheaper than if we ever try to shoot down that F-16 once it's delivered. We can muster all the money we get: if we ever get it, we'll never be able to shoot down that F-16 anyway! So by talking to a few, you know, really moral individuals in the U.S. Congress, we managed to cause such an uproar in the Congress that in the end the Indonesians said they got sick and tired of the whole controversy, and gave up trying to buy the F-16!
>
> And I'll give you another example that is just remarkable. Four old women in England: three were British, one was Swedish. They went into a British Hawk aircraft factory in Liverpool. They went just with kitchen tools, you know, and damaged an entire computer system of one of the Hawk aircraft that had been paid for by the Indonesians and was waiting to be delivered to Indonesia. That factory was supposed to be high security, but somehow they managed to enter, did their job, completed it. They danced around the aircraft, and still the security didn't come!
>
> Only when they finally phoned the media, then the media arrived, and security came. They were arrested, and I was one of the people who finally was allowed to be a defense witness for them in Liverpool. . . . Anyway, one of the women, she spoke in court, and she said, "Well, I read a statement by José Ramos-Horta about the use of the

Hawk aircraft in Timor and that's why I did this." There I was, standing there, and then she said she was motivated by something I said. I felt so bad! She really, you know, ruined my whole day because I thought this woman might be sentenced to twelve years in prison because of a statement I issued.

But finally, against all our expectations, they were acquitted. For the first time in England, in a British court, the invocation of an act of conscience was accepted! The trial lawyer for the four women was that same woman lawyer, Goddard Pierce, who was played by Emma Thompson in the film *In the Name of the Father.* She was the one who acted as the lawyer for these four women, so it was a highly successful case. And . . . according to British Aerospace, it set a very dangerous precedent that if you incapacitate some weapon in England, it is now legal to do it![13]

But anyway, that's just to show that there is in our experience, being a small country at one point abandoned by everybody all over the world—it was the international action that . . . gave us the moral boost, support, that gave us the courage, the faith to continue. And it was the solidarity work in the Congress, the European Parliament, governments, that caused so much damage to the Indonesian side, to the point that it became the most costly foreign-policy issue for Indonesia.

Arias also gave examples of some notable successes he had had—by working at the "demand" end of the arms-transfer chain. Betty Williams had urged him to tell the conference about how he had been able to demilitarize two countries.

"Well, I believe everybody would agree that it's more important, much more important, to convince, to persuade, than to conquer," he said modestly.

Well, that's the essence of leadership after all. When Noriega was ousted in December of 1989, a new president was sworn in, in the Panama Canal Zone. His name was Guillermo Endara. And because he became president as a result of an invasion, no Latin country wanted to recognize the new government in Panama. So I went to Panama City to meet President Endara, and I told him, "Since I'm your neighbor to the north and since I will be leaving office very soon,

I would like to recognize your government under one condition—if you get rid of the armed forces." That's called Costa Rican imperialism!

And he said, "Well, let me think it over." So I raised some funds to initiate the campaign in Panama to persuade the people that this was a good idea—because according to the Panamanian constitution, in order to amend the constitution, there was a need for a referendum. To make a long story short, I was able to persuade the members of Parliament. And the constitution was amended. So as a consequence of that, I tell my friends in Washington that the safest border in the world is that between Costa Rica and Panama!

Arias's other success along these lines came in Haiti. Shortly before the United States helped democratically elected President Jean-Bertrand Aristide return to his country in 1994, Arias met with him in Washington,

and I told him, "You should go back and finish your term, but it is even more important for you to go back and get rid of the armed forces." Haiti, as you all know, is the poorest country in this hemisphere. It is a country which became independent in 1803, before any other Latin American country and the armed forces have been responsible for twenty-six coups d'état since then. The armed forces are corrupt, like in many Latin American countries or Asia or Africa, and they were the main source of instability for that nation.

So again, I raised some funding with some Nordic countries. . . . So we initiated the campaign in Haiti, and again we were able to convince the legislators that they should amend the constitution. So, what I want to say is that Costa Rica's case is not a unique case. It can be replicated in other parts of the world.

Only recently, . . . the Arias Foundation held a conference in Arusha, in Tanzania, with the defense ministers of sub-Saharan Africa; and I'm in the process now of persuading the government of Sierra Leone to get rid of the armed forces. The president of Sierra Leone will be visiting Costa Rica and Panama, next February or March, in order to share with us our own experience.

What we in the developing world need are welfare states, not garrison states. And to govern is to choose, as we all know. We need to choose between the education of our children or pleasing the military people.

OSCAR ARIAS IS an experienced analyst, with a broad understanding of the economic and social facets of today's world. But he is also, in his calm and even way, a powerful persuader. "Democracy is not an end in itself," he argued during the first day of the conference.

> We all know for more than two thousand years that democracy has been a means: the end is always the human being, the mother, the child. And as long as democracy doesn't deliver the goods—and democracy is *not* delivering the goods in many or most African countries, in many Latin American countries, in many Asian countries— so eventually it is going to be questioned. Democracy is going to be questioned by the . . . people, by societies.
>
> I mean, why do we need to praise and struggle for democracy if democracy is creating more and more and more injustice, and poverty increases every day, and inequality increases every day, et cetera, et cetera? It was Berdyayev, a Russian thinker, who said the problem with Christianity is the Christians [audience laughter], but this is true for all religions. We are the ones who are failing, with our indifference.
>
> I don't think we can enjoy peace in the twenty-first century with our ethics of the twentieth century. It has been mentioned here . . . that this century has been the bloodiest century in the history of humankind. I mean, how can we enjoy peace and security and freedom with the values that are prevailing? Selfishness instead of solidarity, so much greed, so much cynicism, so much hypocrisy!
>
> I will be speaking tomorrow about—perhaps it might sound too strong—but about the cynicism of this great nation. I think there is a need for the United States to lead, because the world expects from Washington leadership. But in the right way! Politics goes hand in hand with responsibility and with morality. And certainly, by sending arms to so many countries in the world you are not . . . taking the moral decisions that you should be taking.
>
> This country taught the rest of the world that right is might, and that's what the world expects from this great nation. So . . . I think that the reason why we might not enjoy a more peaceful future is simply because we, as individuals, have failed. *There is a need for a new ethics.* Otherwise, it is going to be very difficult to enjoy peace. I think

there is a need for more compassion, for more generosity, for more solidarity, for more tolerance, and certainly for more love.

On the second day, as he came near the end of the session on the International Code of Conduct, he recalled two great thinkers of earlier ages:

Let me finish by quoting Aristotle. . . . He said, "It is not enough to win the war, it is more important to organize the peace. If you don't organize the peace, then you lose the fruits of victory." Let me add one more quote. This one is from Albert Einstein. I keep telling my friends that the U.S. is the only superpower in the world, the only economic superpower, the only military superpower, but the world expects more leadership from you, moral leadership: the world expects the U.S. to become also a moral superpower. And the quote is from Albert Einstein: "Only morality in our actions can give beauty and dignity to our lives." Thank you.

9

Reconciliation in Action: Bobby Muller and the Anti-Landmine Campaign

Even before he wheeled himself to the podium to make his main presentation, Bobby Muller—with his engagingly direct manner and his trademark shock of white hair—had already emerged as a substantial presence at the conference. He was representing the International Campaign to Ban Landmines (ICBL), which was awarded the 1997 peace prize along with Jody Williams. During the first day of the gathering, he riveted the audience with the story of his personal journey out of the "path of darkness" in Vietnam, and again, when he discussed the issues of accountability and punishment with Archbishop Tutu.

During his own presentation on the second day, one of the most powerful things Muller said connected directly with the themes of personal transformation and reconciliation that ran through those earlier sessions. He was explaining how he first became interested in the issue of landmines, and he recalled how he and his colleagues in the Vietnam Veterans of America were campaigning, back in the late 1970s, to improve the rehabilitative services offered to veterans wounded in the Vietnam War. "As part of the work with the . . . veterans," he said, "obviously, to reconcile with our former adversaries was the key part."

In the excitement and flow of his presentation, it was easy to overlook the insight packed into that small adverb, "obviously." But what Muller was referring to—the obviousness of the need for reconciliation with former foes—is a central tenet of most of the Bible's New Testament, and of theories of nonviolent action in both Eastern and Western traditions, as well as of much of modern psychotherapeutic theory in the West. (It is also a hope echoed by all the laureates represented at the conference: in Aung San Suu

Kyi's hope that one day she can sit down with the leaders of the SLORC and amicably discuss with them the resolution of outstanding problems; in Bishop Tutu's joy—after casting the first democratic vote of his life— in singing the national anthem of his erstwhile oppressors; in the Dalai Lama's conviction that considering your opponent as a potential friend is better for both spirit and body than continuing to harbor hatred for him.)

But how did Robert Olivier Muller get to the point where he saw the need for the transformative experience of face-to-face contact with his former enemies?

Muller was born in Austria in 1946. While still a boy, he migrated with his parents to the United States, growing up on New York's Long Island. He stressed to the audience at his presentation that until his student days at Hofstra University—and after—he was always just a "regular guy."

I wouldn't have been in the audience here, when I was in college! I would've been doing something with an athletic event, or focusing maybe on my studies. I was really the most average student you could ever imagine. And had you suggested that I would one day be appearing on a platform with people such as this, I would've said you're crazy!

What happened? I became an advocate as a result of my life's experiences. And I'm going to say right now, if there's anything I'm going to urge students in particular, it's to get a little less homogenized, and get out there in the world, and expose yourself to different situations. Because I really believe that it's the relatively few among us that can *intellectually* arrive at a certain place of enlightenment: I think most of us need to go out there and get the hard knocks in life, and learn the lessons the hard way, to sort of "get it" a little bit.

I "got it" because when I was a senior in college, the war in Vietnam was going on full-tilt-boogie. It was inevitable that I was going to go into the service! And one day, going into the student union my senior year—I was five-feet-eight, 130 pounds; I was the ultimate runt —and there was a Marine Corps recruiter, and he stood around six-two, 220 pounds, dress-blue uniform, crimson stripe: the ultimate stud. And I said, "Yeah, that's me!" And really, honestly, I hate to admit it, but that machismo thing that kids got: sort of on the basis of that, that impression and that uniform, I joined the Marines.

And I said yesterday you should see the movie, *Full Metal Jacket*, that Kubrick put out, that really the first half of the movie is about Marine Corps boot camp. And it shows you how young guys can be transformed as a result of a process, that we really are very vulnerable, and are susceptible to being altered and manipulated. The long and the short of it is by the time I finished my Marine Corps training, I graduated honor man in my class. I *demanded* Vietnam. I demanded infantry, and my own fear was that the war was going to end before I got a chance to get over and do the right thing.

It was not that he was unaware of the dangers that would face him there. He recalled that during their training, future junior officers were told explicitly that 85 percent of those who went to Vietnam would be wounded or killed. But still, they went.

I went out into the field with seven other lieutenants, all of whom were medevacked before me. I lasted eight months before I took the bullet through the chest. That war was a rock 'em–sock 'em war! And when I got hit I had the good fortune of having called in medevacs, medevac helicopters, for other guys that had been casualties. So I got literally an instant medical evacuation. And with my luck, the hospital ship *Repose* was right off the coast of where I was that afternoon. And they wrote that despite the instant medevac and the extraordinary care, that had I arrived one minute later I would've died. Both lungs had collapsed along with the severed spinal cord.

I was conscious long enough to realize what had happened, and to be absolutely convinced that I was going to die. When I woke up on that hospital ship, even though I had I think nine tubes in me, my response on wakening up was one of absolutely ecstasy, joy, exhilaration! A couple of days later the doctors came by and said, "You know, we've got some good news and some bad news. The good news is that we're pretty sure you're going to live—" And I laughed. I said I could've told you that as soon as I opened up my eyes! "The bad news is you're going to be paralyzed." And I remember saying, "Don't worry about it. That's okay."

I was so grateful to be given a second chance at life! And in that moment of confronting my own mortality, all of what I had put really my future in—business school, corporate America—evaporated! It just didn't seem to have the same meaning anymore.

Muller required considerable treatment for his spine injury, so he was shipped back to his home state. There, he started to discover the sorry condition into which the United States' overstretched system of veterans' hospitals had fallen.

I spent a year in a veterans' hospital in New York City. My hospital was the basis of a scandalous exposé that was on network television, newspapers, and magazines. And it portrayed the extraordinary conditions that at least some of us as returning veterans came back to. And I sometimes say that while the images could convey the overcrowding and the dilapidated facilities, they couldn't capture the despair in that institution. The fact that my closest friend, and ultimately eight of my friends from the spinal-cord-injury [department], committed suicide was better testimony.

I *had* to fight against that system for reasons of my own survival! And by going to a war that was extraordinarily brutal, and having death [all around], and experiencing almost dying, spending a year in a hospital that was as deplorable and as despairing: that's what it took to take the athlete, the dutiful student, and transform him for reasons of his own survival into fighting against that system, and to becoming an advocate.

And it was around that point that President Nixon vetoes a veterans' medical care expansion act on the grounds that it was fiscally irresponsible and inflationary to provide adequate care to Americas' veterans! That was the afternoon that I went to Times Square in Manhattan and blocked up traffic in the middle of the afternoon. And I said, "Wait a minute! I was a Marine infantry officer. I called in hundreds of thousands of dollars a day to kill people. I got shot, and now I come back, and you tell me all of a sudden that it's 'fiscally irresponsible' and 'inflationary' to provide adequate medical care? I don't think so!"

And I said I must be too stupid to know what my rights are, so I went to law school and got a law degree. And I found out that ain't the answer, that what was needed was new laws. And in a very naïve sense—that I now find unbelievable—I figured if somebody simply went to Washington, and *told* the American people what was going on with Vietnam veterans, that with that story being told a compassionate and caring society would have to respond. Come on! This is basic stuff.

He decided to do the telling himself—and was very successful! He won supportive coverage from major, east coast newspapers like the *Washington Post* and the *New York Times*, and appeared on all three of the television networks that dominated American airwaves in those days.

I got a chance to tell my story. That story got amplified and got shared with the American public, and guess what? Not a single thing that we were fighting for was enacted into law. That's a lesson: *simply to argue for something in terms of justice, fairness, equity, doesn't make it in our political process.*

The members of Congress that came forward back then were guys like Al Gore, Tom Daschle, Dave Bonior, Leon Panetta. Yeah, give me those guys twenty years later. But back then they were freshmen! They didn't have any political strength. The veterans' committees in the House and the Senate were controlled by these [other] guys that had been there for a *lifetime,* and they had no resonance with us as the Vietnam generation. I remember going into a Congressional hearing one day, and I think it was about vets' centers, and the *New York Times* very dutifully had done an editorial that morning arguing about the need for vets' centers. And the chairman of the committee holds up that *New York Times* editorial and says, "You know, some people don't get it. Where I come from, which happens to be Mississippi, we don't run in harmony with *New York Times* editorials. We run in opposition to that."

Okay. What we did is we went grassroots. We went into the districts that the members of those committees were elected from, and got into *their* editorial pages, and did *their* radio talk shows, and brought the pressure not from the elite establishment but back into those districts. And finally, incrementally, we started to get the kind of programs that we so critically needed and deserved brought on line. We even got a measure of respect and recognition.

It was through that work, whose focus was to improve the whole range of rehabilitative services—psychological, as well as physical—available to

American veterans, that Muller came to see the need to undertake a reconciliation with his former Vietnamese enemies. *"As part of the work with the Vietnam veterans, obviously, to reconcile with our former adversaries was the key part."* In 1981, he led the first group of American veterans that returned to Vietnam:

> It was an extraordinary meeting, and brought about a whole process of reconciliation which could be another whole discussion. We started humanitarian programs to try and connect the American people with the Vietnamese people. And as part of the humanitarian work, in the eighties, [we found that] the big obstacle . . . between the United States and Vietnam was Vietnam's occupation of Cambodia.
>
> So, we went to Cambodia, and I will simply say what I said briefly the other day: Cambodia changed my life when I went there, more than the entire war experience I had in Vietnam, as brutal as that was. . . . Because what happened in Cambodia was genocide, and it's a whole different order of human experience. The horror that took place on the killing fields there is unimaginable. But Cambodia was kind of unique in another way. It was a country that when you went to the capital city of Phnom Penh you saw people hobbling all over the place, amputees—and you came to understand that there were more than five hundred people every single month getting blown up by landmines. There were more landmines in Cambodia than there were people, and it was considered that Cambodia was proportionally the most disabled society of any country in the world.

In 1980, Muller helped establish a philanthropic foundation called the Vietnam Veterans of America Foundation (VVAF), aimed at fostering reconciliation in war-torn societies and providing assistance to the innocent victims of war.[1] The VVAF decided to set up clinics and rehab centers for landmine survivors in Cambodia. "And by setting up a clinic," Muller said,

> we went through a process of emotionally connecting with an issue that we intellectually understood was devastating. And I think we emotionally connected because the people that came into our clinics were people whose lives we came to understand, and to touch.
>
> And we realized that it was the poorest of the poor, the most vulnerable within the society, that were invariably winding up the vic-

tims of landmines—and that in the majority of the cases it wasn't even military people, but it was civilian people. A couple of years back they did a survey in Cambodia and they found the leading cause of casualty was women going into the forest to gather firewood, because of the economic necessity to do that—and wood is still the primary fuel. It was the kids, either playing or bringing animals out to graze, that were getting blown up.

And we realized, my God, what makes landmines different from all the other kinds of weapons that you can easily say we ought to get rid of—*what makes landmines different is that they're totally indiscriminate*. If you've got a machine-gun, or rifle, or artillery piece, jet fire, whatever, you've got a target and you fire it. There is a command-and-control function with directing that fire. Landmines, there is none! You simply set it, you bury it, you hide it, and whoever happens to step on that landmine becomes the victim. And now we know, after several years here, that in probably over 80 percent of the cases, the people that wind up stepping on those landmines are innocent civilians. Because, again, basically [with] all the other weapons, when the conflict ends, you put the rifles, and the artillery pieces, and the tanks, and the helicopters back into the armories. [But] landmines stay out where you bury them for years and years and years, doing exactly what they were designed to do—to blow off the leg of whoever it is that happens to step on it.

Muller and the VVAF soon became aware that the lasting legacy of land-mines was a problem in many other countries as well as Cambodia—and one that is concentrated almost wholly in poor, underdeveloped countries. Other experts agree. For example, in 1996, researcher Ruth Leger Sivard listed Afghanistan, Angola, Egypt, and Iran as each holding more than ten *million* unexploded antipersonnel landmines.[2] In Egypt, many of these mines have lain dormant in the desert since the great tank battles of World War II—but they continue to kill and maim the unwary, even decades later. In other countries, the mines may be slightly less numerous, but they have been sown in broad swathes in areas that previously were intensively farmed: there, they continue to restrict the ability of local people to return to homes and fields from which they were displaced by the wars of the 1970s and 1980s.

In 1992, the VVAF and the German group medico international decided to tackle the issue of landmines closer to its source, by launching a worldwide effort to *ban* their production, stockpiling, transfer, and use, altogether. That was the birth of the ICBL: Jody Williams was hired to direct it. One of her first projects was to pull together and improve the already-existing body of research on the effects of landmines. In 1995, she and colleague Shawn Roberts coauthored a broad international study titled *After the Guns Fall Silent: The Enduring Legacy of Landmines.* "Landmines are called cheap weapons and in strictly military terms, they may well be. But in humanitarian terms, they are not," the authors argued. They continued with some sobering statistics:

> One hundred million landmines are found in 64 countries—most of them in the developing world. An additional 100 million landmines are stockpiled and ready for use. Landmines disrupt society and severely hamper post-conflict reconstruction. And they kill and maim thousands of people each year. There are already at least 250,000 landmine-disabled people in the world, and that number is growing. Landmines continue to claim 500 victims a week—the equivalent of 26,000 new victims each and every year.
>
> Over 400 million landmines have been deployed since the beginning of World War II, including more than 65 million in the 15 years since the formulation of the 1980 *Convention on Conventional Weapons* (CCW), which attempts to regulate their use.[3]

Regarding Cambodia, the report estimated that 8,000,000 mines continued to contaminate the country, with most of them having been laid between 1979 and 1991. During Cambodia's twenty-three years of war, from 1970 to 1993, the report judged that 200,000 hectares of previously cultivated land had been contaminated by mines, representing a loss of livelihood for some 100,000 farming families. Cambodia, the report stated, "is one of the most mine-disabled countries in the world. The most common figure for the number of amputee landmine victims is 35,000. Current estimates of [new] casualties are 100–200 a month. . . . The health care costs associated with landmine casualties are far greater than the Cambodian medical system can handle. Less than 53 percent of the population has access to health services and the Cambodian government allocates about $0.20 per capita per year for health services." VVAF surveys found that 64 percent of mine victims were civilians, and 36 percent soldiers; but of "military" mine victims interviewed in two Cambodian military hospitals, a sobering 43 percent were child soldiers between ten and sixteen years of age.[4]

When the ICBL and Jody Williams were awarded the Nobel Prize in 1997, the loosely structured ICBL leadership chose Cambodian activist Tun Channareth and British demining expert Rae McGrath to receive the prize on its behalf in Oslo. McGrath ended up giving the ICBL's Nobel lecture. Tun had also reportedly prepared some remarks, but did not end up delivering them. Shortly afterward, however, he was able to publish the text.

> I often say my country is a handicapped country, a country where good land is planted with mines instead of rice, where women collect wood in fear, where children are afraid to run and play freely in the fields, where families are displaced from their homes. The lands of Angola, Sudan, Bosnia, Rwanda, Afghanistan, are victims of mines. They are weeping for peace, wanting the deadly weapon to be lifted from their earth. Our countries remain in terrible poverty, while greedy producers grow rich on our misery. The "mental landmines" of these producers and exporters and fearful governments make them architects of death and destruction. Remember this: We are all landmine victims when we allow this system to continue.

Tun himself is the survivor of a landmine explosion, a double amputee. "My handicaps are quite visible," he planned to say in his Nobel lecture. "They can remind us of the invisible handicaps we all have . . . the 'landmines of the heart.' These landmines inside can lead us to war, to jealousy, to cruel power over others. . . . Together we can stop a coward's war that makes victims of us all."[5]

IN HIS PRESENTATION, Muller gave additional, strong details about the inhumane nature of this weapon:

> When I was on the hospital ship, the guys that cried the loudest were either the guys that were burn victims or victims of landmines, that suffered a traumatic amputation of a limb. And when they changed his dressing on that limb, those guys would cry, literally, I swear, would cry for their mother. The guys in my office come in *today* and

say, "Bobby, I didn't sleep last night. My foot was killing me." He doesn't have a foot! It's called phantom pain: even though the body parts are missing, you can still have these extraordinary, excruciating pains. And because of the nature of what happens with landmines, all this crap gets blown up your limb—shrapnel, dirt, garbage, clothing, et cetera—and you invariably go through a whole series of operations when you're treated like a piece of salami, and you keep getting resected and cut down.

Landmines cause probably the most debilitating, painful kind of injury other than, I would say, the burn cases that you can imagine. Understand that they are *designed to do that*, that they limit the amount of the explosive charge purposely, so that when somebody gets blown up and they're lying on the ground they wind up being a terribly demoralizing factor to those around them. And then you're a burden on the logistical process of getting you medevacked.

You find out that landmines in the millions in [countries like Cambodia] deny the land to the people. You couldn't bring the refugees back from Thailand into Cambodia because land was contaminated. Oh my God, you start to realize—this stupid three-dollar weapon winds up being the major destabilizing factor in these Third World countries, agrarian based societies that are trying to recover. And you realize not just Cambodia, it's Afghanistan, Mozambique, Angola, Kurdistan— And once you sort of, like, really understand this, you say wait a second, *this is a catastrophe*.

Muller and his friends in the VVAF learned valuable lessons from the political battles they had waged earlier. This time, once they had decided to tackle the politics of the landmine issue, they headed as high as they could.

We didn't want freshmen members of Congress: we went to the most powerful guy that we could find. And it's hard to believe that back in '92, there were fifty-seven Democratic members in the Senate. . . . The guy that controlled the money on the Appropriations Committee was Senator Leahy. We said so long as you've got the strength, you're the committee chair, you control the bucks, we want you! And Leahy, thank God, because of his having actually gone out of the country, unlike Jesse Helms—actually having *gone* to areas of conflict, and having *seen* what landmines were doing to victims—said immediately, "I'll help you."

He said, "But Bob, you've got to understand something. It's going to take years." I said, "Senator, that's okay. We're going to stay with you." And he said, "Let me introduce the idea because nobody's talking about landmines. Let me introduce it with a one-year moratorium, just get it on the board and get people to start thinking about it."

In '92, the United States, believe it or not, unilaterally was the first country to outlaw the traffic in antipersonnel landmines. Admittedly, Leahy sort of used a little stealth maneuvering, snuck it into law, but we did it. I was with Leahy when he would talk about this with his colleagues, and he would visualize these children in these areas of conflict, and he would get tears in his eyes. This guy was passionate! He was committed!

A year later, Leahy asked the Senate to extend the moratorium on exporting landmines for three more years. As Muller recalled,

the Senate voted one hundred to nothing to support that. I got to tell you—the Senate doesn't vote one hundred to nothing that the moon circles the earth, for God's sake. This was extraordinary! That inspired the world: the fact that the United States actually was at the forefront of at least the rhetoric to get rid of landmines meant, hey, maybe there's an opportunity here. And other countries started to put together their effort, and said "Let's go!" And Leahy banged our president mercilessly to keep it up. He would introduce legislation each year, ratcheting up the stakes on the landmines issue. He actually got our president to go to the General Assembly of the United Nations and call on the world community to outlaw this weapon, to get rid of it.

The president's problem is that the world community listened to him. And they took him seriously and ultimately delivered an international agreement which, as you probably know, *the United States didn't sign.* We've got 133 countries out there that signed. We, who inspired this campaign, really worldwide and in many ways drove it, wound up at the last minute faltering and not doing it. Fair question: what's going on here?

He said that in 1996 the VVAF took out a full-page ad in the *New York Times*, addressed explicitly to President Clinton, arguing that getting rid of antipersonnel landmines was the militarily responsible thing to do. Among the signatories listed on the page were Gulf War hero General Norman Schwarzkopf, former Chairman of the Joint Chiefs of Staff General David Jones, former NATO Supreme Allied Commander General John Galvin, and General James Hollingsworth, architect of the American defense structures in Korea. "Fifteen of the nation's most respected retired military leaders openly called on the president to get rid of this weapon," Muller said,

> and you should understand one thing—these guys are the ultimate American patriots. They would do nothing, nothing, to compromise the safety, the integrity, and the well-being of U.S. fighting forces anywhere in the world. So the fact that they all leaned into this campaign and argued it should settle any concern that there's a real military issue involved here. The fact is, in Vietnam, landmines were the leading cause of casualties for our own forces. Our peacekeepers, through NATO, UN: the leading cause of their casualties. The leading cause! U.S. soldiers would be better off if antipersonnel landmines were removed from the face of the earth.

Muller recalled how, later in 1996, he accompanied a group of the pro-ban generals in a visit to the White House, to urge President Clinton to support the ban. Most of the political indicators seemed to favor the move. Muller noted that Clinton's opponent in that year's presidential election, former Senator Bob Dole, had come out in favor of the landmine ban—as had his spouse, Elizabeth Dole, the president of the American Red Cross. No one in Congress was standing up to urge retention of the weapon, and the Geneva-based International Committee of the Red Cross, normally renowned for its political neutrality was strongly involved in the pro-ban campaign.

"We've got a crisis out there!" Muller said he told Clinton during the meeting. "Mr. President, what more can we do?"

Muller recalled the president's answer: "You can get the Joint Chiefs [of Staff] off my ass. I can't afford a breach with the Joint Chiefs." The veteran activist added:

What made that comment remarkable was that standing next to him was the *former* chairman of the Joint Chiefs, and he said, "Mr. President, that's why I'm here. I and the other military officers [here] will support you."

"I cannot afford a breach with the Joint Chiefs."

We talk about democracy! Civilian control of the military! The president listened to only one voice, the Joint Chiefs—which our military guys have made very clear, institutionally are incapable of going to the commander in chief and suggesting that you take weapons out of their arsenal. That's not their job. It's the *president's* job, as the commander in chief, to balance off the ultimate humanitarian consequences with whatever marginal military value is there.

And in our meetings over the last seven years with these guys over at the Pentagon, we've closed the door, and said, "Hey, what's going on here?" And they said flat out, "This has got nothing to do with antipersonnel landmines. They're garbage. The point is, we don't want to set a precedent. Because if we let you reach into our arsenal and take out this weapon, in large part because of the humanitarian consequences, then large categories of weapons and munitions systems, cluster bombs, et cetera, would be at risk."

And that's where we stand today.

At the time of Muller's 1996 visit to the White House, the ban movement was already gaining considerable momentum internationally, so the position of the U.S. executive branch, with its constitutional responsibility for the conduct of diplomacy, was becoming more important than that of the legislative branch. In addition, in 1994, the Democrats lost control of the House of Representatives; in 1996, they lost control of the Senate. Senator Leahy was no longer in a position to exert any strong influence on U.S. policy. Thus, between 1994 and 1996, the leadership of the ban movement that Leahy had pioneered so effectively slipped out of the hands of the United States. From this point the ban movement was then ably and energetically taken up by other, smaller governments (see chapter 10).

Muller concluded his presentation by reiterating a couple of key lessons he said he had learned in his adult life so far.

The most significant lesson I've learned . . . is that things don't happen simply because they're right. You've got to get political strength committed to what it is that you're fighting for. And it is a fight. We had the extraordinary fortune of having now a five-term Democratic senator go nuts on this issue and drive it for us. We had the Canadian foreign minister, that Jody will be talking about in a minute, who basically when our years of work on the United Nations on that Convention on Conventional Weapons failed—after years [spent] in getting it brought together to reconvene and examine it. . . . It was the Canadian foreign minister that with great personal courage said, "The hell with the United Nations! We're going to do something totally different: we're going to set a standard, and we're going to invite anybody who wants to, in a year to come and sign this treaty." When he did that, he got pounded. The U.S. went nuts. Our allies berated him. But at the end of the day, a year later, we got it!

So individual leadership counts; political strength has got to be connected to the righteousness of the argument; and a lot of the people here have been just like you—and it's through the experiences in life that you have a role in determining how much you're going to get.

He gestured to the other speakers on the stage with him and said, "They went through the changes that made them advocates, in response to the injustices that they got exposed to." Then he turned back to the mainly student audience. "So each and every one of *you* can be up here in several years. And don't doubt that, please don't!"

THE AUDIENCE LOVED Muller's speech, and his fellow panelists were eager to discuss the issues he had raised. Rigoberta Menchú asked for more information about how mines could be deactivated. Was there not, she wondered, some way that the companies that manufactured the mines could provide something that would help to deactivate them?

Ever the political activist, Muller replied by noting that there had already been demonstrations at several of the U.S. facilities that produce landmines, and that Human Rights Watch could provide information about the companies concerned. "I think putting pressure at all points in the campaign makes an awful lot of sense," he said.

But he also pointed out that deactivating landmines is not an easy task—as he himself had learned after he first became seriously interested in the issue. He told the story of how, back in 1992, first the folks at the Pentagon had sent him over to the State Department for more information on demining contaminated areas—and then, the folks at the State Department referred him straight back to the Pentagon.

It's unbelievable, but as recently as '92, we really didn't have any organized concepts of how to go about demining. Now we do. There are mechanisms, and more times than not it is actually somebody with a very sensitive metal detector going over the ground, getting a signal, and he digs up the landmine. The problem is that I think one of every 125 times that the metal detector gets a signal, is it actually a landmine. All the other times it's a piece of shrapnel, or sometimes even the ferrous content of the soil itself.[6]

But the point is, we now know that it can be done. It costs money to put these people in the field. It's slow and it's dangerous, but it can be done. And countries have pledged millions of dollars. But the difference between the rhetoric and the reality is a substantial difference, and we've got to hold their feet to the fire to get the bucks actually committed. It's a problem that does have a solution, but it requires a commitment of political will, to put the bucks up to get the job done.

Julian Bond asked about the effects of the United States still standing apart from the 135 countries that had signed the landmine ban treaty that the ICBL and the Canadians—led by Foreign Minister Lloyd Axworthy— had pioneered the previous year.

"I think the fact that so many countries have signed the treaty really puts pressure on the United States not to stand outside what is clearly the larger community of nations out there," Muller said. "And the dynamic of having other countries challenge the United States by going forward without it being a mutual deal has been an extraordinary dynamic. However, I think that it is absolutely critical that we continue our efforts, and get the United States [into the treaty]."

He remarked on the fickleness of public attention:

I think one of the ironies that I'm experiencing is we had a hell of a year last year, and you wind up with a [Princess] Diana, that through the tragedy of her death connects this issue with the entire world, really. You get an Axworthy, that basically jettisoned the existing mechanisms and breaks through [new] ground and makes a treaty happen. You get the recognition of the Nobel Prize. And a lot of people think, "Hey, you guys did it. Congratulations. Next!"

And they don't realize that that was a great step but, my God, you still got eighty, ninety million landmines in the ground. You still got hundreds of thousands of victims. You have lots of critical countries that are not signatories, and these things have got to happen. You're not, realistically speaking, I think, going to universalize the support for this treaty by getting India, Pakistan, China, Russia, if you don't get the United States. I think the U.S. is sort of a prerequisite in the process to recruit the others.

And we have differences about aspects of this campaign, but I'll tell you, in my view, the ultimate effect of this effort is to stigmatize this weapon in the public's thinking. So that anybody that does go ahead and use this weapon is branded a pariah, an outlaw. And that means that it has to be universally condemned. You cannot be looking to stigmatize this weapon if the world's superpower, the United States, that has every alternative capability to meet any possible military requirement going, says it's okay to continue to use this weapon. Because what they do in doing that is they undercut the moral imperative of the Ottawa treaty, which says this is an inhumane weapon that the world community cannot tolerate.

So what's been going on puts pressure on the U.S. We have to put pressure on the U.S., get them, get the others, to truly universalize the support and keep it what it needs to be: a humanitarian concern for people, by doing the demining in all of the countries that need to be cleaned up, and providing assistance to the innocent victims around the world.

Harn Yawnghwe noted that in Burma both the military and some of the armed opposition groups were continuing to use landmines. "How does the treaty, in a practical sense, affect areas of conflict?" he asked.

"At the very beginning, somebody said to me, the fact that you have outlaws is not a reason that you don't want to pass laws," Muller replied,

and I think the world is a better place because of the international agreements to prevent the use of poison gas, chemical and biological weapons, and the nuclear limitation agreements that we have—as with the landmines. None of these are going to be the magic wand that's going to make it all better, but they do shift the baseline in the dynamics that underlie a lot of these concerns.

Landmines are . . . a tragedy driven by numbers. And if we can effectively stop countries from manufacturing and exporting, trafficking in the weapon, you're not going to have these situations that we had in the seventies and the eighties, where major producer countries that basically [now] are signatories, or that at least acknowledge no further exports, [were] fueling these third world conflicts by pouring millions and millions of landmines like M&Ms, on top of other weapons deals, into these areas.

So I think, yeah, there are going to be areas of the world that are going to be slower to bring on than other areas. But it's a process, and I think the consciousness around this stuff, the fact that the major producers are basically out of the business, certainly not selling and transporting, are major steps down the road that we have to continue to travel.

Jody Williams agreed with Muller, adding,

part of the issue is that this is such a *new* norm. In one year's time, you know, we achieved the ban treaty. It's going to take time to have that establishment of the norm solidified. But just the pressure that's been brought to bear by the political will of so many countries to sign the treaty, so many countries to ratify: it will become binding international law on March 1, of this coming year, faster than any treaty in history!

That pressure has made countries that are still outside the process even take steps. . . . At least the United States, as Bobby says, says they will sign now.[7] We still need to work on them. But China has announced that they have stopped production for export as of 1996. When we were recently at the UN with Axworthy and others . . . Axworthy was able to tell us he had just had a meeting with the foreign minister of China who for the first time announced that they're giving money to the trust fund for demining in Bosnia, and they're willing to commit demining expertise to train others. So even though they are not as far as we would like them to be, just the fact that they're responding to the global awareness, I think, is very heartening.

Additionally, our own military says that there have been no significant exports of antipersonnel landmines now for over four years. So I think this norm will be firmly established over time, and just the public pressure and the awareness has already made it increasingly difficult for countries to stay outside what is becoming increasingly accepted behavior.

But in order to avoid the Burmas of tomorrow from using mines, what we really need to do is *see the stockpiles destroyed*, and part of the need for this treaty to enter into force as soon as possible was because then the various timetables of the treaty start ticking. Countries that ratified then have four years to destroy their stockpiles. We want the Angolas to sign, and ratify, and destroy, as they teeter on the brink of civil war again. It would certainly be less horrifying if they couldn't have the stocks of antipersonnel landmines to use in the ground again. Cambodia, Kosovo, where they're using mines now. The faster we get this treaty really moving, stocks destroyed, the sooner we have the possibility of diminishing the possibility of use in the future. So, it's part of a process, but we've done a lot in a short period of time, and I'm sure we'll continue.

Julian Bond returned to what Muller had said about the absence of a magic wand. "So many people, many of them young, seem to me to be suggesting that if we can't have magic wands that solve these problems like that, what's the use?" he asked. "What's the use in these long, protracted, twenty- or thirty-year battles? What's the use?"

"Well, you've got to get smart," Muller replied, to much laughter from the audience.

A good friend of mine, Tom Daschle, who's the minority leader in the Senate, . . . said to me, "Bobby, last year, you learned how to play the game." He said, "You take a very small piece of the action, and you stay focused on it for years, and you just keep your focus, you know. And slowly, incrementally, by sticking with it and maintaining a focus, you can get something done." And I really believe that you've got to get into these efforts thinking in terms of, really, decades.

When we started this campaign, I've got to say . . . I had no doubt that we would get there, [but] I thought it would take twenty years. I had no expectation that it would catch hold the way it did, but that's part of the play.

I think one of the things I've learned in Washington is k-i-s-s: "Keep it simple, stupid!" And when you get something that you can explain in thirty seconds, you've got a lot higher chance of success than something that needs a treatment of five minutes to lay out. And the beauty about landmines is I found out when we did telemarketing in the phone banks, guys could get on the phone and in thirty seconds get a commitment for bucks out of somebody on the other end. I said this is a good issue! And I think the fact that it was simple, and people could visualize it, and in fact it was a tragedy on the scale that it was: that helped accelerate the timeline.

But if you want to do something serious, it's not going to happen—unless it's an extraordinary exception—on a short-time basis. You've got to think at least, in my book, ten years plus.

A LITTLE LATER, Bond turned to Oscar Arias and asked how Muller's efforts connected with his campaign for an International Code of Conduct on the transfer of broad classes of "conventional" weapons.

"It's a source of inspiration," Arias said. "It teaches us that we must persevere. If it has taken them such a long time to bring this treaty with a minor, even though very dangerous weapon, how can we be hopeful that we are trying to regulate seven different categories of weapons? . . . If it has taken them six, seven years, perhaps it might take us twenty years, twenty-five years, thirty years. But at least it gives us a lot of hope how an individual can make a difference."

The history of warfare has seen numerous previous efforts to produce and implement worldwide treaties to ban the use, possession, or manufacture of entire classes of weapons on broadly humanitarian grounds. In modern times, those efforts go back to the Saint Petersburg Declaration of 1868, which banned the use in war of explosive or inflammable projectiles weighing less than four hundred grams, on the grounds that they "caused unnecessary suffering."[8] The effort to secure worldwide bans on whole classes of weapons has since then run parallel to two other efforts to limit the damage caused by warfare. One of those was the effort to establish worldwide rules limiting how weapons—even the allowed classes of weapons—could be used, and more broadly, how military campaigns should be fought in order to limit as much as possible the suffering caused to civilians and the "unnecessary" suffering caused to combatants. (The Geneva Conventions of 1949, an important body of rules in regard to such limits, was discussed in detail in chapter 5. In chapter 10, the interesting history of that whole Geneva branch of international humanitarian law will be further examined.) And the other kind of effort to limit the damage caused by war has been bilateral or other less-than-global multilateral agreements to limit arsenals, as witnessed between the two superpowers during the cold war, and also in several regional arms-control agreements.

The Biological Weapons Convention of 1972 was the first international agreement that banned not only the use but also the production, stockpiling, and transfer of a whole category of weapons. And in 1994, parties to the Chemical Weapons Convention agreed not only to ban the use, production, stockpiling, and transfer of all chemical weapons, but also to destroy any facilities under their control in which such weapons could be produced in the future, and to submit facilities in which a broad range of specified "precursor" chemicals might be produced or stockpiled to stringent international controls.[9]

Regarding nuclear weapons, the major existing international agreement that limits their possession and use is the Nuclear Non-Proliferation Treaty (NPT) of 1968, which entered into force in 1970 and was reaffirmed "in perpetuity" in 1995. Under the NPT, discussed earlier in chapter 2, the signatory states signed on to a vague commitment to "pursue negotiations in good faith on effective measures relating to . . . nuclear disarmament" (as well as "complete and general disarmament"). But the treaty notably did not mandate any ban on the possession or use of nuclear weapons. Instead, its signatories agreed to the division of the world's states into two classes, the nuclear weapons "haves" and the "have-nots." The "have" states, those declared nuclear weapons states—the United States, Russia, Britain, France, and China—undertook not to transfer nuclear weapons to the "have-not" states, and also not to use or threaten to use nuclear weapons against them. "Have-not" signatories undertook not to seek to acquire nuclear weapons. There is a further problem with the division of the world along these lines: the five nuclear "have" states are the five states comprising the P-5 group that have permanent, veto-wielding, seats on the UN Security Council.

It is perhaps not surprising if the NPT has not led the world anywhere close to a total ban on nuclear weapons. The five declared nuclear states that are signatories have gained significant political clout in the world along with their possession of nuclear weapons. And the three other states that clearly have the capability to deploy nuclear weapons on very short notice—Israel, India, and Pakistan—remain outside the NPT, and therefore have not even signed on to the treaty's vague general commitment to nuclear (and general) disarmament. As of 1999, therefore, the negotiations toward disarmament that the NPT called for were still nowhere in sight.

The Norwegian Nobel Committee has paid continuing attention over the years to the need for nuclear disarmament. Most recently, in 1995, it divided the peace prize equally between the Pugwash Conferences on Science and World Affairs, a prodisarmament organization founded in the 1950s, and Joseph Rotblat, a former nuclear weapons designer who quit the U.S.-British nuclear weapons program after the fall of Nazi Germany and went on to become one of Pugwash's founders and most venerable leaders.[10]

In the 1997 address in which he formally nominated the ICBL and Jody Williams as laureates, Nobel committee chair Francis Sejersted noted that there are both differences and similarities between nuclear weapons and landmines. "The former are the weapons of the rich, the latter of the poor. Yet they also have something in common. Both hit victims at a vast remove from the actual warfare. They strike mainly at civilian populations, and their effects continue for generations after the end of the armed conflict. . . . At this very time, while nuclear war casts its shadow over us all—and perhaps for that very reason has remained an unrealised threat since 1945—landmines are exploding every single day. Nearly all those killed and maimed are the poorest and most defenceless among us."[11]

At the conference, the Dalai Lama asked both Jody Williams and Muller whether another campaign, similar to that run by the ICBL, could one day succeed in banning nuclear weapons.

Williams's first response was to point to the differences between the two issues:

If the country gives up antipersonnel landmines, it doesn't put its entire existence at threat. And there's still the mentality [in] the handful of nations that have nuclear weapons, [that] if they give them up, they're putting themselves at risk, threatening their entire existence. However, I am increasingly of the belief that more could be done now in the post–cold war period. Part of it was the nuclear standoff between the two blocs of power. I'm not unconvinced that if there were a new approach in this new period more concerted than before, something might be done. It wouldn't be as quick as landmines.

Muller's response was more upbeat. "I think leadership counts and having people that come to the floor and be the catalytic agent and spark movements counts," he said. He noted in particular the vocal antinuclear advocacy that had been pursued by the former commander of the U.S. Strategic Air Command, General Lee Butler (discussed in chapter 2). He added:

> I just tell you that I found it to be an extraordinary factor, to bring the retired military leadership that we were able to recruit into the landmine campaign, and [it undercut] the military's opposition to the campaign when some of their most illustrious and reputable leaders joined our side. When you have somebody who's a four-star retired general officer who had for years been responsible for the dispatch of our entire nuclear capability saying, "You unleash forces which are too dangerous to unleash, you run risks which are too great to tolerate, and we have to walk the nuclear cat down": that is a powerful start for this movement! [This was a reference to Butler.]
>
> And I think that kind of leadership, and the dynamic of what's going on around the world community, including the inability of the Russians to manage their nuclear arsenal, provide extraordinary opportunities. And hopefully, we'll see movement on it soon.

Oscar Arias was then presented with essentially the same question, coming from an audience member: "Can a nongovernmental campaign be effective in ending the use of nuclear weapons?"

"Yes, I believe so," was his reply. "It's very obvious. I mean, civil society is becoming more and more important every day. Civil society is far ahead of governments in pushing issues. This has been shown in Rio, in the case of the environment, this has been shown in Cairo and Beijing on the women's issues, et cetera."

He, too, warned that the fight for nuclear disarmament would not be an easy one to win:

> I know General Lee Butler. I think this is wonderful. His is the minority view, though, in this country—as it is the minority view concern-

ing the seven categories in the International Code of Conduct on Arms Transfers. We're dealing here with the most powerful interest groups on earth, much more powerful than the tobacco industry, than the pharmaceutical industry, whatever you can think of. As I said before, it is not jobs that is behind the sale of weapons, it is profits. So it is a very strong force against peace and humanity, but action is what is needed.

If we all become activists, perhaps this goal of controlling weapons or destroying nuclear arsenals could become a reality, and the dream could become true in twenty years time, thirty years time. So it's a great challenge for the future generations: to have ideals; to understand that the idealists of today are the realists of tomorrow—and that tears become irrelevant if there is no action and commitment.

Muller hammered home a similar point—on the need for citizens to become actively engaged in arms control and disarmament efforts. Reflecting back on his first campaigns for better treatment for wounded war veterans, he concluded,

in this country, the truth is that we are a democracy. We actually have the machinery to exercise that democracy, [but] it's a little rusty. A lot of us have lost faith and confidence in the fact that, you know, you can really engage the gears and make it happen, but I had the good fortune of seeing a real success. . . .

I have a feeling in life that *with knowledge comes responsibility*, and when you know about a situation that obviously 99 percent of Americans had not a clue [about], there's a little bit of an obligation to carry that message home. And when you realize how devastating landmines are, you really have no doubt but that, with an educated populace, landmines will go on that same list as poison gas after World War I, and biological weapons, and chemical weapons, et cetera: that the world community says, yes, these mechanisms might kill people, but the overall cost of putting them into play are too prohibitive and we're going to outlaw [them].

And I, honest to God and strange as it may seem, had absolutely no doubt that we would get there and get this weapon effectively banned. The only question we had was how much time it was going to take.

10

A New Model for Global Action: Jody Williams and the International Campaign to Ban Landmines

When the Norwegian Nobel Committee awarded the peace prize to the International Campaign to Ban Landmines (ICBL) and Jody Williams in 1997, it gave recognition not simply to the substance of their achievement in winning a global anti-landmine treaty but also to the innovative means through which they had won it. When he announced the award, committee chair Frances Sejersted noted that the ICBL made up "a network through which it has been possible to express and mediate a broad wave of popular commitment in an unprecedented way. With the governments of several small and medium sized countries taking the issue up and taking steps to deal with it, this work has grown into a convincing example of an effective policy for peace."[1]

In his address, Sejersted noted the important role the Canadian government had played, acting through foreign minister Lloyd Axworthy, in bringing to such rapid completion the negotiation of a treaty that totally bans the production, transfer, stockpiling, and use of antipersonnel landmines. But he paid tribute, too, to the new role played by a globe-circling coalition of nongovernmental organizations (NGOs):

> When the first International Conference on Landmines was held in London in May 1993, representatives of 40 voluntary [i.e., nongovernmental] organizations attended. The following year, in Geneva, 75 organizations were represented. Today, over one thousand organizations are members of the ICBL. It was by hooking into this popular involvement that the Ottawa process came to mark a new political beginning, lifting the cause out of the backwater it had drifted into.

It is interesting to watch this initiative apparently feeding back into the United Nations and the whole system of international negotiations, and giving them new life.[2]

The presentation that Jody Williams gave in Cabell Hall centered primarily on the role this broad global coalition of NGOs had played—in pushing, feeding into, and supporting the diplomatic efforts made by government representatives at the "official" level. "I'm going to try to explain how a bunch of 'ordinary' people around the world came together to take the challenge of the U.S. president to eventually eliminate landmines, and make it a reality," she said, "and also, in so doing, to create a new model of diplomacy in the post–cold war world that threatens the status quo about how things are done. It has created a new model of diplomacy in the post–cold war world that makes smaller and mid-sized countries working together with civil society a potential new superpower."

But before she started her explanation of how the ICBL won its hard-earned laurels, she asked two of the people who had worked with her and Bobby Muller in the campaign, who had come with them to Charlottesville, to stand up and be recognized. "Ordinary citizens!" she noted, referring to what Betty Williams had said about people who seem quite "ordinary" being capable of making breakthroughs in peacemaking that end up being quite extraordinary.

"Stephen Goose and Susan Walker, please stand up!" Jody Williams said. As they rose to their feet on the left side of the hall, she led the audience in applauding them, and then explained the roles they had played in the ICBL.

> Steve Goose works for Human Rights Watch, another founding member of the [ICBL] organization. Human Rights Watch in 1985 was the first organization to begin the systematic documentation of the impact of antipersonnel landmines: very important, when we went up against governments and militaries to tell them that the weapon was already illegal, to explain to them the *disproportionate* consequence of its use on civilians. Without that documentation, we would not have been able to argue with conviction.
>
> Susan Walker is currently one of the co-coordinators of this campaign. She works for the organization Handicap International which works in twenty or thirty countries, thirty-nine countries around the

world, putting limbs on mine victims. Another organization that came to the belief that it had to join a political movement to ban this weapon because its consequences were too great. There were many like us around the world. It was the people in the field, the organizations doing the work in the middle of the landmine fields who came to the conclusion that the cost of the use of this weapon—the cost to *civilians* for decades after the end of the war—was so severe that it had to be outlawed.

And they were willing to do things which— Many of them, like Handicap International, had never launched a campaign, or participated in one before. Human Rights Watch was great at documentation, but was not real excited about coalition work and being political. But the consequences of this weapon were so great that they believed it was time to take action. So it was these people with real expertise who came together, and in 1992 we formally launched the International Campaign to Ban Landmines.

Williams was a commanding figure at the podium, an informal, self-confident speaker from Vermont—which is also the home state of Senator Patrick Leahy who, as chairman of the powerful Senate Appropriations Committee, was well placed to give the ICBL an early boost. Williams was born in the south Vermont city of Brattleboro in 1950, one of five children of a county judge. Her older brother was deaf and schizophrenic: early in her life, when other kids tried to taunt the boy, she acquired a fierce concern to stick up for him. Later, that concern broadened into a concern for all others whom society might seek to marginalize, scorn, or coerce.

By the mid-1980s, that passion for justice led her to take a poorly paid job as deputy director of Medical Aid of El Salvador, a U.S.-based NGO that aided communities in El Salvador devastated by the fighting between the country's U.S.-backed government and armed, antigovernment insurgents. By then, she was fluent in Spanish and had earned her master's degree in international relations from Johns Hopkins University. In 1992, when Bobby Muller and Thomas Gebauer (of medico international) decided they wanted to launch an international campaign against landmines, Williams was ready for the challenge. She brought to the campaign her own network of contacts, her commitment and other talents as an organizer, and a seemingly boundless fund of personal energy.

"Bobby described really well what happened in the United States," she said during her presentation at the conference.

He very clearly showed the early leadership of Senator Leahy . . . which galvanized much of the world—both the campaign side, and governments—who believed that if the United States, the sole remaining superpower, was willing on its own to stop the export of what was still considered to be a legal weapon, then maybe we could really do something. . . . It might take two decades, like Bobby said, but maybe we really *could* do something!

So our campaign started working at the international level, and the national level—with our various national campaigns, as we grew: the NGOs in the different countries. We're now twelve hundred non-governmental organizations, in seventy-five countries, formed in their own national campaigns, all of us united with the goal of banning the weapon! But each campaign works independently, because each society is different, because each NGO in each campaign works differently. Some are lobbyists. Some are field-workers. There was never this intention of this campaign to dictate from the United States how our Mozambican colleagues, for example, were going to approach their government. Or how our colleagues in Cambodia were going to approach their government. So we each worked independently, but coordinating and communicating constantly toward a common goal.

DURING A LATER discussion period at the conference, Julian Bond (who has had his own long experience of working with social change coalitions) pressed Williams for more details about how the ICBL coalition had operated. "One thing that struck me about your description of the campaign is the pulling together of this coalition of many different organizations, not all of which are prepared to do the same thing at the same time, in the same way. And I imagine that's a difficult process for each of the people gathered around the table. Tell us a bit about how it was done. How did you do it?"

"The idea of dealing with the problem of landmines is not new," the laureate from Vermont replied.

People were trying to deal with the problem of indiscriminate and excessively injurious weapons as a result of the Vietnam War in the mid-seventies, so there were initial steps then. But it wasn't until the end of the cold war, when people were no longer totally obsessed with the possibility of a complete nuclear destruction, that we started to look at how wars had actually been fought on the ground, and the weapons that had been used, and the impact of those weapons.

So by the end of the cold war, [with] the collapse of the Soviet Union, there were lots of groups in the world that were working in heavily mined countries where they had not had access before, such as Afghanistan, Cambodia. [They were] beginning to go into Angola, Mozambique, as democracy was emerging in these countries, and they just saw the amazing devastation of landmines—not just the immediate devastating of the victims, but the devastation caused by millions of landmines. Cambodia has millions of landmines scattered throughout 50 percent of its national territory! How do you repatriate refugees to create a new life when half of your national territory is full of landmines? Laos is full of unexploded munitions from the Vietnam War.

There were, she recalled, a broad variety of humanitarian groups in different countries that were gaining this information, and their members started talking with each other about it. She said that field-workers from organizations like the Belgium-based group Handicap International started saying, "God, everywhere we go we have mine victims, mine victims! We just can't keep putting limbs on them. We have to take political action." In 1992, a group in Australia gathered twenty-five hundred signatures on a petition urging their government to do something about landmines. In the United States, meanwhile, Human Rights Watch and Physicians for Human Rights had produced their report, "Stop the Cowards' War: Landmines in Cambodia," which called for a total ban on antipersonnel landmines. And Cambodian Prince Sihanouk (later, King Sihanouk) spoke at the United Nations calling for a ban. She continued:

> So you had the beginnings of people really recognizing something had to be done. And it just took a couple of organizations—Bobby Muller, the VVAF, and medico international of Germany—to say, "Okay, seems to be something going on here. Let's bring it together and create a political movement."

The only thing that joined us was the common goal of banning the weapon, and every organization that joined then or joins now is free to do whatever they want to contribute to that process. So [the ICBL] doesn't impinge on their own mandate. It doesn't try to dictate to them the form they should take in so doing. But because there is the freedom to do it the way they want, they voluntarily come together all the time.

And every time we have a meeting, we develop an action plan. This campaign has never had a "talking-head" meeting, ever! Every single campaign meeting, whether it's been 450 people from fifty countries in Mozambique during the Ottawa process, or seventy people in London in May of '93, we came out with an action plan, so that our people knew what they should do next. And they could choose to either do it in a big way or a little way, but we always were clear about the next step. That's a combination of letting them be free and giving them a little guidance.

Bobby Muller pulled forward his microphone and added a telling detail of his own about the internal organization of the ICBL:

Can I give a reinforcing comment there? It was just a year ago when the Nobel committee called, and I'll certainly never forget that morning! And this guy Geir Lundestad called, and he said, "Oh, congratulations, Mr. Muller. The International Campaign to Ban Landmines has been awarded the Nobel Peace Prize along with Jody Williams." I said, "Oh, that's great, Mr. Lundestad, but we've got a problem." He said, "Oh, what's that?" I said, "There's no there, there." And he said, "What do you mean?" I said, "Well, there really isn't an International Campaign to Ban Landmines!"

My generational marker is, follow the money! You remember the old Woodward-Bernstein "Deep Throat"? There's a check [that accompanies the peace prize]. "There's no entity to give a check to!" I said. "The International Campaign to Ban Landmines is a *name* given to the collective action of a lot of organizations. It doesn't exist as an organization! There's no president, vice president, secretary/ treasurer. There's no board of directors. We never had these budget meetings. So what are you going to do?"

Muller laughed, and the audience laughed with him at the problem he had described. "And it turned out to be quite a dilemma," he said, "but that's another story. But I think the idea of setting a goal line and saying, Look, all of you out there in whatever way you can, if you agree that that is a deserving goal line to cross, you're a supporter of the campaign. And do whatever you can in your community, in your country, to collaboratively support this collective effort to move [the campaign] downfield— And in that sense, I think that really is a refreshing way of organizing a movement, compared to what I think a lot of us have struggled through in collaborative efforts."

"Perhaps that is the secret of your success?" Bond suggested, to general laughter.

For her part, Williams wanted to stress another aspect of the organizing work, the importance of follow-up:

> People so often ask, "God, how could you organize all this?" It's drudgery: the real nuts-and-bolts work of this campaign is drudgery! It was getting up at 3:30 in the morning every day and faxing people all over the world to say, "This is what the French accomplished today. So when you meet with your government, use it. You know what they're going to be doing." It's making sure, even though everybody was independent to do it their own way, that they cared enough to keep us all informed. So that we all had the power of the smoke-and-mirrors illusions of this huge machinery, right? It was the information. It was the information.
>
> We got so good at the information that governments called *us* rather than other governments to find out what was happening next, because we usually knew before they did. And it was, again, the follow-up, the constant communication, the building of trust, trust, trust. Trust: the most important element in political work. Once you blow trust, you've blown it all! It's hard to rebuild, just as in relationships. You do what you say you're going to do. And if you say you're going to do something and you don't do anything— *Sentiment without action is irrelevant.*

DURING HER PRESENTATION, Williams noted that one of the first things the ICBL did after its establishment was look at the major, already-existing international treaty that addressed the issue of landmines: the Convention on Conventional Weapons (CCW). The CCW (whose full name is the

Convention on Prohibitions or Restrictions on the Use of Certain Conventional Weapons Which May be Deemed to Be Excessively Injurious or to Have Indiscriminate Effects) had been adopted by most of the world's governments during a big conference in Geneva in 1980. The CCW emerged on the heels of a linked pair of international agreements reached three years earlier: additional Protocols I and II of 1977 to the well-known Geneva Conventions of 1949 (see chapter 9).

The 1977 protocols sought to codify in detail the means that military commanders should use in order to protect the rights and interests of civilians living or working in areas likely to be affected by the presence or operation of their forces. For example, Article 35 of Protocol I spells out explicitly, "In any armed conflict, the right of the Parties to the conflict to choose methods or means of warfare is not unlimited." Article 51 states, "Indiscriminate attacks are prohibited. Indiscriminate attacks are . . . those which . . . are of a nature to strike military objectives and civilians or civilian objects without distinction."[3] As Williams noted during her presentation, a large part of the impetus that led to the adoption of the 1977 Protocols, and the 1980 CCW, was widespread disgust at the new forms of weaponry used—and the *ways* they were being used—during the Vietnam War.

In itself, the CCW is a virtually empty legalistic shell: its substance is carried in three attached protocols. These deal respectively with munitions that deliver nondetectable fragments; with landmines and booby traps; and with incendiary weapons, including napalm. When Protocol II, the "landmines protocol," was adopted along with the CCW in 1980, it sought to impose strict limitations on the use of landmines and similar devices, which would prevent them from causing avoidable injury to noncombatants.[4]

The effort to limit the means combatants use in war, called *jus in bello* or the "laws of war," is one with a long tradition in all major world cultures.[5] Broadly speaking, such laws have two general aims, which are pursued concurrently: the first is to establish rules for the way combatants treat combatants from the opposing side in any war; the second is to establish rules to minimize the damage that combat operations have on *noncombatants* in or near the field of battle. In furtherance of this second aim, the laws of war generally seek to establish as clear a separation as possible between combatants and their facilities, on the one hand, and noncombatants and their facilities, on the other.

Specialists on the laws of war have noted that all the world's major cultural traditions have developed sets of limitations on what means are advisable or permissible in the conduct of war. In book 7 of Plato's *Republic*, for example, Socrates tells Glaucon, "If each side devastates the other side's land and burns their homes, conflict comes across as an abomination and neither side can be regarded as patriotic. . . . However, it seems reasonable for the winners to take the losers' crops, and it smacks of aiming for reconciliation rather than perpetual warfare."[6] For his part, British "laws of war" specialist Hilaire McCoubrey has identified codes of limitation that developed within the Hebrew, Hindo-Buddhist, Confucian, Taoist, and Islamic traditions.[7]

In Western Europe, meanwhile, McCoubrey referred to the fact that between the fourth and the sixteenth centuries of the common era, the theory of "just war" generally dominated. This theory, he wrote, "had an unintended negative impact on the development of *jus in bello* [the laws of war], as the general presumption that if one party to a conflict was 'just,' the other must be 'unjust' led to a facile justification for gross cruelties in the conduct of warfare." This had not, he admits, been the intention of founders of "just war" doctrine like Saint Augustine of Hippo or Saint Thomas Aquinas; but, "this appalling consequence nevertheless followed the implementation of the doctrine in practice."[8] By the seventeenth century, C.E., however, the Dutch philosopher and legal theorist Hugo Grotius was starting to formulate laws of war that are recognizable precursors of today's body of such laws. His major work on this subject was the 1625 treatise *The Rights of War and Peace*.[9]

Observance and further codification of the Grotian laws spread throughout Western Europe. After the conclusion of the landmark Treaty of Westphalia of 1648, they formed the generally recognized "ground-rules" for the armed confrontations that continued to occur within the sovereign-state system that was inaugurated, within Western Europe, by that treaty. Then, as the encounters between West European armies spread far beyond their continental homeland to the other parts of the world where the European empires jockeyed for advantage, the Grotian laws of war were still often followed *with respect to other West European armies encountered around the world.* (However, as we saw in chapter 4, they were followed seldom if at all toward those combatants and civilians who were indigenous to the far-flung imperial battlegrounds.)

In the mid-nineteenth century, armies of West European heritage engaged in two clashes, on two continents, whose gruesomeness would have a major impact on the development of the laws of war. In the United States, the excesses encountered during the early years of the Civil War led to the U.S. army's promulgation, in 1864, of the Lieber Code, which clearly codified the humanitarian limitations on combat operation that were mandated by customary views of the laws of war. And in continental Europe, five years earlier, a French army had defeated an Austro-Hungarian army, in an infamously bloody battle at Solferino. A Swiss business executive, Henri Dunant, happened by chance to be a witness to the Battle of Solferino. Horrified by the carnage he saw, he tried to provide ad hoc volunteer medical services to the wounded of both sides. After returning to his home in Geneva, he wrote and started distributing a potent memoir of the battle. He then used the memoir to help mobilize his compatriots into establishing, in 1863, the world's first humanitarian organization devoted to improving the lot of victims of war on both (or all) sides of any armed conflict, *without partisan discrimination among them*.[10] That organization was the International Committee of the Red Cross (ICRC), a Swiss-based voluntary organization that, over the century and a half that followed, played a consistent leadership role in persuading governments to upgrade the formulation of many branches of international humanitarian law.

From the beginning, the ICRC was always associated with the development and activities of "national" Red Cross (and Red Crescent) societies that—like the American Red Cross—operate within national borders to further the humanitarian aims of the broader Red Cross movement that Dunant founded.[11] In 1864, Dunant and his colleagues in the ICRC managed to persuade a number of major governments to take part in a conference that negotiated the first-ever formal (as opposed to customary) agreement among nation-states on the laws of war. This was the 1864 Geneva Convention for the Amelioration of the Condition of the Wounded in Armies in the Field.[12] Five years later, as we saw in the preceding chapter, a similar group of governments adopted the first-ever international agreement mandating a total ban on the use of an entire class of weapon: this was the (still operative) 1869 Declaration of St. Petersburg, which banned the use of explosive projectiles weighing under four hundred grams on the grounds that they would cause "unnecessary suffering," even in combatants.[13] This latter principle, a central tenet of jus in bello, was one to which opponents of landmines would have strong recourse during the 1990s.

Since its foundation in 1863, the ICRC has played a special role as the formally recognized, independent "depositary" for many international humanitarian law conventions and treaties, including the famous Geneva Conventions of 1949.[14] It maintains a strict independence from political entanglement with any government, including the government that hosts its headquarters, Switzerland. Meanwhile, it has continued its close affiliation with the national Red Cross and Red Crescent organizations, which nowadays exist in nearly every country of the world. It must therefore be considered—along with the antislavery societies that were active during the late eighteenth and early nineteenth centuries—as among the earliest and most influential of the secular-based "international" NGOs of the modern era, and thus, an important precursor of the ICBL.

ICRC founder Henri Dunant was one of the first and most influential thinkers and activists of the modern era who saw that war is a *system* of violence that victimizes all who become entangled in it, regardless of the alleged "justice" of the cause for which they fight, or their status as combatants or noncombatants.

In 1901, Dunant was one of the two people awarded the very first Nobel peace prizes.

IN 1995, WHEN the ICBL's activists first came to examine the effectiveness of the 1980 CCW in limiting damage to noncombatants, they found—as Williams noted in her presentation—that "it was weak. It didn't do much to stop the use of landmines, to stop the proliferation. But it was an existing vehicle that we could use as a focal point. And we challenged governments to come together . . . and amend it. And we thought that if we pressed them enough, maybe we could get them to amend it—not to ban the weapon because we knew there wasn't that much political will yet, but at least we could get some movement. We achieved that very rapidly!"[15]

Meanwhile, she continued, the various NGOs around the globe that were affiliated with the ICBL were beginning to have an effect on their own governments:

We had governments begin to recognize that this was an issue that was growing in concern around the world. We had governments that wanted to be seen as the "good guy" in this issue, and they began to compete for leadership on this issue of global humanitarian concern. I said it before: governments have egos, just like individuals. Obviously, theirs are more complex egos, but they do have egos![16]

When Leahy shocked the world with the moratorium on exports, it incensed the French, for example. Considering themselves to be the guardians of human rights, they immediately responded to the challenge and launched their own moratorium. It worked! And then we were able to get our campaigns, for example, in Germany—to get them to say, okay, France has done it, the U.S. has done it, why can't you do it? And then Denmark. And then Norway.

And we kept building, and building, and building. And finally, we got one country to unilaterally ban completely the use, production, trade and stockpiling of antipersonnel landmines: Belgium, in March of '95. The new leader! It was amazing! And then that made other people irritated, so then Austria did the same thing, and then the Netherlands.

All the while we had the United States still *claiming* leadership, as the other countries of the world are moving forward really *being* the new leaders. Words are cheap. Tears, as Betty said, without action are irrelevant. The words of leadership became hollow when other countries took the real lead by action. I can *say* I'm going to do a million things; but it's what I *do* that matters. And unfortunately, leadership remained on [Capitol] Hill and not in the rest of the administration in this country.

But because other countries were willing to do it differently, because they were willing to show leadership—and we worked with them continuously through the process—we were developing a new partnership between governments and nongovernmental organizations in the area of arms control, disarmament, and humanitarian law—which was also a very novel thing to happen.

Generally, she noted, governments seem relatively comfortable having people in the broader "civil society" talk about "tear-jerking issues like children, . . . like women, like trees, the environment: these are 'soft,' easy issues." But government officials prefer to reserve the right to dominate discussions of "the 'manly' issues of war and peace, and armaments," where people perceived as tree-hugging liberals should have no place. But on the landmine issue,

> because we *were* the experts from the field, we were the experts with the documentation, we knew what we were talking about. And they could not disregard us. And because we were always there, dialoguing with them, pushing them, proving time and time again that what we said was right, and doing everything we said we would do—
>
> *The most important thing in many instances in the campaign was follow-up.* Every time we said, we are going to do x, y, or z, we did it, whether it was with our campaign colleagues or whether it was with governments. We did it, did it, did it. That builds trust! You do what you say you're going to do, so people know that when you say it, you mean it. And when this campaign said it, it meant it. And we proved it, and it broke through a little bit the barriers of distrust between government and civil society—which is so odd, because we elect governments, and they should be open to what we have to say. But they're not, generally, especially in issues of arms control and the laws of war.

By October 1996, the intergovernmental "ricochet" effect was going ahead full steam in the direction of a full landmine ban. That was the month Canadian foreign minister Lloyd Axworthy invited fifty governments that were all generally in favor of a ban to send representatives to a conference in Ottawa. The ICBL was represented there, too. As Williams recalled it, the ICBL had

> worked hard to set up an agenda for action which might ultimately lead to the eventual elimination of landmines. Like Bobby said, you know, the U.S. thought they'd run the show in normal diplomatic channels, and it would happen in twenty years—maybe.
>
> So at the end of three days of very difficult work—because we actually made the diplomats work, which was unusual in a conference— Lloyd Axworthy stood up to give the closing address, and to congratulate everybody as politicians are expected to do. "Thank you for all coming, and thank you for this wonderful action plan, and now we have maybe a road map—"
>
> And then he paused, and he said, "But this road map is not enough! It is no longer enough to say we are going to *eventually* elim-

inate antipersonnel landmines. We've been hearing that now for years. The Canadian government challenges you to come back in *one year's time*, having negotiated a total ban on the use, production, trade, and stockpiling of antipersonnel landmines, based on this Austrian draft treaty. And Canada is so determined to set a new international norm that if we're sitting here alone with the International Campaign next year, we are going to sign this treaty to prove that at least one government, two, or ten, are committed to setting a new norm to get rid of this horrific weapon!"

That freaked out the diplomats horribly, because they had not consulted with anyone! They hadn't consulted with the other leaders like Belgium, like Austria, the Netherlands. Normally, you chat with your colleagues, and you discuss whether or not this is a good thing to do. The Canadians knew that if they chatted with their colleagues, they'd be shot down and nothing would happen. So they just did it.

And then, to further horrify the diplomatic community, they said, "Not only are we going to do this, we're going to do it in open complete partnership with the International Campaign to Ban Landmines, and they're going to inside the negotiations. They're going to hear you when you negotiate, so you're not—" And he didn't say these words, but the implication was "So you're not going to be able to stand outside the negotiation doors and pretend you're doing the right thing, [but] go inside and shut the doors and keep civil society out—the same civil society without which this never would have happened—and non-negotiate the ban." So we were in the room!

That is leadership. That is huge risk taking!

Indeed, she noted, the Canadians had taken such a risk with this move that the whole pro-ban effort almost collapsed: "Canada so enraged its partners in the ban movement by grandstanding, by taking the lead, that they could have lost their allies." But once again, the Canadians put actions behind their words:

They didn't just sit back and let it collapse. They went out and lobbied, and pushed, and put their money where their mouth was. . . .

And then, when we went to negotiations, since the most-mined countries in the world are in the developing world, they paid to bring those diplomats to every single negotiation session so that they were part of the treaty. That never happens! Treaties are negotiated in Geneva, where the rich countries have their missions and they send their people who are always stationed in Geneva at the mission. The developing world has not enough money to be there, so they're not involved, and then they're expected to become party to something that they had nothing to do with. Canada said, "Nuh-uh, not this one. These are the guys living with the landmines: they're going to be with us." And they were, at every meeting. We even held a meeting in Africa, to make sure.

And when the world came together a year later to sign the treaty, there were 122 governments that signed in two days. It was incredible! Despite the opposition of the United States, despite end-runs by the U.S. during the negotiations to derail it, it did not happen because the commitment was there. It had been publicly made. We were there with them, and they could not turn back. So we achieved a total ban treaty in one year. Five, as Bobby says, from the launch of the campaign.

It is for that, that this campaign received the Nobel Peace Prize.

The first words of the [Nobel] announcement were for making a utopian dream [come true]   We were called utopians in the early days. It's absurd! [People would say things like,] "Militaries have had these weapons since the U.S. Civil War, since the Crimean War. Every single military in the world has this weapon. You think you're going to get them to give it up? The military's never met a weapon it doesn't like. You're utopian fools."

We took this utopian dream of ordinary fools, and we made it reality.

Like Muller before her, Williams was adamant that, although a lot had already been achieved, a lot still remained to be done. "There's an awful lot of work to be done, and we're still doing it. It's very, very critical that this treaty succeed. As I mentioned earlier, it will become international law more quickly than any treaty ever in history."

BY THE TIME she and Muller came to the conference, Williams had resigned from her formal position as executive director of the ICBL and was working as one of the campaign's three "international ambassadors."

Throughout 1998, the ICBL and its affiliates, the Canadians, and other pro-ban governments continued a broad campaign to get as many governments as possible to ratify the treaty.[17] Article 17 of the treaty required ratification by forty governments before it would enter into force. Those forty ratifications were in place by the end of 1998, and on March 1, 1999, sponsoring governments and ICBL representatives gathered at a ceremony in Oslo, Norway, to celebrate its entry into force. In thirty countries around the world, and some communities in the United States, church bells were rung to celebrate. The treaty's momentum continued. By the end of April 1999, 135 states had signed it, and of these seventy-seven had either ratified it, acceded to it, or otherwise finalized their approval of it. However, the United States, Russia, and China all still stood outside it.[18]

Williams said, "The campaign is working to monitor the implementation by governments in a project called Landmine Monitor to make sure the governments do what they say they're going to do. Just as we did to get them to do the treaty, we're doing the same thing to make sure they obey their own treaty." She said that the campaign was vigilant about the risks of impunity: "We do not want to create another piece of paper that is not adhered to, thus fostering the increasing sense of impunity in this world. If those governments come together and create this law themselves, and they sign and they ratify, they will adhere because *we will be there making sure that they adhere.* Because impunity is a horrific problem, obviously, and we do not want to contribute to impunity."

One main reason the Nobel committee had recognized the ICBL's work, Williams said, was because of the "new model" the campaign had established in the post–cold war period. "This model being civil society working with smaller and mid-sized governments to bring about rapid change to critical issues of concern to the international community. And they said they hoped this model would be used over and over again to deal with critical issues of arms control and peace in the next century."

She said she and many of her colleagues were indeed committed to continuing their work, not just to bring about the successful implementation of the Landmine Treaty, but also to try to ensure the success of their "new model" of international action in other fields, too. "Diplomats around the world are concerned that this model has succeeded," she argued. "It disrupts the way things are done. It disrupts their process. It disrupts their job. It *disrupts the way governments do things.* If we succeed and others are able to use this model, it is threatening to that whole process—so others are already trying to use this model!"

When the news first broke, in October 1997, that the 1997 peace prize would be awarded to Williams and the ICBL, Williams went somewhat famously on record accusing President Clinton of being a "weenie" for having failed to stand up to the Pentagon on the landmines issue and for having stood outside the Ottawa process.[19] A year later, at the conference, she was still firmly—if less undiplomatically—critical of his administration for not working with the new model of international activism. This time, her criticism focused mainly on U.S. opposition to the proposal to establish a lasting International Criminal Court to try cases of "grave breaches" of human rights law and the laws of war.[20]

> The International Criminal Court was another amazing example of the U.S. not understanding that in the post–cold war period, civil society and governments are coming together to do it differently. The U.S. tried to get its interests inserted into the International Criminal Court at the cost of everybody else's beliefs, and the world said no.
>
> Two times: first, the ban treaty, then the International Criminal Court. People are now trying to [get a treaty to ban] child soldiers. The U.S. is against that! People are now trying to do it to limit arms, light arms and small weapons—
>
> We were just with President Arias and José Ramos-Horta in Belgium a couple of weeks ago on a very interesting initiative, trying to use the parts of our campaign that were successful. It's a harder job. This Code of Conduct is a harder job. We said seven categories of weapons [to be regulated by the Code of Conduct]. And I believe that if the model we've developed is applied, and we force governments to continue to accept us as partners, we will succeed. But if we step back and let it become business as usual, diplomacy as usual, power politics as usual, we will be crying, and it will be sentiment without action—which is irrelevant to changing the world.

BY THE END of the twentieth century of the common era, the global "system" based on nation-state sovereignty that had become institutionalized broadly according to the model that had emerged in post-Reformation Europe was still firmly in place. But the classical European principle of near-absolute state "sovereignty" had started to become diluted in a number of significant ways: by the emergence of a system of international agreements mandating protection of the "human rights" of individual persons from abuse by any party, including their own governments; by the voluntary accession of governments to numerous international agreements in technical fields like trade, copyright protection, or arms control; and by the emergence of broad, codified systems of international law regulating both the legality of acts of war, and the means that could be used to wage it. All of these dilutions on national sovereignty tended to draw the citizens of the different states into something closer to a truly global society. And by the end of the twentieth century, none of these dilutions of the state sovereignty seemed easily reversible. Yet there remained a problematic disconnection at the level of the *governance* of the emerging global society. For with the one major exception of the ICRC's special role in overseeing the implementation of some portions of international humanitarian law, all the other systems for global cooperation remained firmly under the control of intergovernmental organizations—primarily the United Nations and its many affiliates, including the World Bank and the International Monetary Fund —in which the voices of government representatives held an unassailable monopoly.

The United Nations has tried, over the years, to mitigate the consequences of this governmental monopoly by fostering the involvement of a broad range of NGOs in various branches of UN activity. But this cooperation has only ever been at the "consultative" level. For example, during the big global conferences organized by the United Nations on such issues as development, the environment, or women's rights, NGOs working in those areas were invited to take part not in the main decision-making bodies, but in parallel "consultative" gatherings. As Williams noted, when Lloyd Axworthy promised that the ICBL would be included in the year of negotiations on the landmine ban treaty, and be *inside the room* during the negotiations, that made a large difference.

Within the domestic politics of different nations, it has generally been recognized—from at least the days of Alexis de Tocqueville—that the kind of voluntary associations that stand midway between families and state authorities play a vital role in helping to build the habits of democracy, and keep democracies vibrant. Two particular roles that democratic theorists see these organs of "civil society" playing are (1) to keep a spotlight of publicity focused on the activities of government and (2) to help to foster among different members of a society those habits of trust that form an essential underpinning of "social" or "public" capital. Both of those essential attributes of democracy-building were explicitly mentioned—but in the context of operations at a global, not national, level—in Williams's presentation.

What she and Nobel committee chair Sejersted both said about the work of the ICBL signaling the emergence of a new model in international relations is borne out, in part at least, by some recent research on the role of transnational NGOs at the global level. For example, American sociologist Jackie Smith has been charting the increased role in global politics of what she terms Transnational Social Movement Organizations (TSMOs), that is, organizations that work at the transnational level to promote social and political change and the development of global civil society. Using one measure of what constitutes a TSMO, Smith indicated that the number of TSMOs grew from 110 in 1953 to 631 in 1993. The largest single issue-area pursued by this array of organizations was "human rights," which was the prime issue for 30 percent of the TSMOs in 1953, and 26.6 percent in 1993. The largest *growth* in issue-area over those forty years was that shown by TSMOs focusing on the environment: their percentage of the total number of groups went up from 1.8 percent to 14.3 percent. Smith noted that in 1953, most of the secretariats of the counted organizations were located in the industrialized world, with only 5 percent of them headquartered in the developing world; but by 1993, that latter figure had risen to 23 percent.[21]

Smith spelled out several important roles that the TSMOs have been playing in the world arena. They "help increase the political resources available to social change advocates. By relating a national or subnational conflict to international laws or norms, they raise the stakes for the government to a new level, where its relations with other states may become part of the cost-benefit equation."[22] She noted that mere pronouncement of a "transnational" or "global" ethic was not in itself sufficient to prevent the breakdown of supposedly transnational organizations along national lines —as happened, for example, to the French, German, and other European components of the Socialist International on the outbreak of World War I. She wrote, too, that "frequently cultural or experiential difficulties complicate the formation of collective identities." Nevertheless, she concluded that the activities of these organizations, help democratize global politics by providing avenues for actors other than governments to influence the public agenda and the decisions taken in global political contexts, by increasing governments' accountability to a global public, and by expanding public debate about the issues considered in international contexts. In other words, they are serving to build up the infrastructures of global civil society and to strengthen them vis-à-vis the interstate system. . . .

TSMOs provide a mechanism for articulating, recognizing, and confronting transnational differences in viewpoints and priorities that are caused by class, race, gender, and national political contexts. The ability to engage in such transnational dialogue—either face to face or via newsletter or e-mail—is a necessary component for the formation of social capital and for the strengthening of a global civil society. . . .

[T]ransnational social movement mobilization promises more than any other contemporary trend to help break down rather than reproduce existing global inequalities.[23]

Jody Williams gave the mainly student audience at the conference her own reflections on the experience of having worked in such a movement:

We didn't set out to change the world. We were ordinary people who saw a problem, [and] believed we could do something to make it better. We never expected that we'd be sitting here with these eminent people because of what we did. We saw a problem, we knew it had to be resolved, *we came together to do it.* Action, not crying. Just ordinary people who have achieved an extraordinary thing, and given activists all over the world the belief that activists anywhere can and do make a difference.

So don't sit back and worry. Don't sit back and cry. And don't sit back and wait for the other guy to make it better. Join in, and help make it better yourself!

11

Toward a Moral Architecture for World Peace

At the end of the conference, before the laureates went to prepare for one final press conference and one final round of formal dinners, Julian Bond read aloud a joint statement they had drafted, the Nobel Peace Laureate Joint Declaration of November 6, 1998. It called for:

- establishing safe havens for children of war, and advancing the cause of children's rights
- universal adoption of the International Code of Conduct on Arms Transfers, and the dedication of resources to erasing the gap between the world's rich minority and its poor majority
- the Chinese government's entry into negotiations over Tibet that would serve the interests of both peoples, with these being conducted expeditiously as an indication of China's sincere intent
- full implementation of UN General Assembly resolutions that call for upholding the results of Burma's 1990 elections, and for the State Peace and Development Council (formerly SLORC) to enter into substantive political dialogue with Aung San Suu Kyi and representatives of Burma's ethnic minorities
- general acceptance of (and respect for) other peoples, communities, and cultures, and integration of the mosaic of languages, traditions, and peoples into the community of nations
- the holding of an internationally supervised referendum to determine the future political status of the people of East Timor, given that their right to self-determination has been recognized by several UN General Assembly and Security Council resolutions
- signing and ratification of the Landmine Ban Treaty by all states that have not yet done so, and the expansion by all governments of their commitments to mine clearance and victim assistance

223

The declaration also urged the international community to "seek new ways of promoting justice, reconciliation and peace in societies making the transition from repression to democracy, and from conflict to civil societies under the rule of law."[1]

THROUGH THE STORIES they brought to Charlottesville as well as the arguments they made there, the laureates showed clearly how these issues connect. Their deliberations also indicated that these interconnections need to be further explored if a sturdy architecture is to be envisioned for the future world at peace.

One main theme throughout the gathering was a plea for boldness, in our actions, our imaginings, and our general ways of thinking. Intellectually, the laureates challenged us to try wherever possible to transcend the existing bounds of our thinking, and to reframe the challenges we face from an ever broader point of view. The Dalai Lama talked about the huge benefits that can be gained by transcending the immediate concerns of the self and becoming more caring and compassionate to others—becoming, as he termed it, "wise-selfish" rather than "foolish-selfish." He also invited us to transcend purely national boundaries to more radically global ways of thinking.

In particular, His Holiness urged people who find themselves in a rights struggle or any other form of conflict to become more aware of the *motivation* (and not just the immediate behavior) of the other party to the conflict, and to focus on taking nonviolent actions that can change motivation. In that way, he said, both parties can cooperate in building peaceable, respectful relations, and even—perhaps—end up as friends. (His words were prefigured, as we saw, by those of Mahatma Gandhi and laureate Dr. Martin Luther King Jr.) His Holiness also issued a potent call for complete external disarmament—including nuclear disarmament—throughout the whole world.

We saw how the various concepts that His Holiness sketched out regarding nonviolent social and political action have played out in four real-world conflicts: those in Burma, Guatemala, East Timor, and Tibet. From Burma, we glimpsed more of the situation and spirit of that remarkable leader, Aung San Suu Kyi, and the example she has set in her ability, through the most dispiriting of circumstances, to find "freedom from fear." Much of what Daw Suu has said and written parallels the approaches of the Dalai

Lama, Gandhi, and Dr. King, including her insistence on not dehumanizing opponents who have sought to dehumanize her, and on continuing to proclaim the possibility of an amicable resolution to the problems between them.

From Daw Suu's representative, Harn Yawnghwe, we heard about the development in the modern era of both the concept of universal human rights and the related international instruments. We also saw vividly how, in the present sovereignty-dominated world system, a repressive government like that of Burma can thumb its nose at requests that it implement the terms of human rights treaties that it has signed and ratified, without facing any serious sanction from the rest of the international community. Human rights treaties may have a positive, long-term effect—especially if they can help to empower those members of any community who want to address these issues within their communities. But in the absence of any formal implementing mechanism at the global level, such change will necessarily be uneven, and slow. For his part, Harn presented a strong refutation of the notion that rulers in Asian societies—or, by extension, anywhere else—should be held to rights norms that are somehow different than those promulgated in the 1948 Universal Declaration of Human Rights.

From Guatemala, we glimpsed the struggle Rigoberta Menchú Tum has endured, surviving and escaping from that country's deep-seated system of intercommunal violence to become an eloquent advocate for multiculturalism and interethnic respect within and beyond her wounded country. Menchú reminded us that building a sustainable peace in a society that has long been ravaged by war is a long-term challenge for all members of that society, not just a simple decision taken by governments or leaders of political factions. "It's not enough to simply sign the peace accords," she said. "What really matters is what happens after those peace accords have been signed." (Betty Williams later underscored this same point when she said, "The absence of violence is only the beginning of the work for peace.")

The Mayan laureate spoke powerfully about the plight of marginalized minorities everywhere, as they struggle to find ways for their voices to be heard, and their votes counted, in a global system still dominated by the powers (and the paradigm) of the existing "sovereign" states. But she spoke, too, about the particular challenge faced by indigenous peoples, as they seek to hang on to their lands and traditions, to determine the course of their development free from coercion by others, and to win respect for their values within the emerging global discourse.

From José Ramos-Horta, we learned more about the situation of what he called "the world's expendable peoples," as they struggle to survive in a world dominated by the brutal, power-balance calculations of many practitioners of "realist" politics. We heard about the inadequacies of the protections that the international system offers to citizens of small, vulnerable states confronting vastly more powerful neighbors—even if such national or protonational communities should, according to the rules of the international system itself, be protected by their own shield of nation-state sovereignty. We heard Ramos-Horta's plaintive assessment that "countries that preached democracy and human rights were the ones that provided most weapons, not only to Indonesia but [to] many dictators around the world." And we learned more about the effects those weapons had on the vulnerable East Timorean community.

In Ramos-Horta, too, we saw the rare sight of a representative still serving a political movement who engaged in honest public reflection about some of his movement's actions of the past—actions that he admitted should perhaps have been different, and should have taken into account the *motivations* of other actors. We glimpsed an engagingly honest reflection on his own personal journey away from espousing, or perhaps condoning, the use of violence. Ramos-Horta told us that when he first heard the Dalai Lama speak, he would have "loved to see someone bombing Jakarta," but that instead he learned from His Holiness's example.

Regarding Tibet, we heard from the Dalai Lama about the need to be steadfast, amidst the most terrible provocations and setbacks, in sticking to nonviolent strategies that always address the *motivation* of the other party. In this real-world context, we heard His Holiness's powerful warning that "from violence there are always negative side effects." We saw the extent to which he is hoping a campaign of friendly persuasion can succeed in convincing China's people and leaders that a noncoerced, self-ruling Tibet can preserve values that are of interest to both peoples. From His Holiness, as from Ramos-Horta, we saw how these smart leaders are prepared, as they seek to formulate a compromise acceptable to vastly more powerful neighbors, to unpack traditional notions of sovereignty and announce significant concessions with regard particularly to the question of a nation-state's "right" to have its own military.

Betty Williams started the more detailed examination of what is needed to transform deep-seated systems of violence into healthier, more constructive relationships. First, we looked at what needs to be done at the personal level—most importantly with the children who have grown up inside conflict-plagued communities, but also, with survivors of conflict of any age. Williams issued a strong appeal to the world community to create safe havens near conflict zones, where the physical and social needs of "the littlest of our citizens" can be fully met. She called for people of all ages to work to give children a political voice that can wield real power in the deliberations of the world's governments.

Exchanges among Betty Williams, Bobby Muller, and other laureates, conveyed their shared conviction that people are inherently good but can too often carry out bad or even horrific acts if they are either trained to do so, are scared into doing so, or are acting out of a spirit of revenge. Archbishop Tutu put his own twist on this: "There is something called original sin, and each one of us has constantly got to be saying, 'There but for the grace of God go I.'" The challenge for peacemakers, the laureates agreed, is to resuscitate the sensibilities and energies of the good person who hides behind the cloak of the perpetrator of vile deeds.

We heard, too, about the importance of engaging women in the struggle to build a more peaceful world. Rigoberta Menchú called on "all of us who *are* the mothers of the world" to unite, and Archbishop Tutu recalled the contribution made to the South Africans' struggle for democracy by the "nurturingness" of the women of their communities. Tutu's remarks resonated with the Dalai Lama's discussion of the importance of "caring" for others if we are to build a peaceful world, and with the many feminist scholars who have emphasized the value of caring in their analyses of social and political action.

Betty Williams—indeed, all the laureates—issued a potent call to action to deal with social ills. She summed up this call eloquently: "Tears without action are wasted sentiment."

We were inspired by Archbishop Tutu's firsthand account of how the South African democrats first negotiated and then implemented a system of "transitional justice" that has charted a new course in the complex task of both dealing with and getting beyond the deeply held grievances of the past. He explained how, under the system agreed on by the South African peace negotiators, the perpetrators of all politically motivated crimes committed during the apartheid era were offered amnesty in exchange for a full telling of the truth about what they did. In an attempt to have a long-term educational effect, this process was intended to elucidate the perspectives of the survivors of political violence as well as its perpetrators.

We sat in on the anguished exploration by Tutu and Bobby Muller of the differences between the *retributive* model of justice, which has dominated in most Western societies, and the *restorative* model of justice, based on some traditional African theories of penology, which Tutu and his colleagues used in their work. Tutu reviewed the considerable experience he has acquired from learning about other societies still riven by deep conflict. He asked, "How do you deal with a postconflict, postrepression period, as most of these countries are going to have to do?" He strongly suggested that a restorative-justice model would be more effective over the long haul for these countries than either a retributive model or, as too often happens, the granting of blanket amnesties.

The South African preacher-laureate also focused on the twin roles that forgiveness and compromise must play, along with accountability, in the search for a lasting peace. Echoing the Dalai Lama's discussion of the need for compromise, he said, "Compromise tends to have a bad press, but it's not always a bad thing."

Oscar Arias Sánchez voiced a powerful plea for people to redefine the concept of *security* in such a way as to restore its full *human* content, along with its customarily recognized military dimension. Then, with his guidance, we explored two structural features of the existing world system that have a huge—and hugely damaging—impact on the human security of the peoples of the world. The first was the present global economic system, in which a gross maldistribution of income and wealth poses a very present threat to the lives, health, longevity, and lifeplans of those billions of "our brothers and sisters" who live in dire poverty. The second feature Arias mentioned was the globe-circling system of arms transfers, in which weapons producers in rich countries that generally already enjoy a high level of military and human security—and first among them, the United States—transfer arms to recipients in poor countries.

"War," Arias argued, "is not just an evil act of destruction, it is a missed opportunity for humanitarian investment." He noted that the present system of large-scale international arms transfers—profit driven and government subsidized—throws fuel on the fire of many local or regional rivalries around the world and vastly increases the damage done when those rivalries erupt into outright warfare. Arias explained that in an attempt to halt this process, he launched his initiative for an International Code of Conduct on Arms Transfers, which seeks to link any international transfer of weapons by a signatory country to the recipient country's compliance with human rights, democratic, and nonaggression norms.

With regard to the "right" of a state to maintain a robust military establishment, Arias gave powerful examples of cases—including in his own country—where the voluntary abjuration by a government of that right can lead to real benefits, while notably *not* leading to the extinction of the country, or of its people's values.

Neither the world economic system nor its present system of international arms transfers is the result, Arias reminded us, of any immutable natural law. Both are products, instead, of centuries of human ingenuity. Human ingenuity—in the form of committed action for change—can therefore set about transforming these systems into more life-affirming structures of global connectedness. "All of you *here* will decide," he told us somberly, "with your activism or your complacency."

Finally, with Bobby Muller and Jody Williams, we had the opportunity to explore various aspects of the campaign they both helped lead, a campaign that in five short years brought into being a widely supported international treaty banning landmines. Muller discussed the rich possibilities for organizing citizen-based campaigns within the United States. From Williams, we heard about the possibilities for globalizing such campaigns through coalitions involving an array of citizen groups from different countries and regions. We learned about the networks of international humanitarian law and arms-control regulations that—along with the body of human rights law discussed in chapters 3 and 4—form a part of the conceptual and juridical foundation on which the concept of a future "global citizenry" can start to be built.

Muller's biography and self-narrative gave us some remarkable lessons about how postconflict reconciliation can work in practice. Muller argued persuasively that it would help the rehabilitation of American veterans of the Vietnam War if they could effect a reconciliation with their former adversaries. (The Dalai Lama's argument that caring for others is good for our "selves" resounded in Muller's speech.) Muller proved powerfully that the dissemination of information is not enough, on its own, to change the world: what is required as well is community organizing and active engagement in the struggle for political change. He also argued that with knowledge there should come a sense of responsibility for using that knowledge to improve the world.

With Jody Williams, we glimpsed the huge potential for good that transnational NGOs have in the present age. These globe-circling coalitions of citizens associations can, we saw, realize concrete goals in the broad peace-building agenda while also bringing about a significant transformation in global power balance and strengthening the long-term ability of people the world over to start seeing themselves as (and acting as) members of an emerging global citizenry.

AT THE END of the twentieth century, the concept of a global citizenry may still seem remote to the daily conduct of international affairs. The world's peoples still live largely confined to the closed, nation-state cubicles to which the post-Westphalian system first consigned them. True, in some cases, nation-states may have started to pool some aspects of their sovereignty into larger, supranational blocs. Some of these blocs, like NAFTA or the European Union, are purely regional. Through their experience, the people who are citizens of European states have been able to learn valuable lessons about the experience and value of transcending their previous "national" identities. But still, the design of regional blocs like the European Union generally excludes most outsiders, rarely aiding in the emergence of truly global structures and institutions for the future.

There are, meanwhile, numerous other bodies and institutions, like the United Nations or the International Court of Justice, that *do* aspire to a truly universal affiliation and jurisdiction. But the right to representation within these global bodies is still monopolized by national governments.[2] As we have seen, nearly all the world's existing governments remain fiercely jealous of both the potential power of nongovernmental entities and any attempt to subordinate sovereign-state powers to those of any emerging globewide jurisdiction. (The United Nations' effectiveness is frequently also paralyzed by the vetoes wielded by the P-5 powers.)

Violence at all levels, from active military combat to prolonged attempts to coerce other groups or nations, remains a dominant reality for far too many of the world's people. Perhaps this should not surprise us. Violence, as Max Weber and others have noted, was historically one defining dimension of the nation-state system. The idea of a fully sovereign state that has *no* military establishment, but depends only on wise diplomacy to defend its borders—a Costa Rica, for example—is still a radically new one that is frequently viewed less as model for the future than a mere curiosity, a strange aberrance from the "normal" theory of the state.

Is there a way out of this situation? All the laureates at the Charlottesville gathering, without exception, counseled the importance of *hope.* As the Dalai Lama said, "If we lose hope, and remain with pessimism, that is the greatest of failure." But in what should we invest our hope?

A first step, as all the laureates indicated, is for everyone, in whatever situation, to start imagining her- or himself as a capable actor, not just a powerless victim of the violence and inequity all around. Indeed, one of the signal contributions that the Nobel Prizes as an institution have made over the past century—in the field of international peacemaking as well as in the sciences—has been an affirmation of the agency and creative power *of the individual.* Governments are not awarded Nobel Prizes, people are.

The laureates also concurred that we need to see ourselves as inextricably connected to the rest of humanity. From Rigoberta Menchú's view of herself as first and foremost a "social actor," to Archbishop Tutu's concept of *ubuntu,* or *botho,* to the Dalai Lama's value of compassion, we see that the laureates all believe strongly that—in the words of John Donne—"No man is an island."

Many of these laureates stressed the value of actively envisioning, or imagining, the kind of world they want to build. For all of them, this would be a world in which the ties of common humanity would be much stronger than what Tutu has referred to as the "irrelevancies" of power, status, skin color, or religious or ethnic affiliation. Indeed, even just *imagining* the world as a single human community can be a jumping-off point from which people can take effective actions that help resolve present conflicts and build toward a shared, cooperative future. When Daw Suu or Harn Yawnghwe spoke about the SLORC generals *also having families,* or when Tutu wrote at length to President Vorster as a fellow family man, those strugglers for peace were reaffirming their own powers of compassion and sympathetic imagination. But they were also reaching out to identify a shared strand of common interest within the existing lives of their current opponents with which they hoped to connect, as a first step toward building a common future.

Beyond imagining cooperative solutions to their own immediate concerns and issues, these laureates have also worked hard at imagining what a future globewide peace will look like. All these laureates subscribe to the goal of the eventual abolition of nuclear weapons and all other categories of major weapons. They seek to build a world, moreover, in which military power itself has become nearly or totally irrelevant.[3] (After all, if a small country like Costa Rica can abolish its standing army, why can't much larger countries do the same?) If the aim is to increase the human security of the world's peoples, however, these laureates realize that any steps toward radical disarmament must be accompanied by a sustained commitment to building new and improved mechanisms for the nonviolent resolution of conflicts at all levels of human society.

At the economic level, the laureates all united to call, in their declaration, for erasing the gap between the world's rich and poor. Realizing this goal will involve investing considerable resources in upgrading the different dimensions of the "human security" of the world's poorer communities. We have every reason to expect that, after a generation or two of such upgrading and with the concurrent conversion of military resources to productive civilian uses, the quality of life for nearly everyone in the world (as measured on something like the UN Development Program's Human Development Index) could be considerably higher than at present. If these upgrades were enacted, the distinction between the range of lifeplans available to the world's poorest people and those available to its richest would be considerably diminished, if not yet wholly erased.

There is still much work to do in all areas of global human governance, including the governance of the global economy. To whom are the existing structures of world economic governance like the World Bank or the International Monetary Fund currently answerable? The answer is: to existing national governments (or more precisely, primarily the governments of the rich nations). Here again, we come up against the problem of the monopoly of nation-states over the levers of global governance, and thus, the absence of mechanisms to protect the interests of groups unrepresented or badly underrepresented within their "national" governments.

In her presentation, Rigoberta Menchú stressed the need to find new ways to integrate the "mosaic" of languages, traditions, and peoples into the community of nations, as well as the need to find ways to bring in to any future global governance structure the various other strata of civil society.

Indeed, it is not too early, as the Dalai Lama and others have argued, to start envisioning how a true "global citizenry" might make its voice heard on key issues in the future. This will certainly involve solving, somewhere along the way, the P-5 problem: the problem, that is, of the concentration of powers within the UN system in the hands of the five states with full nuclear capability. There are many proposals for how that problem could be addressed, primarily through reforming the rules regarding permanent membership of the Security Council, and vetoes. (It would make the most sense to conceive of those reforms as running parallel to a serious nuclear-disarmament campaign: the role of nuclear weapons in world affairs should be deemphasized in both ways together.)

But beyond dealing with the P-5 issue, we need to think of ways to reform the world system in order to break the stranglehold that state sovereignty still exercises over world affairs. Several activists and researchers have already made good headway in thinking through the issues involved. Veterans of organizations like the World Federalist Movement or the World Order Models Project have been doing just this for more than fifty years now.[4] In Europe, where the concept of state sovereignty has started to give way to European Union governance, and a single-layered concept of "national" identity is giving way to a spectrum of European, national, and subnational identities, there has been considerable discussion of the parameters of "post Westphalian citizenship."[5] British professor David Held has called for the establishment of a "cosmopolitan democracy," in which new global political institutions would be created alongside the current system of states and "would override states in clearly defined spheres of activity."[6]

For his part, the Dalai Lama has suggested the establishment of what he has called the World Council of the People. This would, he writes, "consist in a group of individuals drawn, as I imagine it, from a wide variety of backgrounds." Its main task would be to monitor human affairs from the perspective of ethics. The council he proposes would not have any political power. But, he explained, "by virtue of its independence—having no link with any one nation or group of nations, and no ideology—[its] deliberations would represent the conscience of the world. They would thus carry moral authority."[7]

Another interesting suggestion was formulated by Erskine Childers, a twenty-year senior staff member of the United Nations. Childers, who died in 1996, wrote of the need "to bring to life the opening words of the [UN]

Charter: 'We the Peoples of the United Nations.'" To that end, he suggested that alongside the UN General Assembly, where each government currently has one vote, there should be established "a UN Parliamentary Assembly elected by the peoples. This is not sheer utopianism: it is the equivalent of running some seven Indian parliamentary elections."[8] The existing governments would have to agree to this, of course. Childers realized that, and urged a broad, global campaign to persuade them to do so.

Under Childers's plan, the United Nations's existing General Assembly could evolve into something like the upper house of a bicameral system, with the new body acting as the more democratic and accountable lower house. Some system such as this would open up a whole new level of transnational politics among the peoples of the world. It could lead to the empowerment of many groups who are powerless "minorities" under the present system and allow for the constructive reframing of many currently tricky interstate conflicts within broader, suprastate contexts. This plan could also, like the one proposed by the Dalai Lama, act as a dramatic spur to the concept of a "global" citizenship.

Childers was right to note, however, that it would take a big campaign to persuade governments to agree to it—especially the governments of big continental powers like the United States and China, which are especially touchy about any perceived diminution of their own powers to the benefit of a broader polity.

THE BROAD ARCHITECTURE for a future world at peace that emerged from the laureates' discussions is at one level a very simple one: a world without militarism, where differences are resolved and plans made through dialogue, not coercion, and where all human beings are offered equal opportunities to live meaningful, safe, and successful lives. But at a deeper level, it is a world that requires a profound rethinking: a rethinking of the ways many of us have been taught until now to think about the "realities" of world affairs. Of our notions of what is fair or unfair in the world. Of the nature of our connections with, and responsibilities to, people half a globe distant. Of what is required of us if we want humankind to survive and thrive over the centuries ahead. Of what is good and bad about the existing nation-state system, and what the bounds are of the communities with which we identify. In short, a reconsideration of who we are.

At the dawn of the twenty-first century, most or all of these issues are at the forefront of our questioning. The cold war system that dominated global relations between 1945 and 1990 is dead and gone, and we still have no "new world order" to replace it. Attempts to solve problems through military coercion and through the creaking operation of the present world system have been disappointing, to say the least. On both counts, we desperately need to search for better options for the future.

DO SOME OF the ideas mentioned here seem implausible, or totally impractical? The nine laureates in Charlottesville—these heroes for a globewide future—agreed that there is a need for boldness of vision, *and* of action. We should not underestimate the boldness it took for many of these laureates, when the communities to which they belong were still wracked by violence, to step outside that paradigm and start to argue publicly with their colleagues for the use of alternative, nonviolent strategies. "We need a total landmine ban!" Bobby Muller, Jody Williams, and their allies said back in 1992, when all the "realists" still laughed at them. Archbishop Tutu needed boldness, too, as he prayed that night in 1989 and determined that—regardless of the proven ferocity of the apartheid regime—he would invite his defenseless followers to join in a peaceful protest march a few days later.

"In an age of cynicism and greed," Oscar Arias noted, "all just ideas are considered impractical. . . . You are mocked for insisting that we can be more humane!" But Betty Williams suggested a good way to respond to such cynicism: "The insanity of what's going on militarily in the world has got to be challenged—not by me, or Jody Williams, or His Holiness, or anybody else who's supposed to have a 'famous name.' The insanity of that has got to be challenged by every single one of you, *every one of you!*"

Appendix

Recipients of the Nobel Peace Prize

1999   Doctors without Borders, Belgium

1998   John Hume and David Trimble, Northern Ireland

1997   International Campaign to Ban Landmines and Jody Williams, United States

1996   Carlos Filipe Ximenes Belo and José Ramos-Horta, East Timor

1995   Joseph Rotblat and the Pugwash Conferences on Science and World Affairs, Great Britain

1994   Yasser Arafat, Palestinian National Authority; Shimon Peres, Israel; Yitzhak Rabin, Israel

1993   Nelson Mandela and Frederik Willem de Klerk, South Africa

1992   Rigoberta Menchú Tum, Guatemala

1991   Aung San Suu Kyi, Burma

1990   Mikhail Gorbachev, USSR

1989   The Fourteenth Dalai Lama, Tibet

1988   The United Nations Peace-Keeping Forces

1987   Oscar Arias Sánchez, Costa Rica

1986   Elie Wiesel, United States

1985   International Physicians for the Prevention of Nuclear War, United States

1984   Desmond Mpilo Tutu, South Africa

1983   Lech Walesa, Poland

1982   Alva Myrdal, Sweden, and Alfonso García Robles, Mexico

1981   Office of the United Nations High Commissioner for Refugees, Switzerland

1980   Adolfo Pérez Esquivel, Argentina

1979   Mother Teresa, India

1978   Anwar as-Sadat, Egypt, and Menachem Begin, Israel

1977   Amnesty International, Great Britain

1976   Betty Williams and Mairead Corrigan, Northern Ireland

1975   Andrei Sakharov, USSR

1974   Seán MacBride, Ireland, and Eisaku Sato, Japan

1973	Henry Kissinger, United States, and Le Duc Tho, Democratic Republic of Viet Nam (declined the prize)
1972	Prize money allocated to main fund
1971	Willy Brandt, Federal Republic of Germany
1970	Norman Borlaug, United States
1969	International Labour Organization, Switzerland
1968	René Cassin, France
1966–67	Prize money allocated to main fund and special fund
1965	United Nations Children's Fund
1964	Martin Luther King Jr., United States
1963	International Committee of the Red Cross and the League of Red Cross Societies
1962	Linus Pauling, United States
1961	Dag Hammarskjöld, Sweden
1960	Albert John Luthuli, South Africa
1959	Philip Noel-Baker, Great Britain
1958	Georges Pire, Belgium
1957	Lester Bowles Pearson, Canada
1955–56	Prize money allocated to main fund and special fund
1954	Office of the United Nations High Commissioner for Refugees
1953	George Marshall, United States
1952	Albert Schweitzer, France
1951	Léon Jouhaux, France
1950	Ralph Bunche, United States
1949	John Boyd Orr, Great Britain
1948	Prize money allocated to main fund and special fund
1947	The Friends Service Council, Great Britain, and the American Friends Service Committee (the Quakers), United States
1946	Emily Greene Balch and John Raleigh Mott, United States
1945	Cordell Hull, United States
1944	International Committee of the Red Cross
1939–43	Prize money allocated to main fund and special fund
1938	Nansen International Office for Refugees, Switzerland
1937	Robert Cecil, First Viscount Cecil of Chelwood, Great Britain
1936	Carlos Saavedra Lamas, Argentina
1935	Carl von Ossietzky, Germany
1934	Arthur Henderson, Great Britain

1933	Sir Norman Angell, Great Britain
1932	Prize money allocated to special fund
1931	Jane Addams and Nicholas Murray Butler, United States
1930	Nathan Söderblom, Sweden
1929	Frank Billings Kellogg, United States
1928	Prize money allocated to special fund
1927	Ferdinand-Édouard Buisson, France, and Ludwig Quidde, Germany
1926	Aristide Briand, France, and Gustav Stresemann, Germany
1925	Sir Austen Chamberlain, Great Britain, and Charles Gates Dawes, United States
1923–24	Prize money allocated to special fund
1922	Fridtjof Nansen, Norway
1921	Karl Hjalmar Branting, Sweden, and Christian Louis Lange, Norway
1920	Léon-Victor-Auguste Bourgeois, France
1919	Woodrow Wilson, United States
1918	Prize money allocated to special fund
1917	International Committee of the Red Cross
1914–16	Prize money allocated to special fund
1913	Henri Marie Lafontaine, Belgium
1912	Elihu Root, United States
1911	Tobias Asser, the Netherlands, and Alfred Fried, Austria
1910	Permanent International Peace Bureau, Switzerland
1909	Auguste Beernaert, Belgium, and Paul d'Estournelles de Constant, France
1908	Klas Pontus Arnoldson, Sweden, and Fredrik Bajer, Denmark
1907	Ernesto Moneta, Italy, and Louis Renault, France
1906	Theodore Roosevelt, United States
1905	Baroness Bertha von Suttner, Austria
1904	Institute of International Law, Belgium
1903	Sir William Randal Cremer, Great Britain
1902	Élie Ducommon and Charles Gobat, Switzerland
1901	Jean-Henri Dunant, Switzerland, and Frédéric Passy, France

Notes

1. A Gathering of Framers of the Future Global Culture

1. Thomas Jefferson in a letter to Mr. Roscoe, Monticello, December 27, 1820. In *The Writings of Thomas Jefferson*, ed. H. A. Washington (New York: H. W. Derby, 1869), vol. 7, p. 196.

2. Although Luthuli received the prize for 1960, through a quirk of committee procedure it was not awarded until one year later.

3. Text of Norwegian Nobel Committee's citation, as posted on <www.nobel.se/laureates/peace-1984-press.html>. *Apartheid* (apart-hood) is the term in Afrikaans for *segregation*. As a governmental system, it imposed rigid classification of citizens into four official racial categories (White, Colored, Indian, and Black) and totally denied any voting rights to that 80 percent of the population classified as Black. The rights of the Colored and Indian populations were also severely curtailed, allowing the Whites to control all the levers of power in the system.

4. For the text of the proposal, see <www.tibet.com>. See also Sidney Piburn, ed., *The Dalai Lama: A Policy of Kindness* (Ithaca, New York: Snow Lion Publications, 1993), p. 22.

5. Speech by Egil Aarvik on the occasion of the award of the Nobel Peace Prize for 1984, Oslo, December 10, 1984. Text available on <www.nobel.se>. Referring to Tibetans as a "minority" poses some important questions, since Tibetans are only a minority with respect to China's 1.2 billion national population, while in their own country — despite Beijing's intensive efforts to resettle ethnic-Chinese families from inside China in Tibet — they still remain a majority. This question of a dominating neighbor attempting to change the human geography of a dominated but culturally distinct area through massive and discriminatory social engineering — which can be seen as a relatively bureaucratic and slow form of "ethnic cleansing" — is one that was represented at the conference by various participants. It is discussed further in chapters 4 and 5.

6. In the early 1990s, the country's ruling junta, the SLORC, declared in Orwellian fashion that the country's name should henceforth be written in English as Myanmar, and its capital as Yangon. Supporters of the country's democratic movement argue that this step was taken arbitrarily. They prefer to stick with the English-language appellations Burma and Rangoon, which are better known in the global community.

7. The inhumanity involved in maintaining Britain's colonial position in Burma sickened one young Briton sent into the country as a junior administrator. His disgust at the repression he was required to uphold there led young Eric Blair to write — under his pen-name George Orwell — a scathingly satirical exposé of his experiences, *Burmese Days*. His experience in Burma helped turn Blair/Orwell into a lifelong anticolonialist and an exposer of the cant and "double-think" of repressive regimes everywhere.

8. In early 1999, her husband, the British Tibetologist Michael Aris, was diagnosed with advanced prostate cancer. He was not allowed a visa to Burma to visit her, and she was not given any assurance that if she left her country to be with him, she would be allowed back. Within weeks, he died.

241

9. At the end of 1998, Human Rights Watch reported that 194 NLD parliamentarians were still in jail, and one had died there during the preceding year. For updates on this and other aspects of the human rights situation in Burma, visit <www.hrw.org>.

10. An early version of Menchú's *testimonia* was published in a work authored by Elisabeth Burgos-Debray, *I, Rigoberta Menchú: An Indian Woman in Guatemala* (London: Verso, 1984). Some significant aspects of the narrative of that book were contested by the North American anthropologist David Stoll in his book-length study *Rigoberta Menchú and the Story of All Poor Guatemalans* (Boulder, Colorado: Westview, 1999). At the outset of the Burgos-Debray book, the author (who based her text on a series of interviews with Menchú) quotes Menchú stating explicitly, "I'd like to stress that it's not only *my* life, it's also the testimony of my people. It's hard for me to remember everything that's happened to me in my life since there have been very many bad times." (p. 1). A statement on the Rigoberta Menchú Tum Foundation Web site downloaded February 1999 declared, "The testimony of Rigoberta Menchú has the bias and the courage of a victim who, in addition to what she personally suffered, had a right to assume as her own personal story the atrocities that her people lived through. Their dead are still dead, and that is denied neither by the researcher, nor his sources, nor the signers of the peace accords that ended the Guatemalan tragedy." See <http://ourworld. compuserve.com/homepages/rmtpaz/Menu_eng.htm>. Even though Stoll was highly critical of some aspects of the Burgos-Debray book, he still described himself as "someone . . . who thinks the Nobel award was a good idea" (p. viii). Certainly, the questions he raised never caused the Norwegian Nobel committee to consider rescinding the award (telephone interview with committee secretary Geir Lundestad, March 1999).

11. He never had the time, however, to get to New York and have his credentials accepted. That meant that the government he sought to represent never received the formal recognition of other governments.

12. Speech by Francis Sejersted on the occasion of the award of the Nobel Peace Prize for 1996, Oslo, December 10, 1996. Text available on <www.nobel.se>.

13. See Keith Suter, *East Timor, West Papua/Irian and Indonesia* (London: Minority Rights Group, 1997), p. 10.

14. Speech by Francis Sejersted on the occasion of the award of the Nobel Peace Prize for 1992, Oslo, December 10, 1992. Text available on <www.nobel.se>.

15. Suter, *East Timor*, p. 19. Ramos-Horta and others have likened this process to the phased approach inaugurated by the Israelis and Palestinians with their Oslo agreement of September 1993.

16. One good account and analysis of the ICBL can be found in Richard Price, "Reversing the Gun Sights: Transnational Civil Society Targets Land Mines," in *International Organization*, vol. 52, no. 3 (summer 1998), pp. 613–644.

17. See chapter 3 in Charles Taylor, *Sources of the Self: The Making of the Modern Identity* (Cambridge, Massachusetts: Harvard University Press, 1989).

18. Canadian writer Michael Ignatieff has noted of the late-twentieth-century ethnic conflicts he has reported on, "Nationalists are supremely sentimental. . . . There is no killer on either side of the checkpoints who will not pause, between firing at his enemies, to sing a nostalgic song or even recite a few lines of some ethnic epic." See Michael Ignatieff, *Blood and Belonging: Journeys into the New Nationalism* (New York: Viking, 1993), p. 6.

19. Quotes taken from Alfred Nobel's will (see <www.nobel.no/alfreden.html>).

December 10 was Nobel's birthday. In 1948, the Universal Declaration of Human Rights was adopted by the United Nations on December 10. The date seems an appropriate one for people around the world to consider their global connectedness and commonalities.

20. Dunant also originated the first Geneva Convention concerning the treatment of combatants wounded or captured during battle. For a more complete discussion of his role, see chapter 10. For a list of all peace prize recipients, see the appendix to this book.

21. Telephone interview with Geir Lundestad, March 1999. Lundestad admitted that the distinguished (Swedish) secretary-general of the United Nations, Dag Hammarskjöld, was awarded a posthumous peace prize in 1961. The "northern" focus of the selection committee during the early decades of the prize reflected, he said, "the realities of international relations as seen at the time by the north." He added, "We do not claim a perfect record; we claim a respectable record."

22. A number of them also cited President John F. Kennedy as an early role model.

23. P. Jeffrey Hopkins, "Bringing Together Great Hearts and Minds," in the conference program, p. 3. Text available at <www.virginia.edu/nobel/letter.html>. Hopkins served from 1979 to 1989 as the Dalai Lama's translator. He also wrote of the participating laureates, "At the core of their agenda is the conviction that morality is essential for personal, political, social, and economic balance. They believe that without a personal ethic that includes compassion for other human beings, mere self-concern will eventually undo the fabric even of one's own life" (p. 2).

24. Information obtained from <www.wagingpeace.org/nobel.html> on June 18, 1999.

25. These issues are all intimately connected. Working as a journalist in Lebanon for seven years in the 1970s, I saw the operations of one of the Middle East's most deeply entrenched "systems of violence" up close and personal. I saw faction heads and local and international business interests working together to allow the perpetuation of intercommunal killings. I saw how children and teens grew up to consider the violence and hatred quite "normal," and how they were frequently sucked into becoming practitioners of violence, motivated by a deep and understandable desire to get even for brutalities they had seen inflicted on their own close kin. As a working mother with young children, I felt a strong punch in my own gut when, at work in the Reuters office a mile from my family's apartment, I would hear a loud explosion from its general direction and fear the worst.

26. In his latest book, the Dalai Lama has also stressed the importance of using imagination in the struggle for personal and global peace. See chapters 11–16 of His Holiness the Dalai Lama, *Ethics for the New Millennium* (New York: Riverhead, 1999).

27. Benedict Anderson, *Imagined Communities: Reflections on the Origin and Spread of Nationalism* (London and New York: Verso, 1983).

28. Appendix I to Immanuel Kant, "Perpetual Peace," translated in Hans Reiss, ed., *Kant: Political Writings* (Cambridge, England: Cambridge University Press, 1991), p. 125.

2. The Dalai Lama and the Need for Internal and External Disarmament

1. Naomi Tutu, "Introduction," in Desmond Tutu, *The Words of Desmond Tutu* (New York: Newmarket Press, 1989), p. 16.

2. Martin Luther King Jr., *Strength to Love*, 2nd ed. (Philadelphia: Fortress Press, 1981), p. 17.

3. Readers interested in seeing a complete transcript of the conference proceedings can find one through the conference Web site: <www/virginia.edu/nobel>.

4. See William Borman, *Gandhi and Non-Violence* (Albany: SUNY Press, 1986), p. 16. Note that at least two attempts to name the core mission of the U.S. military in the post–cold war world drew directly on the concept of coercion: "strategic coercion" and "coercive inducement." For a good discussion of the relationships among deterrence, compellance, and coercion, see chapter 1 in Lawrence Freedman, ed., *Strategic Coercion* (New York and Oxford: Oxford University Press, 1998). See also Donald C. Daniel and Bradd C. Hayes with Chantal de Jonge Oudraat, *Coercive Inducement and the Containment of International Crises* (Washington, D.C.: U.S. Institute of Peace Press, 1999).

5. Quoted in Mary King, *Mahatma Gandhi and Martin Luther King, Jr.: The Power of Nonviolent Action* (Paris: UNESCO Press, 1999), p. 280. See the other Gandhi quotations in this section of Mary King's book, too.

6. He explores some of these ideas in greater detail in chapter 14 of his book *Ethics for the New Millennium* (New York: Riverhead, 1999).

7. Brodie first published this conclusion in autumn 1945. It is reprinted in Bernard Brodie, "The Development of Nuclear Strategy," in *Strategy and Nuclear Deterrence* (Princeton, New Jersey: Princeton University Press, 1984), p. 3.

8. Martin Luther King Jr., *Strength to Love*, p. 151.

9. "The child's mind" is an apt reference to the subject of Betty Williams's talk (see chapter 6). It was also interesting in light of His Holiness's own childlike quality (*not* childishness), referred to at the beginning of the chapter.

10. Martin Luther King Jr., *Strength to Love*, p. 151. Present author's emphasis.

11. Shortly after Nelson Mandela's historic 1990 release from jail, he succeeded in persuading the ANC's national leadership to suspend the armed struggle that he himself had (not very successfully) spearheaded twenty-nine years earlier. See Nelson Rolihlahla Mandela, *Long Walk to Freedom: The Autobiography of Nelson Mandela* (Boston: Little Brown, 1994), p. 510.

12. For more information on some of those movements, see Mary King, *Mahatma Gandhi and Martin Luther King, Jr.*, chapter 5.

13. For a thoughtful but searing indictment on this score, read Alexander De Waal, *Famine Crimes: Politics and the Disaster Relief Industry in Africa* (London: African Rights, and Bloomington: Indiana University Press, 1997). See also Michael Ignatieff, *The Warrior's Honor: Ethnic War and the Modern Conscience* (New York: Henry Holt, 1997), especially pp. 159–161.

14. For critiques of NATO's 1999 operations around Kosovo, see Michael Mandelbaum, "A Perfect Failure," in *Foreign Affairs* Sept./Oct. 1999, pp. 2–8; Adam Roberts, "NATO's 'Humanitarian War' over Kosovo," in *Survival* Autumn 1999, vol. 41, no. 3, pp. 102–123; and Helena Cobban, "Kosovo Lessons," in *The Christian Science Monitor*, August 12, 1999, p. 11. Actually, the UN's deployment of the UNOSOM force to Somalia had more good consequences on the ground in Somalia than is generally recognized in the United States, where the dominant image remained that of some of the military debacles the force got entangled in. For good descriptions of the UNOSOM deployments, see De Waal, *Famine Crimes*, pp. 159–191, and Mohamed Sahnoun, *Somalia: The Missed Opportunities* (Washington, D.C.: U.S. Institute of Peace Press, 1994).

15. See David R. Smock, *Perspectives on Pacifism: Christian, Jewish and Muslim Views on Nonviolence and International Conflict* (Washington, D.C.: U.S. Institute of Peace Press, 1995), p. 47. Lederach stressed that this should be a multinational force open to members of any religious tradition at all, or none, provided only that they undertook to commit themselves to the principles of nonviolent engagement; he proposed that the Peaceforce be organized under UN auspices, though there might be other ways of organizing it. See also the discussion of the Peaceforce concept in chapter 7 of this book.

16. The Peace Brigades have proven their worth in, among other countries, Guatemala. In Guatemala, they have provided unarmed protective accompaniment that has given several local rights activists, including Rigoberta Menchú Tum, a valuable measure of protection against the local forces of repression and thus enabled them to continue to live and work in their own countries. For more information on their work see Patrick Coy, "Cooperative Accompaniment and Peace Brigades International in Sri Lanka," chapter 5 in Jackie Smith, Charles Chatfield, and Ron Pagnucco, eds., *Transnational Social Movements and Global Politics: Solidarity Beyond the State* (Syracuse, New York: Syracuse University Press, 1997).

17. See for example Fiona Robinson, *Globalizing Care: Ethics, Feminist Theory, and International Relations* (Boulder, Colorado: Westview, 1999). This book contains an excellent bibliography.

18. Article VI of the Nuclear Non-Proliferation Treaty. Treaty text from *Arms Control and Disarmament Agreements* (Washington, D.C.: U.S. Arms Control and Disarmament Agency, 1982), p. 93.

19. See *The Military Balance 1998/99* (London: International Institute for Strategic Studies, 1998), p. 292.

20. The commission was headed by Richard Butler, the Australian disarmament specialist who would later head the United Nation's effort to eliminate Iraq's weapons of mass destruction. Among its other notable members were the French environmentalist Jacques-Yves Cousteau, and Joseph Rotblat, a nuclear physicist and veteran disarmament campaigner who won the Nobel Peace Prize in 1995.

21. *Report of the Canberra Commission on the Elimination of Nuclear Weapons* (Canberra, Australia: Department of Foreign Affairs and Trade, 1996), pp. 24, 25, 22, 58, 7, 71.

22. *Strategic Survey 1997/98* (London: International Institute for Strategic Studies, 1998), p. 45. A thoughtful and very readable exploration of the views of nuclear abolitionists, including many who took part in the Canberra Commission, is Jonathan Schell, *The Gift of Time: The Case for Abolishing Nuclear Weapons Now* (New York: Metropolitan/Henry Holt, 1998).

3. The Individual and the Totalitarian State: Aung San Suu Kyi and the Question of Human Rights in Burma

1. Edward Klein, "The Lady Triumphs," in *Vanity Fair*, October 1995, pp. 120–144.

2. Bertil Lintner, *Outrage: Burma's Struggle for Democracy* (Bangkok and London: White Lotus, 1990), p. 109.

3. "A Conversation with U Tin U," in Aung San Suu Kyi, with Alan Clements, *The Voice of Hope* (New York: Seven Stories Press, 1997), p. 271.

4. See the reporting gathered in Bertil Lintner, *Outrage,* pp. 88–115.

5. "Speech to a Mass Rally at the Shwedagon Pagoda," in Aung San Suu Kyi, *Freedom from Fear* (London: Penguin Books, 1995), pp. 192–198 passim.

6. Bertil Lintner, *Aung San Suu Kyi and Burma's Unfinished Renaissance* (Clayton, Victoria, Australia: Monash University Centre of Southeast Asian Studies, 1990), p. 25.

7. "A Conversation with U Tin U," p. 279. U Tin U commented that "even our jailers voted for us!"

8. *Human Rights Watch World Report, 1999* (New York: Human Rights Watch, 1999). Text taken from their Web site: <www.hrw.org>.

9. Francis Sejersted, "The 1991 Nobel Prize for Peace," in *Freedom from Fear,* p. 234. This collection also prints the speech Alexander Aris gave on his mother's behalf.

10. The group of laureates who went to Thailand in 1993 to try to see Aung San Suu Kyi comprised the Dalai Lama, Archbishop Tutu, Oscar Arias, Mairead Maguire, Betty Williams, and representatives of the Nobel Prize–winning groups Amnesty International and the American Friends Service Committee. The two who went to the White House were Tutu and Williams.

11. In July 1998, Daw Suu and her colleagues in the NLD leadership decided that she should try to travel outside Rangoon to meet with party activists in other areas. Human Rights Watch reported, "On July 7 and 21, she was stopped en route to visit party members and prevented from reaching her destination. On July 24, her car was stopped as she attempted to visit Bassein. This time, the stand-off lasted for six days and ended only after the military forcibly entered her car and drove her back to Rangoon. On August 12, she made another attempt to reach Bassein, and when her car was stopped at the same point, she remained inside for thirteen days with little food or water. Only a suspected kidney infection and jaundice forced her to return to Rangoon" (*Human Rights Watch World Report, 1999*). Text taken from <www.hrw.org>.

12. The conference was held just before the serious illness of her husband was announced. He died in early 1999, without being allowed a final visit with her.

13. Burma, like many countries, discriminates against women by not allowing citizenship to pass automatically from a mother to her children.

14. Aung San Suu Kyi, with Alan Clements, *The Voice of Hope* (New York: Seven Stories Press, 1997), pp. 132–133. I note that Clements, unlike many others who have commented on Suu Kyi's situation, does not engage in obsessive speculation about the effects of her political engagement on her spouse and children—speculation that many in our male-dominated culture seem to focus disproportionately on politically active women.

15. Aung San Suu Kyi, "Freedom from Fear," in *Freedom from Fear,* pp. 180, 184–185.

16. Aung San Suu Kyi, *The Voice of Hope,* p. 46.

17. Ibid., p. 25.

18. Ibid., pp. 152–153.

19. Ibid., p. 29.

20. Ibid., pp. 173–174.

21. For more information on the origins of the Universal Declaration and Mrs. Roosevelt's strategy, see chapter 1 of William Korey, *NGOs and the Universal Declaration of Human Rights* (New York: St. Martin's Press, 1998).

22. The texts of a broad array of global human-rights agreements, including the

Universal Declaration and the two Covenants, can be accessed through <www.unhchr.ch/html/intlinst.htm>.

23. The League of Nations, which existed between the two world wars, had laid more stress on the rights of minority *communities* than on individual human rights. That meant there was a much lower international concern with individual rights issues in those years than there would be in the era of the United Nations. But after Hitler was elected to power in Germany in 1933, he used the issue of the "minority rights" of ethnic Germans in Czechoslovakia and elsewhere to bolster his claim that his invasion of areas where they lived was somehow justified. That led to a substantial discrediting of the idea of "minority community rights" after 1945; but it was an issue that would not go away, as we shall see.

24. Aung San Suu Kyi, "In Quest of Democracy," in *Freedom from Fear*, p. 167.

25. Ibid., pp. 168–170, passim.

26. Ibid., p. 173. Present author's emphasis.

27. Menchú has written of her impressions of her visit with these refugees: "When I saw them I said, 'These are my people!' I felt as if I was in a Mayan camp in Qintana Roo, or in Campeche or Chiapas." See Rigoberta Menchú Tum, *Crossing Borders* (London and New York: Verso, 1998), p. 149.

28. Mohamed Sahnoun, *Somalia: The Missed Opportunities* (Washington, D.C.: U.S. Institute of Peace Press, 1994), pp. 46–47, passim. Sahnoun, who was in effect fired by UN Secretary-General Boutros Boutros-Ghali in October 1992—before things went totally downhill in Somalia—has ascribed much of the blame for the debacle there to the ineptitude and poor organization of the UN leadership.

29. Aung San Suu Kyi, "Empowerment for a Culture of Peace and Development," in *Freedom from Fear*, p. 265

4. The Challenge from the Indigenous World: The Powerful Voice of Rigoberta Menchú Tum

1. The global balance of power would also have been very different if the Chinese had followed up the extraordinary, huge-scale, transoceanic expeditions that Admiral Zheng He organized in the early fifteenth century with a sustained attempt to establish overseas colonies and build a global empire. For more details see F. W. Mote, "China in the Age of Columbus," in Jay A. Levenson, ed., *Circa 1492: Art in the Age of Exploration* (Washington, D.C.: National Gallery of Art, 1991), especially pp. 342–346.

2. Rigoberta Menchú Tum, *Crossing Borders* (London and New York: Verso, 1998), p. 192.

3. Ibid., pp. 71–72.

4. Ibid., p. 170.

5. Ibid., p. 73.

6. Article 7 of ILO Convention No. 169 of 1991, as published in Keith Suter, *East Timor, West Papua/Irian and Indonesia* (London: Minority Rights Group, 1997), p. 2.

7. The text of the declaration can be accessed through <www.unhchr.ch/html/intlinst.htm>.

8. Most indigenous rights activists consider that indigenous peoples constitute a very special kind of minority. One definition, derived from that developed by

UNWGIP, is that "indigenous populations are composed of the existing descendants of the people who originally inhabited the present territory in a country (or countries), wholly or partially, at the time when persons of a different culture or ethnic origin arrived there from other parts of the world, overcame them, either by direct conquest, settlement, or other means, and reduced them to a non-dominant group within their home region or territory" (footnote 2 in Jeff J. Corntassel and Tomas Hopkins Primeau, "The Paradox of Indigenous Identity: A Levels-of-Analysis Approach," in *Global Governance*, vol. 4 [1998], p. 155).

9. Rigoberta Menchú, *Crossing Borders*, pp. 158–159.

10. Judith N. Zur, *Violent Memories: Mayan War Widows in Guatemala* (Boulder, Colorado: Westview, 1998), p. 224.

11. Human Rights Watch report on events of 1998 in Guatemala, taken from <www.hrw.org>.

12. See Douglas Farah, "War Study Censures Military in Guatemala," in the *Washington Post*, February 26, 1999, pp. A19, A22.

13. Charles Babington, "Clinton Regrets Support for Guatemala," in the *Washington Post*, March 11, 1999, p. A1. The next day, the *Post* revealed that as far back as 1968, the second-ranking diplomat in Guatemala City had written a cable to his superiors stating explicitly that "the official squads are guilty of atrocities. Interrogations are brutal, torture is used, and bodies are mutilated" (Douglas Farah, "We've Not Been Honest," in the *Washington Post*, March 12, 1999, p. A25).

14. David Maybury-Lewis, *Indigenous Peoples, Ethnic Groups, and the State* (Boston and London: Allyn and Bacon, 1997), pp. 1–3 passim.

15. Ibid., p. vii.

16. Aung San Suu Kyi, *The Voice of Hope* (New York: Seven Stories Press, 1997) p. 31. Daw Suu also said she agrees with philosopher Karl Popper that she does not believe that people like the dictators of the SLORC are "evil"; rather, they are stupid, or confused.

17. This is a method that has been used to start building interstate confidence in numerous regions of the world, like the Middle East. The idea is that as the representatives of each national military start hearing, in a calm atmosphere, how their counterparts describe the threats they face, they can respond by saying things like, "No, that action of ours that you perceive as a threat is actually intended by us to be a response to some other threat. Maybe together, we can all ratchet down these levels of armament and threat."

18. Fundación Arias para la Paz y el Progreso Humano, *Demobilization, Demilitarization, and Democratization in Central America* (San José, Costa Rica: Arias Foundation, and Montréal, Québec, Canada: International Centre for Human Rights and Democratic Development, 1994), pp. 126–129 passim.

19. See Phillips S. Moulton, ed. *The Journal and Major Essays of John Woolman* (Richmond, Indiana: Friends United Press, 1989), pp. 66, 128–129.

20. Desmond Tutu, *The Rainbow People of God: The Making of a Peaceful Revolution* (New York: Doubleday, 1994), p. 125. Present author's emphasis. Tutu's emphasis on the socially constituted nature of personhood has important parallels with the Dalai Lama's emphasis on "compassion" and some Western feminist scholars' emphasis on "caring"—see chapter 2.

21. From Frost's "The Gift Outright." Frost read that poem at President Kennedy's inauguration.

22. Maybury-Lewis, *Indigenous Peoples*, p. 37. Present author's emphasis. See also Kurt Burch, *"Property" and the Making of the International System* (Boulder, Colorado: Lynne Rienner, 1998).

23. See Timothy Egan, "Poor Indians Who Own Rich Lands Try to Break Out of Vast Federal Maze," in the *New York Times*, March 9, 1999.

24. Maybury-Lewis, *Indigenous Peoples*, pp. 37, 38.

25. Menchú, *Crossing Borders*, p. 182.

26. There is also, of course, an ever-present possibility of a clash between a minority's group rights, and the individual rights of some persons inside or outside that community.

27. Fundación Arias, *Demobilization*, pp. 76–77.

28. Noted during author's visit to Barcelona, June 1992.

29. George Pscharapoulos and Zafiris Tzannatos have estimated that 50 percent of the earnings shortfall suffered by indigenous people in Guatemala results from outright discrimination (cited in UNDP, *Human Development Report 1997*, Box 2.6, p. 43).

5. Resisting the Domination of Stronger Neighbors: José Ramos-Horta on East Timor and the Dalai Lama on Tibet

1. The information in the four preceding paragraphs has been taken from the excellent Web site <www.easttimor.com>, which is run by the East Timor International Support Center, a nonprofit organization of which Ramos-Horta is honorary chairman.

2. Keith Suter, *East Timor, West Papua/Irian and Indonesia* (London: Minority Rights Group, 1997), p. 10.

3. José Ramos-Horta, "A Friend In Need," in *The Age* (Melbourne), October 14, 1996, p. 15, as quoted in Keith Suter, *East Timor*, p. 17.

4. Keith Suter, *East Timor*, p. 11.

5. "Indonesian Integration Attempts," on <www.easttimor.com>, March 23, 1999.

6. Ibid. The quote from Colonel Kalangie is attributed to the *Philadelphia Enquirer*, May 28, 1982.

7. John F. Avedon's classic account of the modern history of Tibet, and the role in it of the Dalai Lama (New York: HarperCollins, 1984).

8. "East Timor Peace Initiative," on <www.easttimor.com>, March 22, 1999.

9. In October 1999, Amien Rais was elected speaker of Indonesia's semidemocratic national parliament.

10. There were clear parallels here with the role Archbishop Tutu was able to play in apartheid-era South Africa. See chapter 7.

11. The information in this paragraph is from Bishop Belo's biography, posted on <www.easttimor.com>, and Keith Suter, *East Timor*, p. 15. See also Arnold S. Kohen, *From the Place of the Dead: The Epic Struggles of Bishop Belo of East Timor* (New York: St. Martin's Press, 1999).

12. Nobel Peace Prize Web site: <www.nobel.no>.

13. Keith Suter, *East Timor*, p. 16.

14. Stephen Weeks, "East Timor Resistance Wants Troops Out before Vote," Reuters wire story, March 18, 1999. Ramos-Horta also warned that over the preceding two months, various agencies connected with the Indonesian military had been distributing large quantities of weapons to "integration" supporters in East Timor.

15. On August 24, Bishop Belo published a powerful piece in the *New York Times*, in which he wrote that over the preceding six months, hundreds of thousands of young East Timoreans had been killed by anti-independence armed groups "created by Indonesian army elements who oppose independence." He urged that "Indonesia's generals, who have longstanding ties to Washington, should be made to understand that Indonesia will not receive any military assistance or . . . loans . . . unless the army ends its campaign of violence." (Carlos Ximenes Belo, "A Day of Reckoning in East Timor," in the *New York Times*, August 24, 1999, p. A19.

16. For more details on this period, see Avedon, *In Exile from the Land of Snows*, (New York: HarperCollins, 1984) pp. 26–30.

17. "Structure of the Tibetan Government-in-Exile," from <www.tibet.com> (the Web site maintained by the Dalai Lama's representatives at the Office of Tibet, London) on March 22, 1999. The U.S. Congress deemed China's presence in Tibet to be "illegal" and to constitute an "occupation" in the Foreign Relations Authorization Acts for fiscal year 1992 and fiscal year 1993.

18. These guerrilla operations received some help from the CIA, but this ended before Washington normalized relations with Beijing in 1974. See "World News Briefs: Dalai Lama Group Says It Got Money from C.I.A.," in the *New York Times*, October 2, 1998.

19. "The Statement of His Holiness the Dalai Lama on the 40th Anniversary of the Tibetan National Uprising Day on 10 March 1999," <www.tibet.com> on March 22, 1999.

20. For the text of the proposal, see <www.tibet.com/proposal/5point.html>.

21. See <www.tibet.com/DL/10mar99.html>.

6. Transforming Systems of Violence at the Personal Level: Betty Williams and the Rehabilitation of Survivors of Violence

1. More details of the summit, and the WCCC, can be found on the WCCC Web site: <www.compassioncenters.org>.

2. This is a fine example of what Sigmund Freud called "the narcissism of minor difference." See his *Civilization and Its Discontents* (New York: Norton, 1961), and Michael Ignatieff, *The Warrior's Honor: Ethnic War and the Modern Conscience* (New York: Henry Holt, 1997), pp. 34–71.

3. This point has been eloquently made by others, too, including Cambodian landmine survivor and ICBL organizer Tun Channareth—see chapter 9.

7. Transforming Systems of Violence at the Intergroup Level: Desmond Tutu and Reconciliation in South Africa

1. Desmond Tutu, *The Rainbow People of God: The Making of a Peaceful Revolution*, ed. John Allen (New York: Doubleday, 1994), pp. 6–7.

2. Ibid., pp. 7, 12.

3. Egil Aarvik, "Presentation of the Nobel Peace Prize," in *The Nobel Peace Prize Lecture: Desmond M. Tutu* (New York: Anson Phelps Stokes Institute, 1986), p. 17.

4. Desmond Tutu, *The Rainbow People of God*, p. 191.

5. See Nelson Mandela, *Long Walk to Freedom: The Autobiography of Nelson Mandela* (New York: Little Brown, 1994), pp. 481–486.

6. Article 3 of Act No. 34 of 1995, Promotion of National Unity and Reconciliation Act, 1995. Taken from the TRC's Web site, <www.truth.org.za/legal/act9534.doc>, on April 6, 1999.

7. Desmond Tutu, *The Words of Desmond Tutu* (New York: Newmarket Press, 1996), p. 77.

8. See Desmond Tutu, *The Rainbow People of God*, p. 267.

9. Ibid., p. 229. Necklacing was a punishment sometimes meted out to political opponents or suspected government informers by young black activists in the townships. It involved placing a tire filled with gasoline around the opponent's neck and setting fire to it.

10. The Bisho massacre occurred in September 1992, during the twilight of the ill-fated "Bantustan" system.

11. Nelson Mandela, "Foreword," in Neil J. Kritz, ed., *Transitional Justice: How Emerging Democracies Reckon with Former Regimes* (Washington, D.C.: U.S. Institute of Peace, 1995), vol. 1., p. xi. Mandela (like Gandhi before him) had studied law in South Africa's British-derived legal system.

12. Nagel's and Weschler's views, as referenced in Lawrence Weschler, "A Miracle, A Universe: Settling Accounts with Torturers," in Neil J. Kritz, ed., *Transitional Justice*, vol. 1, pp. 491–492. There is also, of course, a strong relationship between the intended targets of dissemination of knowledge (in this case, the public) and accountability: "To whom does a government official consider him- or herself answerable?"

13. David Becker, et al., "Therapy with Victims of Political Repression in Chile: The Challenge of Social Reparation," in Neil J. Kritz., ed., *Transitional Justice*, vol. 1, p. 589.

14. José Zalaquett, "Balancing Ethical Imperatives and Political Constraints. The Dilemma of New Democracies Confronting Past Human Rights Violations," in Neil J. Kritz, ed., *Transitional Justice*, vol. 1, p. 205.

15. "Tutu Says Amnesty Process Exposed Previous Regime," Johannesburg, SAPA (South African Press Association) in English, June 23, 1998; reproduced in Foreign Broadcasts Information Service, *FBIS-AFR-98-174*, June 23, 1998.

16. "'Atrocious Things Were Done on All Sides'" (excerpts from the TRC final report), published in the *Washington Post*, October 30, 1998, p. A32. Also available through the TRC Web site: <www.truth.org.za>.

17. Pumla Gobodo-Madikizela, "Facing the Truth in South Africa," in the *Washington Post*, November 1, 1998, p. C7. Present author's emphasis. See also the commentary in Martha Minow, "Justice Beyond Punishment," in ibid., p. C1.

18. Lynne Duke, "S. African Report Draws Bitterness," in the *Washington Post*, October 30, 1998, p. A1.

19. A good short introduction to the "laws of war" can be found in chapter 1 of Hilaire McCoubrey, *International Humanitarian Law: Modern Developments in the Limitation of Warfare*, 2nd ed., (Aldershot, England: Dartmouth/Ashgate, 1998). These laws are discussed at greater length in chapter 10 of this book.

20. Veteran peace-builder John Paul Lederach has written, "The basic paradigm of reconciliation . . . embraces paradox. It suggests, for example, that . . . providing space for grieving the past permits a reorientation toward the future and, inversely, that envi-

sioning a common future creates new lenses for dealing with the past." See John Paul Lederach, *Building Peace: Sustainable Reconciliation in Divided Societies* (Washington, D.C.: U.S. Institute of Peace, 1997), p. 29. See also his exploration of the relationships among peace, justice, truth, and mercy in the process of reconciliation, in the same section.

21. The "restorative justice" approach has been tried at the community level in at least one crisis-torn Western city—Northern Ireland's Belfast. See Jane Lampman, "Halting Force and Intimidation," in *The Christian Science Monitor*, June 10, 1999, p. 13.

8. Oscar Arias Sánchez and Structural Aspects of the Struggle for Human Security

1. The text of the Esquipulas-II agreement can be viewed on the Arias Foundation's Web site: <www.arias.or.cr>.

2. From the Nobel Web site: <www.nobel.se> on June 18, 1998. President Reagan's special envoy to Central America, Philip Habib, had asked Reagan to support the agreement, but Reagan chose not to, so Habib resigned from his position. See text of an interview conducted with Arias in July 1995 on <http://theodore-sturgeon.mit.edu:8001/peacejam/sanchez/interview.html> (downloaded June 18, 1998). In Charlottesville, in a seeming reference to U.S. policy at that time, Arias remarked at one point, "In this country, it's murder to kill one person, but if you kill 100,000, then it's 'foreign policy.'"

3. The text of the Code of Conduct can be obtained from the Arias Foundation's Web site: <www.arias.or.cr>.

4. From the introductory memorandum preceding the text of the code, ibid.

5. Both of the figures for what it would cost to provide basic public services worldwide are taken from *Human Development Report 1997* (New York: UN Development Program and Oxford University Press, 1997), p. 112, box table 6.4. This publication contains numerous equally informative aggregated (as well as particularized) statistics.

6. Figures from Ruth Leger Sivard, *World Military and Social Expenditures 1996* (Washington, D.C.: World Priorities, 1996), pp. 44 and 45. See also tables 19 and 38 (pp. 188–189 and 215) of *Human Development Report 1997*.

7. The *Human Development Report 1997* estimates that for a total of around $80 billion per year, appropriately targeted, the world's poorest people could be both lifted out of poverty and set on the path to real long-term development. The report notes, "That is less than 0.5% of global income." It says that $30 billion of the total sum could come from national budgets (i.e., in the countries concerned), provided they were appropriately restructured. In another section, the report stated that in 1995, industrial countries spent $182 billion on subsidies to their own producers and exporters, and that the effect of these subsidies is, in many cases, to wipe out any possibility that producers in developing countries might have to compete. Clearly, the global economy is not built on anything like a level playing field. The report states baldly that "lack of political commitment, not financial resources, is the real obstacle to poverty eradication. Eradicating absolute poverty is eminently affordable." (*Human Development Report 1997*, box 6.4 [p. 112], and box 4.2 [p. 86]).

8. The numbers produced by the UN Development Program more or less bear him out. This organization reported that in 1995, the United States gave 0.10% of its GNP in ODA, compared with Denmark (0.96%) and Norway (0.87%). Per capita ODA from the United States in 1994/95 was $33, compared with Denmark ($273) and Norway ($255). That year, American ODA totaled $7.37 billion, while that from Japan came to $14.49 billion, from France, $8.44 billion, and Germany, $7.52 billion. The amount of ODA given *per capita* of the U.S. national population was $33 (Denmark's was $273). Ibid., table 37 (p. 214).

9. *The Military Balance 1998/99* (London: International Institute of Strategic Studies, 1998), p. 269.

10. Ibid.

11. Ibid., p. 270.

12. The Quai d'Orsay is the location of the French Foreign Ministry.

13. The incident he described took place in January 1996 and was launched by a group of peace activists who came to be known as the Ploughshares Four. For more details, see Keith Suter, *East Timor, West Papua/Irian and Indonesia* (London: Minority Rights Group, 1997), p. 17.

9. Reconciliation in Action: Bobby Muller and the Anti-Landmine Campaign

1. The VVAF has an informative Web site: <www.vvaf.org>.

2. Ruth Leger Sivard, *World Military and Social Expenditures* 1996 (Washington, D.C.: World Priorities, 1996), p. 15.

3. Shawn Roberts and Jody Williams, *After the Guns Fall Silent: The Enduring Legacy of Landmines* (Washington, D.C.: Vietnam Veterans of America Foundation, 1995), p. 3.

4. Ibid., pp. 20, 22.

5. Tun Channareth, "Peace, Step by Step," in the *Nation* (New York), January 5, 1998, vol. 266, no. 1, p. 7.

6. International humanitarian law prescribes that commanders who order the laying of mines should take pains to give public notice of the general whereabouts of mine fields, as well as to retain detailed records of the location of the mines, to aid their subsequent removal. In many cases, these rules have been totally ignored.

7. The United States has said that it plans to be able to configure its forces in such a way that it will able to sign the treaty by 2006.

8. The United States did not ratify this agreement until 1974.

9. Information about all these agreements except the Chemical Weapons Convention from Shawn Roberts and Jody Williams, *After the Guns Fall Silent*, pp. 491–492. Find information about the CWC on its homepage: <www.opcw.nl>.

10. The Pugwash group took its name from that of the summer residence of Canadian business executive Cyrus Eaton, who hosted the group's first few meetings at his Pugwash estate. More information about the group is available on their Web site: <www.pugwash.org>.

11. "The Lecture Given by the Chairman of the Norwegian Nobel Committee Francis Sejersted," Oslo, December 10, 1997. Text posted on <www.nobel.no>.

10. A New Model for Global Action: Jody Williams and the International Campaign to Ban Landmines

1. Announcement of the Nobel Peace Prize for 1997. See <www.nobel.se/laureates/peace-1997-press.html>.

2. "The Lecture Given by the Chairman of the Norwegian Nobel Committee Francis Sejersted," Oslo, December 10, 1997, pp. 1, 2. Contact Nobel Institute for text.

3. The full text of these important articles, as well as all the major treaties and agreements in the field of international humanitarian law, can be viewed through the International Humanitarian Law section of the excellent Web site maintained by the International Committee of the Red Cross, at <www.icrc.org>.

4. For the text of Protocol II, see ibid.

5. *Jus in bello* rules are distinct from—though related in important ways to—*jus ad bellum*, which sets out the whole set of considerations that govern the right to wage war against another state in the first place.

6. Plato's *Republic*, sections 470d–e, in Robin Waterfield's translation (Oxford: Oxford University Press, 1993), p. 188. Many other interesting limitations are described between 469b and 471c. Socrates was portrayed as arguing, in particular, that the limits on what belligerents could do in wars with other Greeks should be much tighter than those on what they could do to non-Greeks.

7. See Hilaire McCoubrey, *International Humanitarian Law: Modern Developments in the Limitation of Warfare*, 2nd ed., (Aldershot, Hants: Dartmouth Publishing, and Brookfield, Vermont: Ashgate Publishing, 1998) pp. 8–13.

8. Ibid., pp. 11, 12.

9. See Hugo Grotius, *The Rights of War and Peace*, translated by A. C. Campbell (Westport, Connecticut: Hyperion Reprint, 1993).

10. As Jody Williams said, "Information, information!" Margaret E. Keck and Kathryn Sikkink have also focused on the role of "information politics" in the emergence of international NGOs. See especially chapter 2 of their book *Activists Beyond Borders: Advocacy Networks in International Politics* (Ithaca, New York: Cornell University Press, 1998).

11. For more details about the organization and workings of the Red Cross movement, see David P. Forsythe, *Humanitarian Politics: The International Committee of the Red Cross* (Baltimore, Maryland: Johns Hopkins University Press, 1977). See especially the organizational diagram on page 6.

12. For an excellent account of this conference and its sequelae, see Martha Finnemore, "Rules of War and Wars of Rules: The International Red Cross and the Restraint of State Violence," in John Boli and George M. Thomas, eds., *Constructing World Culture: International Nongovernmental Organizations since 1875* (Stanford, California: Stanford University Press, 1999).

13. See Hilaire McCoubrey, *International Humanitarian Law*, pp. 16–20.

14. For more information on the international Red Cross movement, see David P. Forsythe, *Humanitarian Politics*, or the ICRC Web site, <www.icrc.org>.

15. In 1995, legal specialists from Human Rights Watch contributed to Shawn Roberts and Jody Williams's seminal book *After the Guns Fall Silent*, an analysis in which they judged the effectiveness of the CCW and its attached Landmines Protocol against the standards laid out in Additional Protocol I of 1977 to the Fourth Geneva

Convention of 1949. The 1977 protocol had explicitly prohibited attacks deemed to be "indiscriminate," for example, between combatants and noncombatants. "On a practical level, the treaty has been a failure," the HRW memorandum said of the CCW. "It is a failure on a theoretical level as well; the Landmines Protocol does not conform to customary humanitarian law, particularly as set forth in Articles 51(4) and 35(1) and (2) of Additional Protocol I. In the view of . . . Human Rights Watch, these laws require a total ban on landmine use" (p. 489).

16. Richard Price, in his study of the ICBL, concluded that "the case of [antipersonnel] land mines suggests that moral proselytism is apt to be relatively more important in gaining a transnational network of policy advocates and allies in the earliest phases of a campaign. . . . Once states perceive that an incipient norm has reached a certain level of support among other states, a second social systemic process—emulation—is likely to play a relatively stronger role as key decision makers embrace the new norm in order to avoid outlier status." See his article, "Reversing the Gun Sights: Transnational Civil Society Targets Land Mines," in *International Organization*, vol. 52, no. 3 (Summer 1998), p. 640.

17. Its formal name is the Convention on the Prohibition of the Use, Stockpiling, Production and Transfer of Anti-Personnel Mines and on their Destruction.

18. Some U.S. participants in the ICBL have noted wryly that their organizing work proved more effective at the international level than within their own country. Up-to-date information about the status of signatories, ratifications, and the like is available from the ICBL Web site: <www.icbl.org>.The site has well-organized background material and some fascinating links to other related sites.

19. See, for example, Mary McGrory, "Clinton in the Mine Minority," in the *Washington Post*, October 16, 1997, p. A2.

20. It was this court whose establishment Bobby Muller had been advocating in his discussion on transitional justice issues with Archbishop Tutu (see chapter 7). The proposed court would be a permanent body, unlike the international criminal tribunals dealing with war crimes in Rwanda and the former Yugoslavia, but its work would certainly build on the precedents being established in those two 1990s-era courts. For more details on the ICC, see Alton Frye, ed., *Toward an International Criminal Court?* (New York: Council on Foreign Relations, 1999), and chapter 21 in William Korey, *NGOs and the Universal Declaration of Human Rights* (New York: St. Martin's Press, 1998).

21. For the fuller table, see Jackie Smith, "Global Civil Society? Transnational Social Movement Organizations and Social Capital," in *American Behavioral Scientist*, vol. 42, no. 1, September 1998, p. 97.

22. Ibid., pp. 98–99.

23. Ibid., pp. 101–105, passim.

11. Toward a Moral Architecture for World Peace

1. The text of the declaration can be viewed at <www.virginia.edu/nobel>.

2. In the European Union, by contrast, there are direct elections by voters to a European parliament. Citizens of the European Union are also the only people in the world who can bring claims against their own governments for violations of internationally recognized human rights. They do this through the European Court of Human Rights, whose first president, René Cassin, was awarded the Nobel Peace Prize in 1968.

3. In chapter 14 of his new book *Ethics for the New Millennium* (New York: Riverhead, 1997), the Dalai Lama has called for the disestablishment of all the world's militaries.

4. For the report of an interesting, broad-ranging investigation of many of these issues undertaken under the auspices of the World Order Models Project, see Richard Falk, *On Humane Governance: Toward a New Global Politics* (University Park: Pennsylvania State University Press, 1995). The World Federalist Movement, which claims adherents in twenty-two countries, is headed by the actor and thinker Sir Peter Ustinov. For more information, see their homepage: <www.wfa.org>.

5. See for example, Andrew Linklater, "Citizenship and Sovereignty in the Post-Westphalian State," in *European Journal of International Relations*, vol. 2, no. 1 (1996), pp. 77–103.

6. David Held, "Democracy and Globalization," in *Global Governance*, vol. 3 (1997), p. 264.

7. His Holiness the Dalai Lama, *Ethics for the New Millennium*, p. 216.

8. Erskine Childers, "The United Nations and Global Institutions: Discourse and Reality," in *Global Governance*, vol. 3 (1997), p. 275.

Further Resources

THIS BOOK COVERS such a wide range of topics that readers interested in learning more will need to rely strongly on their own research skills and the expertise of the reference staff in libraries. What follows are some ideas for further research, grouped into categories: 1. The International System; 2. War and Peace; 3. Countries Studied.

Most of the citations given in the notes to the text are *not* repeated in this section. If you want to know more about nonviolence, or East Timor, or any other specific aspect of the book, look for some of the sources cited in the relevant portions of the end notes. (The corresponding chapters are indicated in the list that follows.)

New information sources are becoming available all the time. The ideas here were compiled in September 1999 and include suggestions for on-line resources and for locating hardcopy publications. In many of the relevant fields of study, a small number of Web sites are particularly well maintained and provide timely and reliable information. In addition, some Web sites distinguish themselves by providing broad links to other sites that provide information in relevant areas. Where possible, I have attempted to indicate those sites.

Regarding hardcopy publications, I have tried to identify some subject headings, according to the widely used Library of Congress system, that will lead you to lists of relevant books.

1. The International System

Structure and Reform of the International System (chapters 1, 11): The journals *Global Governance* and *International Organization* deal centrally with these issues. Look, too, for the annual journal *Ethics and International Affairs*. The UN associations of the United States and other countries maintain useful Web sites: see <www.wfuna.org> and <www.unausa.org>. The UN's own enormous Web site, <www.un.org>, is becoming better organized and more usable. In a library search, look under headings like *Ethnicity, International organization,* or *International relations—Moral and ethical aspects.* Look for works by Richard Falk or Stanley Hoffmann.

Human Rights (chapter 3): Both Human Rights Watch and Amnesty International maintain good Web sites: <www.hrw.org> and <www.amnesty.org>, respectively. Both groups now put their annual reports and many of their other materials on-line in a user-friendly way, as well as publish them as books. Amnesty International (which won the 1977 Nobel Peace Prize) has good links to other sources. Visit the UN High Commissioner on Human Rights Web site, <www.unhchr.ch>, for the texts of human rights treaties and much more. A library search under *Human rights* will bring up an unwieldy amount of material. Try breaking the category down by country or region.

Human Security and Elimination of Global Poverty (chapter 8): The two main sources of country-by-country data on poverty-related issues are the UN Development Program's annual *Human Development Report* (HDR) and the World Bank's annual *World Development Report* (WDR). The WDR, available through <www.worldbank.org>, gives standard economic data. The HDR focuses on the human development aspects of the data: highlights of its text are available through <www.undp.org/hdro>. The UNDP site also provides many links to other organizations concerned with poverty: <www.undp.org/poverty/links/links.htm>. In a library search, use headings like *Economics —Moral and ethical aspects* or *Poverty—Developing countries*. Look for works by Nobel economics laureate Amartya Sen.

Indigenous Peoples (chapter 4): Many indigenous rights organizations have a good presence on the Internet: <www.nativeweb.org> has many productive links. (Those available through the Minority Rights Group's <www.minorityrights.org> also seem good.) Other interesting addresses are those for the Unrepresented Nations and Peoples Organisation: <www.unpo.org>; the UNDP's Indigenous People's Network: <http:// nywork4.undp.org/info21/sector/s-c-indi.html>; and Cultural Survival Inc.: <www. cs.org>.

International NGOs (chapter 10): The Brussels-based Union of International Associations publishes a four-volume *Yearbook of International Organizations*, as well as other directories of materials and the journal *Transnational Associations*. It posts some of that information on its Web site, <www.uia.org>, which has thousands of links; not all of them are fully developed. The many NGOs that have consultative status with the United Nations can be accessed through <www.un.org>, or more easily through <www.conferenceofngos.org>. Jackie Smith, Charles Chatfield, and Ron Pagnucco, eds., *Transnational Social Movements and Global Politics: Solidarity Beyond the State* (Syracuse, New York: Syracuse University Press 1997) contains much useful analysis: it also has an extensive bibliography.

2. War and Peace

Strategic Affairs, the Arms Trade, and Disarmament (chapters 2, 8): The International Institute for Strategic Studies (IISS) publishes two much-respected annuals: a worldwide factbook *The Military Balance* and the analytical *Strategic Survey* (which has good maps). It also publishes the journal *Survival*. None of these publications were on-line in September 1999. The Stockholm International Peace Research Institute's more peace-oriented and analytical annual *SIPRI Yearbook* is available both as a book and on-line, through <www.sipri.se>, which also has good links to other organizations. The NGO Committee on Disarmament has many good links from its site: <www.peacenet.org/ disarm/>. Look there for the well-written "The ABCs of Disarmament." The *Bulletin of the Atomic Scientists* has good information on many nuclear-weapons issues: <www.bullatomsci.org>. The Arms Transfer Working Group has an informative site with links to many action-oriented organizations: <www.fas.org/asmp/atwg>. From the Arias Foundation's Web site, <www.arias.or.cr>, look at some of the pages for its Center for Peace and Reconciliation. In a library search, check under headings like *Nuclear strategy, Nuclear weapons, Arms control, Arms transfers,* or *Disarmament*.

Landmines (chapters 9, 10): The ICBL's site, <www.icbl.org>, has good information and good links. So does the Mine Action Information Center at James Madison University: <www.hdic.jmu.edu/hdic/demining.htm>. MAIC also publishes the *Journal of Mine Action*. For a significant new book, see Maxwell A. Cameron, Robert J. Lawson, and Brian W. Tomlin, eds., *To Walk without Fear: The Global Movement to Ban Landmines* (Toronto and New York: Oxford University Press, 1998).

International Humanitarian Law (chapters 9, 10): The International Committee of the Red Cross has a huge Web site that is clear, user-friendly, authoritative, regularly updated, and trilingual: <www.icrc.org>. You can easily find the texts of all IHL treaties, lists of which states have signed and ratified each one, well-written analytical pages on subjects like the status of women under IHL, or the environment and war. You can also read or download full-text articles (in English or French) from the ICRC's journal, the *International Review of the Red Cross*. In a library, check under headings like *Laws of war, War (International law)*, or *War—Moral and ethical aspects*.

Nonviolence, Peace Education (chapters 2, 6): Look for numerous journals including *Peace Review* and *Peace and Change*. The Nonviolence Web has a huge library of Internet links that is not well organized but can be very productive with a little effort: <www.nonviolence.org/links.htm>. Try the (Swedish) Life and Peace Institute's site, <www.life-peace.org>, which also has good links; or the Carter Center's site, <www.cartercenter.org>. In a library, look for good books by or about Mahatma Gandhi, Dr. Martin Luther King Jr., His Holiness the Dalai Lama, or other advocates of nonviolent social change; check under headings like *Multicultural education* or *Nonviolence*.

Transitional Justice, Reconciliation (chapters 6, 7): The South African TRC has much of its documentation available on-line: <www.truth.org.za>. The Center for the Study of Violence and Reconciliation, also in South Africa, has a well-organized site with many excellent links worldwide: <www.wits.ac.za/csvr/>. The U.S. Institute of Peace has an on-line library of documents relating to (and issued by) truth commissions around the world: <www.usip.org/library/truth.html>. Restorative justice approaches are being applied in a domestic context in many places, including Canada, Australia, and Native American communities: for useful links to some of these programs, visit the Quaker site <www.web.net/~cfsc/qcjjlink.htm>. For library research in these areas, check under headings like *Amnesty, Conflict psychology*, or *Reconciliation*.

3. Countries Studied

Hardcopy Publications: After you have checked out the most interesting-looking books cited in the text, do a catalogue search under the relevant country name, perhaps followed by *—Politics and government*. The folks who compile the Library of Congress subject headings still use *Burma*, but you may still need to use the heading *Timor Timur (Indonesia)*. You can also try main headings like *Mayas, Quiché Indians*, and *Shan (Asian people)*.

On-line Suggestions: For Burma, try <www.freeburmacoalition.org>, which supports Aung San Suu Kyi and promises more educational material to come. For East Timor, try José Ramos-Horta's <www.easttimor.com>, which has broad, up-to-date news coverage, or <http://etan.org>, from the East Timor Action Network. A great place to access English or Spanish links on human rights and political issues in Guatemala is <mars.cropsoil.uga.edu/trop-ag/social.htm>. For Northern Ireland, you can access the group Betty Williams helped found at <www.peacepeople.com>. The Web site <www.irishpeace.com> has excellent links. For Tibet, the Dalai Lama's representatives in London have a broad range of solid documentation and up-to-date information at <www.tibet.com>. The Tibet Online group runs <www.tibet.org>. The site <www.tibetinfo.net> is run by the Tibet Information Network and has pages in Chinese and Tibetan, as well as English; it also includes a broad range of links.

Index

Vietnam Veterans of American Foundation (VVAF), 9, 10, 180, 185–88, 187–88, 190, 207
Vietnam War, 10–11, 116–18, 146, 180, 181–83, 185, 191, 206, 207, 210, 229
violence, 230–31; breeding violence, 119–20; ignorance as ultimate cause of, 121; motivation and (see Motivation and violence); distinguished from nonviolence, 20; negative side effects of, 29; rehabilitation of survivors of, 104–27. See also Nonviolence
Voice of Hope (Aung San Suu Kyi), 119
Voltaire, 157–58
von Ossietzky, Carol, 39
von Suttner, Baroness Bertha, 12
Vorster, John, 130–31, 132, 134, 231

Walesa, Lech, 39, 164
Walker, Susan, 204–205
war-crimes trials, 135, 141, 143
warfare, 118; Dunant's definition of, 213; laws of war, 143, 210–13; opportunity costs of, 159, 228; as unwinnable, 21–22, 23
Washington Post, 184
wealth, inequalities in distribution of, 156–58

weapons. See disarmament; specific types of weapons
Weber, Max, 230
Weschler, Lawrence, 140
West Timor, 83
Wiesel, Eli, 4, 163
Williams, Betty, 104–27, 148, 176, 204, 227, 235; biographical sketch of, 2–3; International Code of Conduct on Arms Transfers and, 4, 14, 153, 163; "Tears without actions are wasted sentiment," 104, 124, 125, 214, 227
Williams, Jody, 14, 67, 82, 110, 113–14, 119–20, 125, 164, 200–201; biographical sketch of, 9–10, 205; ICBL and, 1, 11, 180, 187, 188, 196–97, 203–22, 229, 235
Witness for Peace, 30
Woolman, John, 73
World Bank, 220, 232
World Centers of Compassion for Children (WCCC), 3, 109, 116
World Council of People, proposal for, 233
World Federalist Movement, 233
World Order Models Project, 233
World Trade Organization, 56–57

Zalaquett, José, 141
Zur, Judith, 65–66